Surnames, DNA, and Family History

JUL 1 6 2013

SALINA PUBLIC LIBRARY

1701 9100 293 652 7

P9-BYS-064

WITHDRAWN
Salina Public Library

Surnames, DNA, and Family History

GEORGE REDMONDS,
TURI KING,
AND
DAVID HEY

OXFORD
UNIVERSITY PRESS

OXFORD
UNIVERSITY PRESS

Great Clarendon Street, Oxford OX2 6DP

Oxford University Press is a department of the University of Oxford.
It furthers the University's objective of excellence in research, scholarship,
and education by publishing worldwide in

Oxford New York

Auckland Cape Town Dar es Salaam Hong Kong Karachi
Kuala Lumpur Madrid Melbourne Mexico City Nairobi
New Delhi Shanghai Taipei Toronto

With offices in

Argentina Austria Brazil Chile Czech Republic France Greece
Guatemala Hungary Italy Japan Poland Portugal Singapore
South Korea Switzerland Thailand Turkey Ukraine Vietnam

Oxford is a registered trade mark of Oxford University Press
in the UK and in certain other countries

Published in the United States
by Oxford University Press Inc., New York

© 2011 George Redmonds, Turi King, and David Hey

The moral rights of the authors have been asserted
Database right Oxford University Press (maker)

First published 2011

All rights reserved. No part of this publication may be reproduced,
stored in a retrieval system, or transmitted, in any form or by any means,
without the prior permission in writing of Oxford University Press,
or as expressly permitted by law, or under terms agreed with the appropriate
reprographics rights organization. Enquiries concerning reproduction
outside the scope of the above should be sent to the Rights Department,
Oxford University Press, at the address above

You must not circulate this book in any other binding or cover
and you must impose the same condition on any acquirer

British Library Cataloguing in Publication Data
Data available

Library of Congress Cataloging in Publication Data
Data available

Typeset by SPI Publisher Services, Pondicherry, India
Printed in Great Britain
on acid-free paper by
MPG Books Group, Bodmin and King's Lynn

ISBN 978–0–19–958264–8

3 5 7 9 10 8 6 4

SALINA PUBLIC LIBRARY
SALINA. KANSAS 67401

Contents

Foreword   vii
Preface   ix

   Introduction   1
1 By-names   21
2 Hereditary Surnames   41
3 Expansion and Decline   62
4 Distribution and Migration   84
5 Linguistic and Social Factors   106
6 Meaning and Method   127
7 DNA and Surnames   148
8 The Link between Surname and Y Chromosome Type   173
9 The Wider Picture   194
   Conclusion   215

Bibliography   218
Index of Names   225
General Index   241

Foreword by Sir Alec Jeffreys

What is in a name? Quite a lot, as this book from three leading experts will tell you. We are all intrigued by our origins, and one of the most powerful proxies for our family identity is our surname, at least in those societies where surnames are inherited down the generations. As the authors discuss, the wonderful diversity of surnames in Britain has a surprisingly recent origin and can give fascinating clues about the wheres and whens of surname adoption and the origins, sometimes comical or bizarre, of our names and how they have evolved and migrated around the British Isles. But historical, etymological, and geographical surveys of surnames tell only part of the story. Over the last few years an alternative approach using modern molecular genetics is beginning to shed major new light on our names. This book explores this new science and shows how DNA can identify clans of men sharing the same recent male ancestor, and can give tantalizing clues about the age of a surname and levels of historical marital fidelity. This can be fraught, as for example when I was recently asked to review a Y chromosome analysis of same-surnamed men from a distinguished Arabian dynasty which, to my great relief, showed that they all shared the same Y chromosome!

DNA is not a panacea and the key message from this book is the importance of marrying history with genetics. So for those who would spend good money on sending a mouth swab off for Y chromosome testing – this is now becoming big business and a significant part of the DNA identification world – I would strongly recommend that you read this book first and understand what DNA might be able to tell you and just as importantly what it cannot.

Of course, this book is not the end of the story. We are in the middle of a technological revolution that is seeing the cost of reading information from DNA plummet. I foresee in the not-so-distant future that a global genetic readout will become the must-have birthday present. The driver will not, I suspect, be for medical reasons (which could make for a gloomy birthday) but for ancestry. By definition, this readout will, for men, contain huge amounts of information on their Y chromosome, allowing them all to be linked together in a giant family tree on which surnames can be superimposed. This in turn will identify male clans, when and maybe where surname switches took place, and perhaps even the identities of those involved in this historical hanky-panky. I look forward to the 2030 edition of this book with bated breath.

Alec J. Jeffreys

Department of Genetics
University of Leicester
June 2010

Preface

'What's in a name?', asked Shakespeare. 'That which we call a rose by any other name would smell as sweet.' His own surname is a puzzling one that seems to have been some sort of nickname, but its original meaning is uncertain. Like many of the names discussed in this book, it appears to have had a single-family origin. It began to spread in the fifteenth century but for several generations it was confined to a few Warwickshire parishes. The Shakespeares are still found principally in Warwickshire and the neighbouring counties of Staffordshire and Worcestershire. A fashionable theory in recent years is that the young William Shakespeare moved to a south Lancashire Catholic house-hold, where a William Shakeshafte was recorded as a 'player', but this claim illustrates the unfortunate tendency to make facile, erroneous assumptions about surnames. It ignores the fact that several Shakeshafts were recorded in neighbouring Lancashire parishes from at least 1381 and that this surname is mostly found in south Lancashire and Cheshire to this day. The Lancashire Shakeshafts have no proven connection with the Warwickshire Shakespeares.

The aim of the present book is to assess the evidence for the origins and spread of surnames in a far more rigorous way and to argue the need for an approach that combines linguistics with genealogy, local history, and genetics. The different approaches to the study of surnames that are brought together here began with doctoral theses at the University of Leicester. George Redmonds and David Hey finished theirs in the Department of (now the Centre for) English Local History in the early 1970s, whereas Turi King completed hers in the Department of Genetics in 2007. George Redmonds was concerned with the origins, spread, and distribution of the surnames of the West Riding; Turi King examined the relationship between British surnames and Y-chromosomal haplotypes; and David Hey reconstructed the family histories of all the seventeenth-century inhabitants of the Shropshire parish of Myddle. These different specialisms are reflected in the title of the book, but we are all agreed that a multi-disciplinary approach is vital to a true understanding of the surnames that British people bear today, and that surnames can shed light on many different aspects of social history.

Surname studies have been advanced enormously in recent years by the use of Stephen Archer's CD, *The British 19th Century Surname Atlas* <www.archersoftware.co.uk> (2003), which provides distribution maps and frequencies for every name recorded in the 1881 national census. Steve has kindly given us permission to use some of his maps here. George Redmonds and David Hey have also benefited from the professional assistance of archivists in national and regional record offices, from the comments and questions of those who have attended conferences and meetings of local and family history societies, from friends and colleagues who share our interests, and from Ann-Marie and Pat's good-humoured tolerance of their husbands' longstanding interest in surnames. Turi King thanks Professor Mark Jobling, who initiated a comprehensive study of the link between British surnames and Y chromosome type and who has become a very dear friend as well as a wonderful supervisor and advisor, and Professor Sir Alec Jeffreys, who acted both as an internal advisor and PhD examiner; his invention of the technique of DNA fingerprinting forms the foundation of the genetic component of this work. Professor Kevin Schürer kindly provided a great deal of information about the frequencies and geographical localization of surnames in Britain. Turi also wishes to thank Rob and the children, family and friends (especially Patricia Balaresque), who have had to listen to her burbling on about surnames and the Y chromosome for over ten years. She did not inherit her father's Y chromosome but she inherited his love of science. Oh, and his surname!

We also thank the team at OUP for their advice and support at every stage of the book's production: John Davey, Elmandi du Toit, Jennifer Lunsford, Michael Janes, and Francis Eaves.

HUDDERSFIELD VETERANS. In August 2009, a Rose Bowl was presented to the Huddersfield and District Bowling Veterans by Ian Armitage, accompanied by the President of the Association, Frank Lockwood. The bowlers in the photograph had the surnames: Bray, Crowther, Firth, Haigh, Hoyle, Pogson, Sheard and Sykes. It is a remarkable fact that all ten names can be found in local parish registers from 1538 and that no fewer than nine of them had their origins within a six-mile radius of Huddersfield. That takes their history back to the thirteenth and fourteenth centuries. Sheard was the exception, having moved into the Calder Valley by 1538, probably from Lancashire where Adam del Sherde was taxed in 1379. The continuity of families in the former textile towns, on both sides of the Pennines, has had a striking impact there on surname development.

Introduction

Just about all of us know someone called Smith. Theirs has always been by far the most common surname in Britain. In the 1881 national census no less than 422,733 men, women, and children bore this name. Today, the Smiths account for 1.3 per cent of the British people. Back in the Middle Ages when surnames were being formed, most villages had a smith, but few had more than one; a smith was easily identified by his occupation. Some were men who smelted the raw material, turning iron ore into pig iron, but mostly they were blacksmiths who turned their hand to making whatever their neighbours wanted. They were skilled men who enjoyed real status in the community, and they paid tax at a higher rate. This widespread surname clearly has many origins in different parts of the country. Their numbers were increased later when compound names, such as Combsmith or Smithson, were abbreviated to Smith.

It might be expected that the most common surnames would be spread evenly across the country, but that is not quite true. The Smiths can be found in every part of England, but if we look at the figures from the 1881 census, both as actual numbers and in terms of numbers per 100,000 of the population in each registration district, they were much less common in the south-western counties of Cornwall, Devon, Dorset, and Somerset than in the rest of the country. Even in counties where the name was a familiar one it remained rare in some parishes for centuries. Of course, several of our most common surnames are found chiefly in Wales, which did not begin to adopt the English naming system until the sixteenth century, and often much later. The Welsh formed most of their surnames from fathers' personal names, and as only a limited range of personal names were in use at the time a very high percentage of Welshmen acquired surnames such as Jones, Evans, Thomas, and Roberts.

The next most common surnames in 1881 were Jones (339,185) and Williams (215,163), largely because of their strength in Wales, followed by Brown, Taylor, Davies, Wilson, Evans, Thomas, Roberts, Johnson, and Walker, all with counts over 100,000. These twelve surnames are still the most common ones in Britain today, though their order at the bottom end of the scale has changed a little. Clearly, they all have many different family origins. In 1881 the most common 500 surnames in Britain were shared by 40 per cent of the population and the top 1,000 surnames by 60 per cent. Yet at the same time over 30,000 British surnames were borne by only 10 per cent of the inhabitants. Paradoxically, it was – and still is – very common to possess an uncommon surname.

One of the rarest British surnames at the time of the 1881 census was Ellel, which was shared by just twenty-seven Lancashire people, living within a few miles of each other. The name was derived from a small place in low-lying land within the parish of Cockerham, near Lancaster. In 1379 a John of Ellel (*Johanne de Elale*) paid poll tax at Walton-le-Dale, a mile or two to the south of Preston, and another *Johannes de Elleall* was taxed in Gisburn, just across the border in the West Riding of Yorkshire. In Victorian times, this rare surname was still firmly rooted within the neighbourhood where it had arisen back in the Middle Ages. In 1881 three households lived in Chatburn, three in Blackburn, and one in Accrington, and the heads of households in Blackburn had each been born in Chatburn, a little further north and only four miles away from Gisburn. As we will see, Ellel is typical of very many British surnames in appearing to have a single-family origin. Its concentration in a particular part of the country in the Victorian era prompts genealogical research that tries to link the medieval and the modern evidence and directs DNA testing to see whether genetics supports this suggestion.

The origins and spread of surnames

Before the Norman Conquest no-one in England possessed a surname. People were known simply by an Old English (Anglo-Saxon) or Old Scandinavian (Viking) personal name, sometimes with the addition of a nickname or another type of non-hereditary by-name. Only a few of the Norman barons who introduced the fashion for surnames into England already had one when they arrived and none of these went back far in time. Although nicknames were a common addition to a personal name, even amongst the royal family, they had not yet developed into hereditary surnames. The spur to the adoption of names that were passed on to children seems to have been the barons' desire to identify families with their estates back in Normandy or with their newly confiscated lands in England, but the practice took a long time to become entrenched. Indeed, during the twelfth and thirteenth centuries some junior members of baronial families assumed different surnames, while the convention that married women acquired their husband's name took time to become established. At the next step down the social scale, most knights in the south of England possessed surnames by about 1200, but the process took much longer in the north of the country, where some knights were still without one a century later. Even at this top social level the adoption of fixed, hereditary surnames was a slow and irregular process.

The ordinary people of England, who formed the vast majority of the population, took much longer to follow the lead of their social superiors. Twelfth- and thirteenth-century deeds referred to or were commonly witnessed by merchants, craftsmen, or peasants who possessed only a personal name. The richer commoners of London sometimes had hereditary surnames by the second half of the twelfth century and soon afterwards their counterparts in leading provincial cities such as Norwich or Exeter adopted them, but in the late thirteenth century many wealthy burgesses still managed with just a personal name, usually coupled with a non-hereditary by-name. In the countryside the fashion for surnames started to spread amongst free-tenants and serfs alike across southern England and East Anglia from about the middle of the thirteenth century. Firm, statistical evidence is lacking, but it seems that the first half of the fourteenth century was a particularly formative time. Even so, some families, especially in the north of England, still did not have a surname when the various poll taxes were collected in 1377–81; many Lancashire people, for instance, were recorded simply as the son or daughter of someone. By the early fifteenth century few English families were still without a surname, but some of these names continued to evolve and were sometimes changed out of recognition.

The major disaster in the mid-fourteenth century that we know as the Black Death not only wiped out numerous surnames across the country but resulted in the spread of some of the surviving ones to new places where vacant farms enabled men with ambition to start anew with a better chance of becoming prosperous. This shake-up of names in parishes throughout the land continued for a generation or two before families settled in their new homes. This helps to explain why some of the locative surnames that are easy to spot in the poll tax returns of 1377–81 were no longer very close to their points of origin. Nevertheless, despite this shake-up, most families remained within the neighbourhood or 'country' that had been so familiar to their ancestors.

Although the majority of the English population had acquired hereditary surnames by about 1400, new surnames continued to appear in later centuries. The levying of another poll tax in 1381, shortly after the first two, was a major cause of the Peasants' Revolt in that year. The ferocity of that uprising caused the abandonment of taxes on polls (heads) for almost three centuries. An unfortunate result for the historian is the lack of comparable records during the fifteenth century. We have no further lists of surnames until the the lay subsidies of Henry VIII's reign and they are far less comprehensive. Some of the new surnames that appear in sixteenth-century records may well have been in existence, unrecorded, for several generations. Others may have been mutations from a name that can be recognized only, if at all, by the use of genealogical methods which can spot when and where a name changed its form.

Reaney's *Dictionary of English Surnames*

Since its first appearance in 1958, the standard work on the etymology or meaning of surnames has been P.H. Reaney, *A Dictionary of English Surnames*, now available as P.H. Reaney and R.M. Wilson, *A Dictionary of English Surnames* (revised third edition, 2005). Traditionally, surname dictionaries have been compiled by philologists with expertise in old languages. Their concern has been to provide an explanation of the meaning of a name. Commendably, they have searched for the earliest recorded instances of names, a proper technique if the proposed etymology is to be valid. It is now recognized, however, that many of their earliest examples were merely by-names that never developed into hereditary surnames. Many other names that appear in the dictionaries were lost not long after they were formed because the Black Death of 1348–50 reduced the English population by more than one-third, perhaps one-half. Before this disaster a larger variety and number of English surnames were used than at the present day, even though the population was less than one-tenth of what it is now. Many of the surnames and by-names recorded by Reaney were once more widespread than at present because only one or two families with these names survived. As the population level dropped dramatically, some surnames became more regional in their distribution than they were before. Many other surnames never had more than one source.

Reaney's dictionary often quotes early examples of surnames in districts other than those where they were found in the post-medieval period; he thus sometimes gives a misleading impression of where a surviving family name originated. For instance, he suggested that the surname Ramshaw had the same derivation as surnames derived from place-names such as Ravenshaw (Warwickshire) and Renishaw (Derbyshire). In fact, Ramshaw is a County Durham surname which is derived from Ramshaw Hall, Evenwood, near Auckland. The Durham hearth tax returns of 1666 list five households of Ramshaws in Chester-le-Street ward, two in Darlington ward, and one in Stockton ward. Of the 739 people who bore the surname in the 1881 census,

396 lived in County Durham and 149 in Northumberland; none was found in the heartlands of the Renshaws and Renishaws. Although he knew that his own name came from Ranah Stones Farm in south-west Yorkshire, Reaney usually missed the point that uncommon names are associated with particular districts and often have single-family origins.

Reaney's achievement was considerable. His dictionary is still a first port of call. Yet his conclusions about the etymology of a name can often be shown to be wrong. He had no interest in the geographical distribution of names, nor in the ways in which medieval surnames continued to evolve in later centuries. His opening words in his Introduction were: 'The purpose of a Dictionary of Surnames is to explain the meaning of names, not to treat of genealogy and family history.' Yet by ignoring genealogy his explanations of the etymology of a name are often incorrect. Every family name, however common, had a single progenitor and every effort must be made to identify him and his immediate descendants if we are to understand how a name arose and perhaps evolved into something different. The expertise of the philologist in interpreting the earliest recorded form of a surname cannot by itself be trusted to offer a proper account of the meaning of a modern name. A multi-disciplinary approach is necessary for a proper understanding of the etymology of a surname and its subsequent development.

The present (third) edition of Reaney's dictionary has been shown to have a very large number of names that either never developed from by-names into hereditary surnames or which died out in later centuries. D.K. Tucker has calculated that no less than 2,972 names in the current edition, that is 11 per cent of the total, were no longer in existence by the time of the national census of 1881. Conversely, the dictionary missed some common regional surnames such as Oakes and Winterbottom. Reaney's pioneering work was valuable at the time and can still be useful, but his real purpose seems to have been to explain the meaning of medieval names, whether or not they became hereditary and whether or not they survived. Nor was he much concerned with the ways that surnames might evolve over the centuries. Unfortunately, many of Reaney's flawed explanations are repeated in other dictionaries and are accepted as accurate in a variety of historical publications, despite all the new work of the past half century.

The *English Surnames Series*

A different approach was tried not long after Reaney's dictionary first appeared. In 1965 the Marc Fitch Fund endowed the English Surnames Survey in the Department of (now the Centre for) English Local History at the

University of Leicester, and Richard McKinley was appointed as Director. The survey was less concerned with philology than with the historical origins, evolution, and spread of surnames. McKinley produced a steady stream of county studies, starting with Norfolk and Suffolk and continuing with Oxfordshire, Lancashire, and Sussex, and *A History of British Surnames* (1990), which became the basic textbook on the Leicester approach. Meanwhile, George Redmonds's 1970 Leicester PhD thesis was published as *English Surnames Series, 1: Yorkshire, the West Riding* (1973). This book was the first to champion the idea that very many English surnames have a single-family origin. Some of these have remained rare, but from the sixteenth century onwards, as the population grew, families that produced numerous sons spread from their point of origin into the neighbouring towns and countryside, and occasionally much further.

The Leicester approach emphasized genealogical methods in the context of the growth of local communities and stressed the fluidity of development in the centuries after surnames first became hereditary. In the post-medieval period, numerous surnames changed in minor ways and some altered out of recognition in the course of only two or three generations. Genealogical methods have to be used to link modern names with those recorded in historical sources and to establish the variant forms of a surname before plotting them on distribution maps. This is easier said than done, for some names became unrecognizable while others shaded into each other and even assumed the forms of local place-names and personal names with which they had no real connection. It is unwise to guess the meaning of a family name simply from its modern spelling.

For ordinary people whose surname has changed from the original medieval form, the most likely explanation is that an ancestor migrated to a new neighbourhood where the name was unfamiliar and patterns of speech were different. The origins of some family names are puzzling because both the surname and the place-name from which they were derived have changed in spelling and pronunciation over time. For example, the surname Shufflebottom comes from a place near Bury (Lancashire) that is now known as Shipperbottom. The first record of the surname occurs in 1285 as Richard de Schyppewallebothem, which can be explained as 'sheep – well – valley bottom', a similar name to Ramsbottom, not far away. The 1881 national census listed 542 Shufflebottoms, 617 Shufflebothams, and 150 people with many other spellings of this name, most of them in south Lancashire and Cheshire. A further 112 Shipperbottoms were recorded in the census: 108 of them in the Bolton registration district (which included Bury) and the other four nearby in Haslingden. All the bearers of this unusual name, whatever the spelling that they prefer, perhaps share a common ancestor, unless they are descended from what geneticists call a non-paternity event.

Identifying the source of a surname is often a straightforward task for a knowledgeable local and family historian, but equally often it is fraught with difficulty. An interesting example is the surname Depledge, which in 1881 was shared by 477 people, of whom 335 lived in the West Riding of Yorkshire, 47 in Lancashire, 30 in Derbyshire, and 17 in Cheshire, with the others scattered elsewhere. Depledge sounds like a place-name, but where is it? Early spellings of the name include Deplache, Deplatch, Deplytch, Deplish, and Deepleach, as well as Depledge. The Depledges had arrived in the West Riding by the Elizabethan period, when a William Depledge was recorded at Barnsley in 1570, but no such place-name was known and no medieval records of the name were found east of the Pennines. The spread of the name within Yorkshire could have been the result of a single migrant having a number of sons. Although Cheshire had only 17 Depledges in 1881, most of the pre-1600 references to the name came from Mottram-in-Longdendale, on the Cheshire side of the Pennines. This provided the vital clue that led to a search of the English Place-Name Society's volumes on Cheshire, which noted Depleach Hall, near Cheadle, a 'deep, boggy stream' that was recorded as Depelache in 1366. The home of this family name had been identified.

Another example is the rare surname Fernihough. In the 1881 national census 57 of the 144 people sharing this name were recorded in Staffordshire, especially in the Leek (26) and Cheadle (20) registration districts, and most of the others were in neighbouring counties. A generation earlier in 1842–46 nearly half the 95 Fernihoughs whose deaths were registered came from Staffordshire. Back in 1666, the Staffordshire hearth tax returns recorded 15 householders with this name, of whom 12 lived in Totmonslow Hundred, so it is in the Staffordshire Moorlands that we must look for a minor place-name meaning the 'ferny ridge'. Strong clues are provided by the will of Elizabeth Fernihough of Fernihough in the parish of Leek, which she made in 1619, and by the naming of Adam de Fernihaleugh in a 1327 lay subsidy return for Endon township within Leek parish. With these references in mind, the exact source of the name can be identified from a map of Endon township in 1816, which marked a farm named Fernihough on its eastern border. The distribution of the surname, centuries after it had been formed, leads us to its source.

Rare names such as these immediately suggest a single-family origin, but others are so common that multiple origins are often assumed until a distribution map suggests otherwise. Greenwood is perhaps the best example of this. In 1881 no less than 23,256 British people bore this name. Surely, we think, there must have been many green woods up and down the country that gave rise to this popular surname. Yet when we look at how the surname was distributed in 1881 we find that 10,612 of the Greenwoods lived in the textile district of the West Riding of Yorkshire and another 7,304 lived in neighbouring parts of Lancashire. The Halifax registration district alone had 3,015 Greenwoods, high in the Calder Valley. Further west, Todmorden had 2,960, and to the east Bradford had 1,754, Keighley 862, and Dewsbury 509. On the Lancashire side of the Pennines, Rochdale had 1,307 Greenwoods, Burnley 1,046, Haslingden 956, Blackburn 543, Ashton-under-Lyne 516, and Oldham 455. The concentration in these neighbouring registration districts is remarkable. It is known that many surnames in the West Riding and Lancashire ramified considerably from the Elizabethan period onwards. Names derived from farmsteads and hamlets that were shared by only a few families in the Middle Ages now became prolific as the textile industries spread across the hills and down the valleys. In medieval England the Greenwoods were thin on the ground. The first record of anyone bearing this name is that of John del Grenwode in Sowerby in 1275. His name seems to have come from the hamlet of Greenwood Lee in the neighbouring township of Heptonstall, high in the Calder Valley. In 1379 Richard de Grenewod and three Thomas de Grenewods paid poll tax in Halifax, a John de Grenewode occupied Bradley Grange further down the Calder Valley, and the John de Grenewod who had set up home across the Pennines in Lancashire probably shared the same family origin. The Thomas Grenewod of High Greenwood, recorded in 1430, shows the link between the surname and a minor place-name. The Greenwoods became the most prolific of all the families in this part of Yorkshire and over the moors in the neighbouring townships of Lancashire. Heptonstall churchyard contains numerous tombstones of Greenwoods and of people who took Greenwood as their Christian name, presumably because of family connections. There is even a gravestone for a Greenwood Greenwood.

When we turn to P.H. Reaney and R.M. Wilson's dictionary we find that the explanation offered for the etymology of Greenwood is simply 'dweller by the greenwood'. The explanation is correct in a general way, but it offers no clue that the name is probably derived from a single green wood high above the Calder Valley. Likewise, Patrick Hanks and Flavia Hodges, *A Dictionary of Surnames* (1997 edition) offers 'topographic name for someone who lived in a dense forest', an unlikely landscape feature in the moorland district around Halifax.

Local and family historians can make a substantial contribution to a subject that has long been the domain of the linguist. The *English Surnames Series* has shown that distributions of surnames at different points of time across the centuries, linked by genealogical research, and an emphasis on local historical context in searching for the origins of surnames often produce different etymologies from those offered in the standard dictionaries. Many surnames have changed over the centuries. Simply finding a medieval example of a likely sounding name is not enough.

Mapping surnames

Plotting the geographical distribution of surnames at various points of time is a development that is now a key tool for investigating their origins and spread. It began in a simple way with the publication of H.B. Guppy, *Homes of Family Names in Great Britain* (1890), which extracted the names of farmers from current Kelly's *Post Office Directories* on a county-by-county basis, but the idea was not followed more thoroughly until the 1960s, when telephone directories were used to show modern distributions of surnames. In the 1990s maps were constructed from data collected from the civil registration of deaths in England and Wales between 1 January 1842 and 31 December 1846, using contemporary maps of the new poor law unions, which were mostly the same as the civil registration districts. These maps provided many examples of surnames that were still concentrated in particular localities at the beginning of the reign of Queen Victoria. Very often, these distinctive groupings of names pointed to the places where surnames had been created several centuries earlier. The 1840s were chosen for these studies in order to capture patterns just before the railways made it much easier for ordinary people to travel further than before, but then research by Colin Pooley and Jean Turnbull, published as *Migration and Mobility in Britain since the Eighteenth Century* (1998), showed that cheap rail travel had only a modest impact on where the majority of people chose to live in Britain, even if a minority moved far from home and, over the centuries, hundreds of thousands migrated to distant lands.

The release of Stephen Archer's CD, *The British 19th Century Surname Atlas* (Archer Software, 2003), which provided instant maps of all the surnames recorded in the 1881 census, aggregated by counties and by poor law unions, showed that the distribution patterns in the late Victorian era were little different from what they had been a generation earlier before rail travel became common. Precise measurements are now available at the click of a mouse. Information technology has made the old, laborious methods obsolete though it has not challenged the accuracy of their results. More recently, a website at University College, London, <www.spatial-literacy.org>, has provided free maps of the most frequent 25,000 surnames in the 1881 census, but these are arranged only by counties and many interesting but rare names are not included. Archer's poor law union maps provide the local detail that is essential in locating the homes of all of our family names.

The <www.spatial-literacy.org> website also provides surname distribution maps, colour-coded by counties, of names taken from the 1998 electoral registers. Quick comparisons of the patterns revealed by the 1881 census and the modern era can now be made. At present, the website does not include names such as Ellel which have less than 100 people on the electoral registers, but in many other instances the information is instantly available. A clear conclusion is that, despite the increased mobility of modern times, most British families have still not moved very far from the neighbourhoods that were familiar to their distant ancestors. Today's picture is more blurred than it was in 1881 but the old pattern is still discernible.

The geographical spread of surnames recorded in the 1881 census returns helps us to identify the origins of a particular name whatever its category. The homes of locative names are generally the easiest to identify, though we have to be alert to variant pronunciations and spellings. Similar place-names can cause confusion by giving rise to two or more separate family names. Some of the Derbys who lived in Lancashire in 1881 may have moved from the county capital of Derbyshire but most of them are more likely to have been natives who took their name from West Derby, near Liverpool. The largest number of Hampshires were found in South Yorkshire, but that is because the surname there is a shortened form of Hallamshire, the ancient name for the cutlery district around Sheffield. Locating the home of a locative surname is bedevilled by the tendency for the place-names of villages and minor settlements to be replicated elsewhere. Some, such as Norton and Sutton or Bradford and Bradwell, can be spotted quickly, but other duplicates are obscure. The uncommon surname Osgathorpe, for example, was derived from two small places, one in Leicestershire and the other on a hill within modern Sheffield. In some cases where different places have the same name, only one of these settlements gave rise to a surname.

The 1881 census returns show that some Scottish surnames, too, were restricted in their distribution. The Dalgleish family were Borders landowners who took the name of their medieval residence in the parish of Ettrick in Selkirkshire as their surname. A Symon de Dalgles lived there in 1407. The surname proved difficult to spell, so in the 1881 census we find 1,349 people recorded as Dalgleish, 549 as Dalglish, 414 as Dalgliesh, and another 112 with thirteen other spellings of the name. Selkirkshire had 147 people with various forms of Dalgleish, but Midlothian had many more with 380 and Lanarkshire had 100, for families had moved there in search of industrial employment. The name remained absent or very rare in the Highlands and Islands and it was scarce in the western lowlands. Even Perthshire had only seven Dalgleishes and Dunbartonshire just five. Meanwhile, 186 Dalgleishes had moved south across the border; 24 had settled in Northumberland and 21 in Lancashire, while another 62 had gone all the way to London. What is not clear is whether everyone with this name is descended from the medieval landowners or whether the surname might also have arisen independently when someone of more lowly status left Dalgleish during the period when surnames were being formed.

Many examples of surnames that Reaney classified as personal names and which appear to have had just one origin can be quoted from up and down the country. In 1881 Adlam, which Reaney said meant 'noble protector', was the surname of 772 people, of whom 258 lived in Wiltshire, 130 in Somerset, and 66 in Gloucestershire; the Warminster registration district accounted for 121 of the Wiltshire Adlams. In contrast, 138 of the 298 Adlards lived in Lincolnshire; Reaney was content to give the meaning of the name as 'noble, hard'. On the other side of the country, in Lancashire, the Prescot district accounted for 269 of the 543 people named Anders (probably from Andrew) and many more people with this name lived nearby in Wigan and Leigh. Allpress, which Reaney derived from 'the old priest', was a name borne by only 239 people in 1881, most of whom lived in Huntingdonshire (especially St Ives) and Cambridgeshire; a Thomas Alprest was recorded in Cambridgeshire back in 1278. A final example is Dodds, which perhaps has more than one origin but which is a north-eastern name. In 1881 the 6,309 people named Dodds included 1,927 from County Durham and 1,390 from Northumberland. The personal name Dodd, from which Dodds is derived, became a more widespread northern surname, with large numbers of bearers in Lancashire, notably Ken Dodd of Knotty Ash, Liverpool.

Pet forms or diminutives of personal names have multiple origins in such surnames as Hancock or Marriott, but here too, judging by the 1881 census returns, we can find names in these categories that seem to be limited to just one or two families. For example, Elkin, thought to have been a diminutive of Elias, is principally a Staffordshire name; 234 of the 610 Elkins in 1881 lived in that county, with 76 in Stoke-on-Trent, 73 in Stone, and 35 in Wolstanton. The etymology of Burdekin, a Peak District name that has spread a little into Yorkshire and Lancashire, is problematic as the first record is to a Burdekan. Reaney regarded the name as a diminutive of *burde*, the Middle English predecessor of 'bird'. He concluded that the diminutive meant 'little young lady' and was 'undoubtedly derogatory', but this was not necessarily so. In 1881 the Burdekins numbered only 242 and their largest number was in the Hayfield registration district on the north-western side of the Peak District. This is not many miles from Castleton, where John Burdekan was living in

1381, and close to the places where his descendants were taxed on their hearths in the early 1670s: Hope (3), Edale (2), Tideswell and Charlesworth, and just across the Yorkshire border at Dungworth. Soon, they had found their way to Sheffield and Wigan, then in the early nineteenth century Thomas Burdekin sought his fortune as a merchant in Australia; his wife had a river named after her in Queensland and their son became Mayor of Sydney. We have to keep these long-distance migrants in mind when we emphasize the point that most members of a family did not move very far.

Peter McClure, the leading modern expert on the etymology of English surnames, has concluded that pet forms of personal names must be studied by looking at all the historical records that deal with the same communities in order to decide which personal names were current in a locality when surnames were formed, and with what frequency. This approach is similar to that of the local and family historian. It also highlights the variant forms of personal and pet names which have arisen in different parts of the country. In a series of articles in the scholarly journal *Nomina*, McClure has demonstrated that many pet forms or diminutives of personal names have different origins from those proposed by Reaney.

While occupational names such as Smith, Taylor, Wright, and Turner are among the most common in the land, a number of specialist occupations have produced surnames that appear to have had a single origin. They include Frobisher, a polisher of armour, from Altofts, near Wakefield; Jagger, a pack-man whose horses carried heavy loads of coal or lead and whose surviving members may all be descended from a John Jagger who paid poll tax in 1379 at Stainland, near Halifax; and perhaps Watchorn, possibly a musician with the town watch, who had 342 descendants (with six different spellings of the name) in 1881, chiefly in and around Melton Mowbray. In contrast to these small numbers, the Rimmers, descendants of a rhymer or poet/musician, had increased to 4,794 in 1881, of whom 4,211 lived in south Lancashire and north Cheshire. The Rimmers were particularly numerous in the Ormskirk district, where they numbered 2,089. The earliest references to the name are found further east in Eccles and Withington in the late thirteenth century, by which time it had become hereditary. Richard McKinley concluded that the medieval references to Rimmers all seem to concern a single family in that part of Lancashire.

Distribution maps of surnames before the nineteenth century have to depend on less perfect data. We do not have the necessary information to construct maps on a national scale. We have to be satisfied with county maps that highlight local concentrations of names and which guide us back further into the past. The best source that is available for making distribution maps is the collection of hearth tax returns for England and Wales from the 1660s and 1670s, which provides a great deal of information on the whereabouts of family names halfway between the period of surname formation and the present day. The tax was the chief source of revenue for Charles II's government. The returns for each county were arranged by ancient subdivisions known as hundreds or wapentakes, which in turn were divided into parishes or townships, or sometimes into even smaller units. The head of each household in a particular settlement was named and the number of hearths in his or her house was noted. However, the returns are not yet readily available in print or on websites for every county, though a project led by Roehampton University and the British Record Society is aiming to fill this gap over the next decade or so. Nor are the lists that are presently accessible always complete. In particular, the names of those poorer householders who were exempt from the tax were not always listed. Nevertheless, the great majority of the householders of England and Wales were recorded in the places where they lived at a certain point in time, just like a census. The Staffordshire hearth tax return for 1666, for example, named 20,648 householders, the Nottinghamshire return for 1674 listed 11,959, and the Cambridgeshire return for 1664 recorded 13,563. These are large samples, dating from nearly two centuries before census enumerators' books record nearly every person in the country on the same day, once every ten years.

Hearth tax returns show with great clarity that in the second half of the seventeenth century very many surnames were confined to particular districts, which were generally the ones where the name originated in the period of surname formation three or four hundred years earlier. Armistead is derived from a farmstead in the parish of Giggleswick in the Yorkshire Dales. People with this name were recorded in the neighbouring townships of Giggleswick and Langcliffe in the poll tax returns of 1379. Three centuries later, their numbers had grown considerably to 72 households, nearly all of which were resident in or near Ribblesdale, where the name originated. The Armisteads formed 26 households in the parish of Giggleswick and 18 in other parts of the dale. All but three of the rest lived within Staincliffe and Ewcross wapentakes, the administrative districts that covered north-west Yorkshire. Armistead was a common surname in Ribblesdale but it was hardly found in other parts of Yorkshire before it spread into the textile district of the West Riding and across the border into Lancashire from the fifteenth century. The story of the Armisteads is typical of many other families in this part of England.

In some cases, the place-name has changed over time but the surname has preserved the original pronunciation. The surname Belk does not lead us quickly to the conclusion that it came from Belph, a small place in the parish of Whitwell on the Derbyshire–Nottinghamshire–Yorkshire border. The 1881 national census recorded only 297 people with this name, of whom 121 were living in the borough of Sheffield, about twelve miles to the west. Further back in time, the hearth tax returns of 1664–72 for the three neighbouring counties show that the Belks had not yet set up home in Sheffield. Six households were established in three South Yorkshire villages, less than five miles from Whit-well, three households had moved further east into north Nottinghamshire, one household lived in a neighbouring Derbyshire village, and just one family had moved about twenty miles west into the Peak District. This restricted distribution three centuries or so after the formation of the surname points to the neighbourhood where the name probably originated. The English Place-Name Society's volumes on Derbyshire reveal that Belph (as it is now known) was recorded as Belgh in 1179 and as Belk in 1273. The surname appears regularly in the early Whitwell parish register.

The County Durham hearth tax assessment for Ladyday 1666 provides many examples of surnames that were derived from place-names, though some of these, such as Breadnell, Blenkinsopp, Harbottle, and Shaftoe, had spread south from Northumberland. For example, the rare name Elstob, which comes from a south Durham village between Darlington and Sedge-field, was shared by twelve south Durham householders: eight in Stockton ward, three in Darlington ward, and one in Easington ward, a rather compact distribution. Two centuries later, the 1881 census recorded 198 Elstobs, of whom 103 lived in County Durham and 52 in neighbouring parts of the North Riding of Yorkshire and Northumberland; another 85 were recorded as Elstub, a variant favoured in the West Riding, particularly in Dewsbury, where 54 were listed. This is a straightforward example, where past distribu-tions of a surname point to the place of origin. It is often the case, however, that either the place-name or the surname changed its form or that the village, hamlet, or farmstead from which the surname sprang has disappeared. In such cases, the 'home' of a family name is more difficult to find. In South Yorkshire the surname Brewell comes from a local pronunciation of Braithwell, in Derbyshire the village name Brailsford was corrupted to the surname Brelsforth, and in Staffordshire the surname Huntbach is derived from the settlement now known as Humbage Green. Many surnames, some of them numerically very important, are derived from places that have disap-peared or have changed in status. Yorkshire examples of surnames derived from place-names that have not been identified on modern maps include Hemingway, Hinchcliffe, and Crabtree. The place-name that has produced the surname Rawnsley is commemorated today only by a field name.

Surnames that were familiar to people in Kent had a very different sound from those in north-east England. The Kent hearth tax returns for 1664 and the 1881 census enumerators' books locate many family names in particular parts of the county. Those that were derived from local place-names are the easiest to identify. For example, in the 1881 census 241 of the 309 Kingsnorths lived in Kent, particularly in and around Ashford, close to the village of Kingsnorth, and in neighbouring registration districts. In 1664 hearth tax was paid by 23 householders with this distinctive surname. Blaxland was a much rarer name, one that was derived from a farm on the edge of West Blean Wood, near Canterbury. The William Blaxland who was exempt from payment of hearth tax in 1664 lived nearby at Wickhambreaux; he appears to have been the only person with this surname at the time. By 1881 some of the 118 Blaxlands who were recorded in the national census had moved away from the family's original neighbourhood, but 83 of them still lived in Kent and 18 had gone no further than Surrey; they were found mainly in the Milton (20) and Eastry (19) registration districts. Some other types of names remained just as local. Saffery, which was probably derived from an Old English personal name, may have had a single-family origin, for 69 of the 112 bearers of this name in 1881 lived in Kent and another 25 were settled in London. Twelve Safferys were recorded in the Kent hearth tax returns of 1664, in the same north-eastern parts of the county, extending from Canterbury to Sheppey and the Isle of Thanet. Rigden, thought to be a diminutive of Richard, gave rise to another surname in this part of the county. In 1881 no less than 454 of the 560 Rigdens lived in Kent, particularly in the neighbouring registration districts of Blean (132), Eastry (80), Dover (64), and Elham (51); 27 Rigden households paid hearth tax in the same parts of Kent in 1664. A final example – though very many more could be provided – is Hogben, which originated as a nickname for a man with a crooked leg, or 'hokebone', meaning a haunch or hip bone. Reaney quotes Thomas Huckebone (1479) and Peter Hugbone (1500), both found in Kent, and by the early seventeenth century Hugben, Hogbin, and Hogbyn were variants. By-names and surnames are lexical items that are often in evidence before the vocabulary items that are used to explain their meanings. This name seems likely to have had a single-family origin, but by 1664 the Hogbens had multiplied to 40 households in Kent. Two centuries later, the 1881 census recorded 1,012 Hogbens, of whom 841 lived in Kent, 52 in Middlesex, and 45 in Surrey, no doubt mostly in London and its suburbs.

In the third quarter of the seventeenth century, wherever the hearth tax was levied in England and Wales, the concentration of surnames near their point of origin was more evident than when the national census was taken in 1881. Although the national population had recovered to the highest level that it had achieved in the Middle Ages, it had not yet begun to rise spectacularly. The hearth tax returns are a crucial source of evidence for the distribution of surnames before the Industrial Revolution. Time after time, they point unerringly to the places where surnames originated three or four centuries earlier.

When we venture back even further in time the available data for mapping surname distributions is less reliable, yet it can still offer powerful evidence. The recording of baptisms, marriages, and burials in the 11,000 or so ancient parishes of England and Wales began in 1538, though few parishes have registers that go back as far as that. Members of the Mormon Church have assembled a vast amount of genealogical information by transcribing parish registers or the copies that are held in diocesan archives. This they have made freely available in a variety of forms, the most accessible of which is the website <www.familysearch.org>. The entries are arranged alphabetically by surname (including variant spellings which may or may not be connected) and by county. A trawl through these extensive lists will provide very many examples of the whereabouts of a particular surname between the sixteenth and nineteenth centuries. The earliest references are particularly useful in identifying the parishes where a surname was found a century or more before hearth taxes were first levied. The downside is that the transcriptions were made by amateurs, who often made mistakes in deciphering difficult handwriting, and all entries that say 'about' a certain year should be ignored as these as merely guesses based on estimated ages and places of residence at the time of marriage. We must also remember that the coverage is incomplete. Nevertheless, as we will see, the website provides a most useful and ready source of information for studying the spread of surnames in the Tudor and Stuart period.

By far the best medieval source for the distribution of surnames during the period when they were being formed is now available in print in three substantial volumes as Caroline Fenwick, ed., *The Poll Taxes of 1377, 1379 and 1381* (1998–2005). These taxation lists for people over the age of sixteen are arranged like the later hearth tax returns: by counties, then by hundreds or wapentakes, then by parishes or townships. Unfortunately, the extant returns are far from comprehensive. They do not survive for some counties and are incomplete for others, but where they do exist they provide essential evidence about the homes of family names. The laborious task of searching through scores of thousands of (unindexed) names is enlivened by the discovery of amusing examples such as Thomas Chesandbred at Litcham (Norfolk) and Roger Gotobed at Sandy (Bedfordshire) or by finding that one of the poll tax payers in Hemlingford hundred (Suffolk) was a woman named Margaret Thatcher. By 1377–81 most English surnames had been formed. We are back to their period of origin. It is common to find that the more distinctive surnames in the poll tax returns were borne by very few people, sometimes by just a single taxpayer and his family. We cannot be certain that Roger Gotobed was the ancestor of the 345 people with this surname in 1881, but they were found mostly in neighbouring counties, especially Cambridgeshire, where 110 of the 145 Gotobeds were living in or near Ely. Two centuries earlier, 21 of the 24 Cambridgeshire householders bearing this name in the hearth tax returns of 1664 lived in the Isle of Ely. Unfortunately, the poll tax returns for 1377–81 do not survive for Cambridgeshire.

These then are the main sources for mapping surname distributions over time. This approach has made a major contribution to our understanding of how and where our surnames originated and how they spread. Many of the conclusions made by compilers of dictionaries have been shown to be mistaken. However, it must be stressed that mapping surname distributions must be combined with other methods of enquiry, including the traditional ones of linguistic analysis and genealogy. Only by tracing a family name back over the generations can we see whether or not its modern form is the same as the original one.

A multi-disciplinary approach

It has become clear that more than one approach is needed if we are to obtain a proper understanding of how a surname was formed and how it spread or declined over the centuries. Knowledge of old languages is still vital to an understanding of the meaning of a name, even if many of the solutions that are offered in dictionaries can be shown to be mistaken. A linguist can demonstrate that Osmond was an Old English personal name whereas Tuki was a Viking one, but genealogical methods are needed to prove the connection between Tuki and the surname Tookey. A knowledge of Middle English helps to explain surnames that were created from pet forms or diminutives of personal names, such as Wilcock or Watkins. It would also help to solve the problems associated with the origins of nicknames such as Nice and Yapp. It is vital too in identifying surnames that came from obsolete occupations, such as Alabaster (a maker of crossbows) or Kember (a comber of wool or flax).

The difficulty with the purely linguistic approach of the compilers of dictionaries is that they have rarely tried to link the earliest forms of medieval names to the modern stock of British surnames. Many of their early examples were simply by-names that never developed into hereditary surnames. We can now see that distribution maps of surnames at various points in time are essential to a proper understanding of how and where a name arose in the

Middle Ages. These maps must be used alongside the dictionaries to verify or question the explanations that are on offer. Distribution maps point family and local historians in the right direction, suggesting the places where an investigation should begin. The techniques of genealogy should then be called into play, for it is important to trace a family name back in time, step by step, to see whether it ever changed form and to take the researcher to the district where the surname arose. The modern linguistic approach of such scholars as Peter McClure is in tune with that of local and family historians in emphasizing the need to search for evidence in all the various local records that are available.

The most important conclusion that has arisen from detailed studies across the land is that uncommon names often have just one origin and in other instances no more than two or three. This is not too surprising when we consider the wide range of names that were available to a relatively small national population in the thirteenth and fourteenth centuries. The suggestion that everyone with the same rare surname shares a common ancestor has, however, to be tempered with the knowledge that at certain times in the past illegitimacy rates were high. The data are hard to collect and for the early modern period it relies heavily on parish register entries which indicate that a child was 'base born'. For most of the late sixteenth and seventeenth centuries illegitimacy rates were no higher than 1 or 2 per cent, though they did reach 3 per cent between 1590 and 1610. They then fell back to the old level and did not reach 3 per cent again until the 1750s. Parish registers may not always be an accurate guide, but the picture is consistent across England and Wales. From 1837 the civil registration records of births provide firmer data alongside those of the parish registers. Together they show that, as the national population level rose dramatically, illegitimacy rates soared to 7 per cent in the 1840s but then declined steadily to 4 per cent by the last decade of the nineteenth century. It is clear that the chances of a present-day person having an illegitimate ancestor in the male line at some point in the past are considerable. We also have to take account of other forms of 'non-paternity events'. Death rates were much higher than today, so it was common for a widow to remarry. Sometimes, the children from the first marriage assumed the surname of her new husband. In other cases, an adopted child would acquire a new surname. We might reasonably argue that 'non-paternity events' are of little importance in the cultural, as distinct from the biological, history of a family, but as we will see they do create problems when we come to interpret the evidence of the latest approach to the study of surnames: the analysis of the DNA structure of the Y chromosome, which like a surname is passed down from father to son.

In 2000 Brian Sykes and Catherine Irven published a paper in the *American Journal of Human Genetics* on the DNA that they had extracted from a group of men with the surnames Sykes. As over 50 per cent of the samples had a similar genetic structure and all the others were not linked into clusters, the authors concluded that there was just one 'original Mr Sykes'. This conclusion had an enormous impact, but it surprised local and family historians for, although the surname is now largely concentrated in the Huddersfield district, people named Sykes were recorded in different places in early West Riding records and, as a syke was simply a 'stream or ditch, often on a boundary', the word had given rise to several minor place-names. In 1379 men named 'del Syke' or 'del Sikes' were taxed in six different townships in the West Riding and once at Butterworth (Lancashire). Historians had assumed that the surname had more than one origin. This pioneering test, however, used only four genetic markers. Since the year 2000 DNA-testing techniques have advanced rapidly and far more markers are now used. This new tool for the study of surnames, which at first seemed to provide clear-cut answers, needs evaluating. We will see that geneticists are making a major new contribution to the study of the origins and development of surnames in Britain, Ireland, the United States of America, and elsewhere but that DNA evidence is not a magic wand that will solve all problems.

COWGILL: distribution in 1881. The surname Cowgill is derived from a minor place-name in the Yorkshire Dales, near where John de Colgyll was taxed in 1379. The 754 Cowgills in the 1881 census lived nearby or in the adjacent industrial districts of Lancashire and the West Riding. A one-name study undertaken by Perry Cowgill has proved both genealogical and genetic links between American and Yorkshire members of the family. Ellen Cowgill, together with her three sons and two daughters, is named on a certificate from the Quaker Meeting at Settle (Yorkshire) that authorized the removal of a number of local families. She appears to have been the widow of Edmund Cowgill, who was buried nearby at Slaidburn in 1675, and her son John was the indentured servant of Cuthbert Hayhurst from Slaidburn. The family arrived in America with the Penn fleet in 1682 and two of the sons have present-day descendants in the USA. When nine Cowgills in the USA and three from the original district in England had DNA tests using 25 markers, two of the Englishmen were judged to match the US Cowgills with 23 markers and the other with 22.

1

By-names

Scholars who have studied surnames have placed great emphasis on the related topics of meaning and etymology and have, understandably, concentrated on names which have survived, but they have had less to say about the numerous by-names which never became hereditary. P.H. Reaney made the first systematic collection of by-names, but as many of his assumptions about their links with modern surnames have been shown to be wrong his errors have tended to overshadow the value of his research into the by-names themselves. The by-names of our medieval ancestors probably outnumbered the surnames that survive in present-day Britain. They were still in common use in the late fourteenth-century poll tax returns, though the distinction between a by-name and a hereditary surname in these records may not always be obvious to the modern reader. The return for Redenhall in Norfolk in 1379, for example, lists about eighty taxpayers, several of whom were not given a second name but were identified simply as the servant, son, or brother of another taxpayer. These people, together with those whose second names were identical with their given occupations, such as John Taillour and John Turnour, are unlikely to have had hereditary surnames at the time. On the other hand, William Thunder, senior, and William Thunder, junior, provide clear evidence of a hereditary surname and some of the dozen or so other names that occur more than once in Redenhall were probably hereditary by that date. They include Angketel, a possible source of the surname Anketell which is derived from a personal name, and 'de Mendham', which refers to a Suffolk place-name. By-names in both these categories have long been studied by scholars who specialize in place-name and personal name studies. Less work has been done on occupational names and nicknames, represented in the Redenhall list by Robert Stringere and Walter Heyr (literally the 'heir'). The origins and meanings of some other names in the list are unclear. These include Cokerose, Godknape, Buntyngflyth, and Klyngbell, interesting but puzzling local by-names which find no mention in standard works of reference. They attract our attention because they are unusual, but even apparently commonplace by-names can be of interest. Among the Redenhall taxpayers were two weavers, named as Constancius and Reginaldus Flemmyng, whose distinctive first names suggest that they had recently arrived from Flanders. The by-name Fleming occurs in other parts of Britain as early as *c.*1150, and yet evidence for the word in the *Oxford English Dictionary* goes back only as far as *c.*1430. The Nicholas and Richard Brabon who were recorded in the same list at Redenhall were probably natives of the Duchy of Brabant.

Scholars have tended to emphasize the large proportion of the population which acquired hereditary surnames in the course of the thirteenth and fourteenth centuries, but the Redenhall list is a reminder of how unstable many names continued to be as late as 1379. It has much in common with poll tax returns right across the country. The potential value of by-names as lexical items has been largely ignored by contributors to the *OED*, but as they provide many insights into the development of the English language and the acquisition of hereditary surnames they are examined in some detail here.

Occupational by-names

Abundant evidence survives to show that surnames derived from occupations were often late to stabilize and that many by-names of this kind persisted well into the mid-fifteenth century; a few were still not hereditary in the sixteenth century. Typical examples include John Clockmaker of Beverley, who was paid twelve shillings in 1436 for repairs to the clock of Holy Trinity, and William Organmaker of Ripon, who mended the organ and the bellows in 1455. These by-names, together with Waterleader (1455) and Breadseller (1463), stand out because they are distinctive occupations, but more familiar names are also found in similar contexts. For example, John and Richard Teyllar of York were paid for supplying 'v hundredth walle teylle' in 1518 and William Carver spent five days in Ripon *c.*1520 'framyng panelles et carvyng by hynde the hy alter'. We can infer that James Brigendermaker was literally a maker of briganders, that is body armour for foot soldiers, for when he took up his freedom to trade in York in 1453 his occupation was unrecorded, unlike the entries for those around him. Clearly, many such by-names were vocabulary items, not stable surnames, and in some cases they throw light on the early history of obscure words and phrases.

Crafts and trades

Detailed study of medieval evidence from Yorkshire reveals that a record of a by-name can quite often predate the evidence presented in the *OED*. For example, the earliest entry in the dictionary for the word 'sword-sliper' refers to its use in Scotland and the north of England, and a York document of 1478–79 is quoted in which a 'swerdsliper' was paid for making a sword sheath. John Swerdslyper of Ripon (1379) and William Suerdsliper of Wakefield (1313) take the history of the term back much earlier. Similar evidence exists for a few occupational terms that are not recorded in the *OED*. One example is 'comb-smith', presumably a word for the man who made the combs that were used to comb wool. He was evidently a metalworker and the occupation features in records from the fourteenth century at least. For example, John Cok of Bradfield in Norfolk was taxed as a 'coomsmyth' in 1379 and the by-name occurred in Richmond in 1395 as John Kamesmyth. The hereditary surname is recorded in Wakefield from at least the late fifteenth century, but appears to have become extinct before 1800, though it may survive as Smith, since the Combsmith family of Batley sometimes used this abbreviation.

The word 'board', which we now use in the general sense of a piece of timber, was more specifically a thin plank in the Middle Ages, one suitable for furniture or flooring. In 1379 Henry de Werldlay of Follifoot was described as a 'bordclever', a term which suggests splitting rather than sawing. Boards were referred to as 'clift burde' in 1478 and the tools that the cleavers used were probably the 'mell and wedge' of the lath-river. It is not clear whether sawing marked a step forward in the process or was simply an alternative practice, but 'sawn boards' are referred to frequently in fifteenth-century records. The by-name is found in Selby in 1441–42 when Richard Bordclever worked for 1½ days on a house in Gowthorpe and again, as late as 1497, when William Burdclever lived in York. It has been suggested that Adam Bordewright of Wakefield (1330) made 'boards' or tables, but he may have been a specialist who worked with the sawyer. The by-name or surname was recorded again in 1431 when Robert Burdwryght witnessed a grant of land in Calverley.

The earliest *OED* reference to a 'kit', a circular wooden vessel made of staves, is from 1365, but Kittewritt was the by-name of a Norland tenant in 1275. Less straightforward examples of occupational by-names include Clouter, Dishbinder, Wyndelester, and Floyter. Adam Clouter of Wakefield (1307) was probably a cobbler, for 'clouts' were leather patches, and in 1589 the cordwainers of York were ordered not to 'coble or clowte any old shoes'. However, 'clouts' could also be iron plates, attached to axletrees and the like in order to prevent wear. The will of the archdeacon of Richmond, in 1400, recorded a debt to Alan Quelewright (i.e. wheelwright) for 'iiij cloutez...pur le charet', so it is possible also that the 'clouter' was an ironworker. The occupational by-name 'dishbinder' occurred several times in Sowerby, near Halifax, in the fourteenth century, but the meaning in this case, if not the etymology, is obscure. John le Dishbinder and Richard Dissher were neighbours in 1331, and both men were doubtless involved in making dishes, but it is unclear just what part 'binding' might have played in that process. William Disshebinder was a tenant in the same township in 1339. In neighbouring Hipperholme, Thomas Wyndelester was fined 12d. for non-attendance at the manor court in 1275. This name does not appear again in the rolls, but it seems certain to have been based on 'windle', a word that had several meanings: a basket; a measure, usually of corn; or an appliance for winding yarn. The last of these terms seems the most likely one to have given rise to 'Wyndelester' and the term can perhaps be compared with 'spinster', for it has the suffix -ster that was originally associated with a feminine form of the noun.

Just occasionally, by-names can help to throw light on medieval practices that are otherwise poorly documented. In 1379, for example, two men called Henry Floyter were living at Newton in Bowland in the parish of Slaidburn. It seems possible that they were related to Roger Floyter alias Bowland of York (1415) but this spelling of the by-name has not been recorded since that date. It is tempting to link the term with the dialect word 'floyt', used in early Yorkshire documents for a dyke or watercourse. It occurs in 1482 in Rowley near Lepton, where 'le common floyt' was on a flood plain near Fenay Beck; a previous mention of 'le floytyate' in 1465 probably referred to a 'gate' or sluice that controlled the flow of water onto the land. This word was later confused with 'floodgate', and it gave rise to a local place-name; a Lepton farm called Floyd Green now occupies the site of the 'Flowtegren' in 1596. The Lancashire historian Mary Higham described the flood plain in Newton in Bowland as a site where flax was processed on a large scale in the Middle Ages and she was able to identify not just the former water courses but also the site where a sluice would have allowed water from the river Hodder to flow on to the land. It seems a distinct possibility, therefore, that the system in Newton was controlled by the 'floyters'. Elsewhere, floating was associated with encouraging the early growth of grass in water meadows. The rare surname Floater, with a total of just twelve in 1881, all of whom lived in Holderness, may have a quite separate origin, though the name has the same meaning.

Animal husbandry

Farmworkers also acquired by-names whose meanings are now difficult to determine. To 'lib' an animal was to castrate it, and the verb occurs as early as 1395, when the disbursements for Whitby Abbey included a payment '*pro libbyng porcorum*', that is for libbing swine. The occupational by-name is on record from 1339 when Elias, the son of Robert Swynlibber was fined 40d. in Sandal, near Wakefield. Thomas, another son of the same Robert, was referred to in the same rolls as either Swynlibber or Grislibber; as 'grice' refers to young pigs the two terms are identical in meaning. 'Geld' meant the same as 'lib' but was used more frequently and was found in the by-name and hereditary surname Geldhird. Robert Geldegrise of Scotton and Hugh Geldehogg of Malton were both recorded in 1301; in many parts of northern England 'hogg' was the usual word for castrated male swine. References to the occupation of 'sowgelder' occur as late as the eighteenth century.

Some of the terms for the numerous specialist herdsmen who are mentioned in medieval rolls are not listed in the *OED*. For example, William Quihird of Bainbridge (1301) and William le Quyhird of Sowerby, near Thirsk (1327) were herdsmen who were responsible for the heifers. The prefix in this word has a Scandinavian origin and it was in use from the fourteenth century right across the counties of the North, the north Midlands, and Scotland. A frequent York-shire alternative to 'quy' was 'why', as in 1486 when the vicar of Felixkirk left 'a whye of ij yere age' to his servant James, 'a whye of the same age' to Mergery Halidaye, and 'ij whyes that is at Boltbe with calfe' to villagers called John Thomson and William Richardson. References to a 'whye styrke' (1485) and a 'quye stirke' (1553) are slightly confusing since the word 'stirk' was also used of a heifer. In Yorkshire, though, it seems to have been applied to young animals of either sex so the compound term merely put the emphasis on the animal's age. The use of 'stirkherd' as a by-name was recorded in the fourteenth century, for example Adam le Styrkehyrd of Goathland (1301) and John Styrkhyrd of Long Preston (1379). The name became hereditary and can be found in parts of Yorkshire as late as 1598. It may survive as the surname Strickett, a spelling recorded from 1576, although this word was also used as a diminutive of 'stirk'.

Nowtherd is listed in the *OED*, but the by-name Elias Nouthirde of Skeeby, near Richmond (1301) provides an earlier example of its use. 'Nout' derives from a Scandinavian word for cattle, the equivalent of the English 'neat', and it is at the heart of a rich local vocabulary: 1426 le Nawtmerkette; 1442 twynter-nawt, stirkenawte; 1502 the nowte . . . fayre; 1538 nawtte herre (i.e. hair); 1557 two naut gayth (sic for gaytes); 1610 nawtehouse; 1642 noutheard wages and sesses and layes. It also gave rise to the by-name Noutfot in Richmond (1301). In most of these the meaning is absolutely clear but 'naut gaytes' requires some explanation. These 'gates' were not ways for cattle but the rights a tenant had in a stinted pasture.

The term 'twynternawt', quoted above, is just one example of a vocabulary that can be traced back to the fourteenth century at least. In 1362, for example, five bullocks that belonged to a Mitton farmer were called 'tuynters': the animals in question were 'two winters old', just as 'thrinters' or 'trinters' were three winters old. Most examples of these words are found in north-country or Scottish sources and yet L'Estrange Ewen found the by-name Twowynterold in Essex even earlier, in 1327. Both twinter and thrinter were used attributively, and early examples include 'threnter stotts' (1466) and 'twenter neytte' (1545). It seems that a term meaning 'of three winters' was in use in Old English, but the lack of examples over the following 500 years led the editors of the *OED* to suggest that it may have been formed anew in the sixteenth century. The records of Fountains Abbey contain references to 'trynters' in the 1440s, and these, in conjunction with the uses of 'twinter' already quoted, point more to its continuous use.

A rare survival is the Scottish surname Phimister, found principally in Caithness and Moray as a variant of the less common Femister or Feemister; together they throw light on another aspect of animal husbandry. In George F. Black, *The Surnames of Scotland* these names are traced back to Alexander Feemaister (1458), who owed his name to the occupational term 'fee-master', the title of the man responsible for herds of cattle or flocks of sheep. Significantly, Black noted that Melrose Abbey had a 'fee-master', and he quoted a Scottish source of 1553 which makes explicit the connection with livestock. The *OED* has examples of 'fee' as a word for cattle or livestock, and 'fee-house' meaning a cattle-shed, but no reference to 'fee-master'. The words that are in the dictionary have an Old English origin but they are not seen as having any connection with 'feeman' and 'feemanship', which are entered separately and said to derive from 'fee' in the feudal sense. The term 'feeman' is thought to mean 'vassal'. A series of Fountains Abbey documents throws new light on all these words and on the Scottish surname. A lease of 1508 required one tenant to deliver 'all the styrkis . . . yerely to the feamayster', an abbey officer who was responsible for the 'feemen' on the individual granges and farms. They were all subject to customary practices which are expressed in a range of leases by such words as feemanly, feemanlike, and 'femasterscepe' (1537). There is no doubt that the term feemaster has a much longer history, for it would translate the earlier Latin phrase '*magister averiorum*'.

Quarrying

The word 'quarry', in the sense of a place where stone is mined and cut, is on record from *c.*1420, and the occupation of 'quarrier' from *c.*1375. The occupational by-name, on the other hand, is found in several counties from the thirteenth century; Reaney noted it in Worcestershire in 1275 and it occurs also in the Wharfedale village of Embsay from 1297. The name was given to the man in charge of a quarry, and it is unlikely to have had the same meaning as the more modern term 'quarryman'. This seems to be implicit in the fabric rolls for York Minster, where the expenses for stone brought from the specialist quarries in Tadcaster detailed payments in 1400 to the '*Custus*

Quarerarum', Henry Quareour. Occupational by-names could remain un-stable for centuries, and Black notes that John Querreour was quarrier to the bishop of Dunkeld as late as 1507–12. Like Feemaster, it draws attention to the role of the great religious institutions in this area of naming.

Clear evidence of heredity is provided in the case of the Embsay family, mentioned earlier, who were connected with Bolton Priory until the Dissol-ution. Ralph le Quarreur was recorded on various occasions between 1297 and 1311, and entries include money paid to him in 1309–10 *'pro fractione lapid[um] apud Bolton'*. The same by-name was recorded in Embsay at regular intervals until at least the 1540s, with Richard Querrier identified as a Priory tenant in 1539. Different spellings of his surname around that time include 'Wharrear' and 'Warrear', both occurring in tax rolls for Embsay. Reaney thought that similar examples derived from the word for 'warrior', but in northern England they are characteristic variants of Quarrier.

Some of these early by-names are transparent in meaning, whereas others cannot yet be explained. Among those which have an obvious meaning is 'Bakstoneman', found in the poll tax returns for Lonsdale in 1379 and Saddle-worth in 1377. The two Saddleworth men who had the by-name were obvi-ously quarrying bakestones, the large flat stones on which oatcakes were baked. The Saddleworth writer, Ammon Wrigley, referred to these quarries as 'Backstone Pytts', a term that he found in a lease dated 1553. The *OED* has references to bakestones from 1531, but the by-names in the poll tax returns take the word back to the fourteenth century, and minor place-names to well before that: an undated thirteenth-century deed for Burton Constable men-tions a place named 'Bacstanegraues', surely a site where the stones were 'graved' or dug out. Similar names were recorded at Barforth-in-Teesdale in 1301 and at Thorner in 1438.

Wood management

In the case of the by-name Richard Wandehagger, recorded in the Holderness parish of Wawne in 1297, there can be little doubt that the occupation referred to a specialist woodman. 'Wands' were the pliant young shoots of trees such as the willow or hazel, which were employed in a wide variety of ways by medieval craftsmen and farmers. They were used in hurdles, as the term 'flekewandes' indicates (1364), and their pliancy is clear from terms such as 'wynding, watlyng and writhing wands' (1617). In Ripon, in 1399, the fabric accounts for the minster record the expenditure of 21s. for 'lxvj wandschothis' (that is wand shoots), whilst similar accounts for Beverley in 1446 note the payment of 11d. for 500 wands used for binding the thatched roof of a barn. A 'wand-bushell' in 1490 was presumably a wickerwork basket, and frequent later references include items such as 'wanded' bottles, chairs, skeps, creels and arks. In 1600 the Settrington farmers employed 'small writhing wandes for tying up ther cattell and making harrow wythes'.

The more frequent by-name 'hagger' referred to the man whose task it was to care for the 'haggs' or coppice woods. Both words were used in the court rolls of Wakefield manor as early as 1315, when tenants were fined for 'escapes in the Hagge' and Robert the Hagger lived in Stanley. 'Hagg' may already have had the meaning that is explicit in later woodland documents. In a survey of 1540, for example, Hampole Wood was said to contain 'eighteen coppices called haggs' which were to be felled in succession over a period of eighteen years, a coppice cycle that was usual in South Yorkshire. In 1524 a Fountains Abbey lease permitted the tenants to 'make a copye and hagge' of their woods. Such woods had to be protected. It was not an uncommon offence for tenants to carry off loads 'of wood called wandes' (1598) or sell 'wands unlawfully taken from the woods' (1558), so a careful landlord might grant privileges to a trusted tenant who was then responsible for 'the fostership' of the hagg (1524). The Great Ouseburn place-name 'Wandhagg' indicates that certain haggs were specifically set aside to provide wands and the by-name of Richard Wande-hagger of Wawne takes that practice back into the late thirteenth century.

The word 'snag' is now generally used of an impediment or obstacle, but its earliest history is obscure. It is probably of Scandinavian origin but no references have been noted earlier than the late sixteenth century. The modern meaning of 'snag' dates only from the nineteenth century and it masks the word's earliest associations with wood management, although the semantic history seems clear enough. In the nineteenth century, chiefly in America, it was the word used for a tree imbedded in the bottom of a lake or river, with one end or one large branch directed upwards, forming a hazard to passing boats. It has been said that paddle-steamers had their wheels in the stern to avoid coming into contact with 'snaggs' (1822). Previously, the word 'snag' was used to describe the short stumps that projected from the trunk of a tree after the branches had been lopped as part of the felling or pruning process. This meaning is implicit in a Brandsby document of 1608 that mentions 'stubbes and snagges' of wood. A by-name, however, takes the history of the word back to 1339, when William Snaghasel was a tenant in Sowerby, near Halifax. If the name can be interpreted literally, he is likely to have been the woodman whose task it was to cut off the hazel wands that were employed by local craftsmen.

In Old English *impa* had to do with the young shoots of plants and then of grafted shoots, and it clearly retained those meanings in the post-Conquest period, when it occurred in both by-names and place-names. The oldest place-name seems to be 'Impecrofte', mentioned in an undated Nottinghamshire document of the twelfth century, and a similar place-name gave rise to a by-name in the fourteenth century, for in the poll tax returns of 1379 John Impcroft was taxed as a resident of Salford (Lancashire). It seems reasonable to infer that imp crofts were enclosures where young trees were nurtured, a kind of specialist market garden or plantation. In 1414, for example, a Methley man called John Cook was indicted at the manor court for stealing saplings from the imp yards that belonged to the lord of the manor, and the clerk helpfully added the words 'to wit young oaks'. The only reference to an impyard in the *OED* is to one in Durham in 1337–38, but in other northern counties references to an alternative term with the same meaning include 'Ympegard' (*c.*1250) in Cumberland, and 'Impegarde' in Follifoot near Harrogate (1259). We do not know how old the practice was, nor when the term imp croft began to fall into disuse, but it was apparently in decline by the sixteenth century, when fields named Imp Croft and Imp Yard were typically being used for crops or for livestock, but certainly not for young trees. Their changing role is reflected in the field name 'Cowe close otherwise Ympyarde', listed in the Dissolution survey for Hampole Priory in *c.*1540. Chaucer demonstrated how the figurative use of the term paved the way for later meanings when he wrote, 'Of feeble trees ther comen wrecched impes', emphasizing that not all chips off the old block inherit good qualities.

Ironworking

Industrial archaeologists take special note of the minor place-name 'Cinder Hills', since it refers to the heaps of slag that accumulated in metalworking, and which can therefore indicate the site of an early forge or bloomery. It is actually a very common minor place-name in counties such as Cheshire and Yorkshire, and the earliest examples date from the thirteenth century. In Handsworth, near Sheffield, the place-name is recorded as 'Sindirhil' in a charter of 1200–18 and it gave rise to a surname that survived into the mid-fifteenth century at least. Among the first men to be so called were Richard de Scynderhill, taxed in Handsworth in 1297, and John de Synderhill who witnessed a Handsworth deed in 1396. Thomas Syndrell was a tenant on the manor of Sheffield in 1441, after which the name appears to have become extinct. The particular interest in this case is that 'cinder hill' is not mentioned at all in the *OED*, although the name evidence suggests that it was a word in fairly frequent use, and one or two examples have been noted in documentary material. For instance, in a manorial survey of Almondbury, in 1584, a freeholder called Nicholas Fenay was said to hold 'a parcel of waste at Fenay Bridg end, being a synder hill', whilst in 1750 the Almondbury overseer of the highways went to John Brooksbank's 'about bying a part of Sinderhill' to be used in road mending;

this second example suggests that the word was already on its way to becoming a place-name. In all these early references the first element is 'sinder' not 'cinder' and that may seem strange, but 'sinder' is a word of Old English origin and has no connection etymologically with the French word *cendre*, meaning ashes. Almost inevitably, though, the close connection in both spelling and meaning ensured that the two were linked in the popular perception. When the antiquarian Ralph Thoresby wrote in his diary in 1703 that he had 'seen great heaps of slag or cinders overgrown with moss ... now often dug into for mending the highways' he clearly saw a link between the two words and that influenced his spelling. Incidentally, he confirmed why so few cinder hills have survived, despite the frequency of the place-name.

In those parts of the North where the surname Stringer is most numerous the by-name is on record from the thirteenth century. Thomas, called le Strenger, who is mentioned in an undated document from that period, was living in Bramley, near Leeds, and John Strynger of Thornhill near Dewsbury was taxed as a nail-maker in 1379. These were iron-working areas at that time, so it seems that these men operated a 'string hearth'. This interpretation also throws light on the name Stringfellow, for iron forge accounts of 1547 refer explicitly to the responsibility that the 'stringefelloe' had for 'breakeinge and feyinge of synders and breakeing of the blowme'; the 'bloom' was the lump of wrought iron produced at the forge, before it was drawn out into bars. The *OED* notes the use of this word in Old English, but has no other examples until the end of the sixteenth century, and no record at all of the occupational term 'bloomer'. Nevertheless, the occupational by-name Bloomer is on record from the thirteenth century. Reaney has references from 1202 in ironworking parts of Derbyshire and Staffordshire and Adam le Blomer of Dewsbury was fined for illegally cutting wood in 1285. Bloomer certainly became a hereditary surname and was noted by Edgar Tooth in a Betley document of 1298. It seems likely to have stabilized in that part of England, for Staffordshire was the main 'home' of the surname in 1881.

Occupational nicknames

One further aspect of by-names that has received little attention is the direct link between occupations and nicknames. P.H. Reaney discussed surnames such as Garlick, where the name of the article made, or the commodity dealt in, was used for the maker or dealer, via the process that is called metonymy. Evidence for such interpretations is not easy to locate but occasionally the context clearly supports the inference. For example, Reaney's explanation of Plant as a by-name for a gardener received little support from John Plant in his recent article on the surname and yet 'William Plant, gardiner' was a Hull taxpayer in 1379. The modern spellings of the Lancashire surnames Masheder and Mashiter probably conceal a connection with brewing. The earliest known example of the name is John Masshrother of Lonsdale (1379), which seems to derive from the 'mashrother', an implement used to stir up the malt in the mash tub. The *OED* has references to this word from the mid-fifteenth century.

A number of similar examples were quoted in volume 1 of the *English Surnames Series*, although in these cases the association was rather more specific; that is John Pike, fishmonger (1378) and Richard Pepercorne, spicer (1379). It was only a short step from names coined in that way to nicknames based on the occupation, for example William Sharpe, sawer (1444), and Hugh Skarf, *piscator* (1305): 'skarf' derived from the Scandinavian word for the cormorant. In 1332, John Ferrer was the Snaith blacksmith, whereas his son Henry was named in deeds as Henry Dynthard; that is 'strike hard'. In both Sharp and Dynthard there is already a hint of the humour that can occasionally be more explicit in the bestowing of nicknames. In this category are Henry Scrapetrough, miller (1293), William Whitebrow, plasterer (1333), John Nevergelt, goldsmith (1431), Henry Gourdskyn, a seller of wine (1445), and William Hetblak, baker (1460).

Although very few names of this type became hereditary, the practice may throw new light on some established surnames that have disputed etymologies. The nickname Drinkall was said by Reaney to derive from 'drinc hail', a customary reply to a pledge in drinking, with the meaning of good luck or good health. He maintained that 'as ale was the usual drink, there was no point in a nickname drink ale'. In general it seems unwise to reject an apparently straightforward interpretation on those grounds alone and the literal meaning in this case is supported by an example in the Bradford court rolls. In 1362 William Drynkale was the elected ale-taster, a manorial office like that of the leather searcher or pinder. The frequency of the by-name over a wide area may indicate that 'drink ale' became something of a traditional nickname, parallelled by 'good ale'. In 1332, for example, Robert Godale was elected as the ale-taster for Horbury. Scattered examples of the by-name 'Sourale' seem likely to be derogatory nicknames for people with that office.

Nicknames derived from by-names, derogatory or not, are frequent in early sources and have proved irresistible to some writers. L'Estrange Ewen, criticized for his etymologies, nevertheless drew our attention to a range of fascinating examples. In Gloucestershire he found Richard Boltupright in 1335, an early use of this term and one that is quite difficult to interpret as a nickname. 'Upright' had two apparently contrasting meanings, either 'erect on the feet' or 'flat on the back', both in use in the fourteenth century. In 1275 Ralph Uprit was a tenant of Crigglestone, near Wakefield. The compound 'bolt upright' was used at least twice by Chaucer with reference to love-making. In the Reeve's Tale are the lines: 'As I have thryes, in this shorte night swyved the milleres doghter bolt-upright'. The inference here is clearly that the girl was on her back and if the term was customarily used in such contexts it may tell us what lay behind the by-name.

Another example quoted by L'Estrange Ewen is Thomas de Lodelowe *dictus* Whirlinthecole (1351), the name of a Norfolk man and more obviously a nickname. The word 'whirlecole', later 'whirlicote', apparently referred to a coach or carriage, although the precise meaning of the suffix is unknown. 'Whirl' can probably be taken at face value, bearing comparison perhaps with 'spin' in the phrase 'going for a spin'. Robert Whirle was one of the carters who served Bolton Priory in the period 1296–1308. L'Estrange Ewen noted a similarly complex 'phrase name' in the same Norfolk source: Henry Bonde son of Nicholas Bonde *dictus* Trilontheberye (1351). The *OED* references to this phrase are from much later, starting in 1519: 'Make rome, syrs, and let us be mery, with huffa galand singe tyrll on the bery'. The meaning of the by-name remains obscure but it seems to refer to merry-making and it provides evidence for the use of the expression from a much earlier period.

By-names of this kind are sometimes found in the work of writers whose contribution to surname etymology has been unmercifully criticized, but that does not invalidate the examples they identified in early sources. It is perhaps time to look again at the by-names collected by writers such as Weekley and L'Estrange Ewen and to add names that are recorded in more recently published source material. Numerous volumes of the court rolls of the manor of Wakefield have been published over the years, more than a dozen of them quite recently, and among the colourful examples from 1331–33 are the following: Thomas Bochcollock, Matilda Bullyfrogge, Robert Cokespur, Henry Comberkichyn, John Fyndyrne, Robert Ilhore, John Lekeblade, Robert Oldeschreu, John Pike-scull, Michael Sekilwethir, Robert Soutermogh, John Swetliglade, Roger Taun-teliry, William Twentipayr, William Whiteserk, and Richard Wythehoundes.

In these same volumes the domestic cock appears to have been responsible for numerous compound by-names and the evidence for these is generally much earlier than the examples in the *OED*. The names of several tenants from the Wakefield area illustrate the point, for they include German Cok-spore (1284) and Henry Cockeshank (1323), the latter possibly derogatory. 'Cockspur' became hereditary in Stanley and Robert Cokspour was taxed there in 1379, but the name may have become extinct soon afterwards, for no later references have been noted. The *OED* has no entry for 'cockshank' and the first reference to 'cockspur' as a vocabulary item is from 1591. A third tenant was Thomas, the son of Christiana Skot, called Cockehakel, a common thief, apparently an isolated example of the by-name. It may have originated in Lancashire, for Christiana was from Extwistle, near Burnley. The 'hackles' of the cockerel were the long, shining feathers on its neck, which were erected when the bird was angry. The *OED* evidence goes back no further than *c*.1450.

It can be shown that some by-names of this kind occurred in numerous localities and were given to individuals who were probably unrelated. Such expressions were in widespread and everyday use. Inevitably, not least because they were sometimes uncomplimentary, few of them became hereditary and even fewer have survived. Nevertheless, it is possible to trace the history of a small number of them and in the process raise questions about some of the previous etymologies that have been suggested.

Hurlbat

The *OED* evidence for this word emphasizes its obscurity, whilst making it clear that a 'hurlbat' was some kind of club, used either as a weapon or in a game. The earliest reference to the term is from *c*.1440: 'Pleying at þe two hande swerd, at swerd & bokelere, & at two pyked staf, at þe hurlebatte'. Reaney noted examples of the by-name in Essex (1327) and Hampshire (1333) and it recurred in both those counties in the poll tax returns of 1377–81. It was also found in Berkshire in 1381, where Thomas Hurlebat was taxed at Marsh Benham. The surname was rare in England by 1881, confined to a few small groups and with different spellings. Hurlbatt (16) was closest to the original word and occurred mostly in Surrey, whereas the most numerous was Hurlbutt (31) dispersed in places far apart such as Leicester (10), Chester (9), and Barton-upon-Irwell (5). Other uncommon variants were Hurlbut (13), found in Leicester, and Harlbutt (5) in Tynemouth. The surname is also found in the USA, taken there as early as 1635. Its variants there and in Leicester include Hurlburt and Hurlbert, suggesting that it was linked in both countries with names such as Hubert and Albert.

Go fair

The *OED* has no headword for this phrase, but it seems certain to have been widely used in England in earlier centuries, possibly as an alternative to 'fare well', with the wish that a departing friend's journey should be 'fair' or trouble-free. Just what the by-name meant is unclear but among the earliest examples are Robert Gafayre of Leathley, Yorkshire (1290–93) and Jul' Gofayr of Childrey, Berkshire (1381). These can perhaps be compared with the name of John Rydefare, a York brewer (1401). In Yorkshire, the hereditary surname was found in the fifteenth and sixteenth centuries in townships in the neighbourhood of Selby and Howden, for example Robert Gafare of Wistow

(1469), who was possibly a descendant of James Gafare, a servant of Thomas Saltmersh, esquire, in the poll tax return of 1379. Documents for Howden, especially title deeds and parish registers, reveal how the surname was eventually transformed, apparently under the influence of the name Garforth, established in the parish from the 1580s. The first 'Goforths' were recorded soon afterwards and in the hearth tax returns of 1672 this was the only form of either surname listed in Howden. The confusion is no doubt explained in part by the tendency of dialect speakers not to pronounce final 'th' but it may also be that the adverb 'far-forth' (meaning further ahead, in time or space) was an influence. In the USA the name is sometimes said to be an English version of a German surname but the 'progenitor' was William Goforth, a Quaker who sailed from Hull in 1677.

Derne love

The now obsolete 'dern', meaning 'hidden' or 'secret' lay behind this expression which is recorded several times in the *OED* from *c.*1300. It probably referred to an illicit or deceitful relationship, and Chaucer appears to have used it in that way in the Miller's Tale, saying of the clerk, 'of derne love he cowed and of solas'. The by-name may therefore have been customarily used of philanderers, similar in origin to Blandamore. The numerous early examples of the by-name range from Hugh Dernelove in Oxford (1279) to John Dernelof who was taxed at Upholland in Lancashire in 1381. The earliest names on record, though, are William Derneluue (1206) and Thomas Dernelof (1275), both Yorkshire examples: Thomas was a juror at Wakefield manor court and may have passed the name on to Robert Dernelove who was a tenant of the same manor in 1296. However, it was in the Knaresborough area that the change to Dearlove took place, removing any derogatory allusions the name may have had. The priest Robert Derelove, whose will dates from 1534, was probably the Robert Dernluff, chaplain, who surrendered land in Birstwith in 1506. The loss of the 'n' later allowed some writers to take the surname at face value, and interpret it more favourably. Weekley, lacking the benefit of the early spellings, linked it with Sweetlove. The distribution of Dearlove in 1881 reflects its early history, with the most significant totals in two districts, one in Berkshire and Oxford, the other in West Yorkshire. It was particularly well established in Wallingford and the area around Knaresborough.

Kigelpening

By-names provide the only evidence of this compound noun, whose meaning remains a mystery. Several examples of the name have been found in the fourteenth century in both Yorkshire and Nottinghamshire: Robert Kygulpeni, for example, was taxed in West Leake in 1327 and Robert Kygelpeny in New Malton in 1301. Almost a century earlier, in 1218, William Kigelpening of Leeds was involved in a court case that had to do with a robbery and breach of the peace. Peter McClure has speculated that the first element may be a Scandinavianized pronunciation of the word 'cudgel' and that it may have also denoted a skittle, as does the cognate German word 'kugel'. If that were the case 'kigelpening' may have been the name of a game in which pennies were used as projectiles or a pile of pennies formed the skittle.

Just when and where the name became hereditary is not yet known but it seems certain to be linked with Kicklepenny which is on record in and around the Yorkshire parish of Snaith from the fifteenth century. Typical examples are Robert Kykylpeny (1495), Robert Kicklepenie (1575), and Elizabeth Kickle-penny (1640). This was a rare surname and probably meaningless to those who heard it, even people in the local community, and it seems to have led to the variant Kittlepenny, noted in the Hull hearth tax return of 1672. 'Kittle' is the word in north-country dialects for 'tickle' and a further change saw Ticklepenny established as a Hull surname. Linguistically, this is an example of metathesis but the change also made the name more intelligible, the sort of re-motivation that we loosely refer to as popular etymology.

Although one or two authors have attempted to explain the origin of Ticklepenny, it remains an unusual surname and is not mentioned in the most recent dictionaries. Lower suggested that it derives from a locality in Lincolnshire, possibly linking it with Ticklepenny's Lock on the Louth canal, but this was presumably named after the lock keeper. Ernest Weekley was scornful of Lower's theory but did not suggest an alternative, simply comparing it with the German surname Küstenpfennig. In 1881 over fifty Ticklepennys and Tickelpennys were still living in Hull and parts of Lincolnshire, but the name is missing from the current Hull telephone directory and may be even rarer now. However, a recent article in the *Hull Daily Mail* brought confirmation that it has survived and that it still has associations with East Yorkshire and north Lincolnshire.

By-names and place-names

A very large number of by-names and surnames derive from place-names, and scholars have long been aware of that in their search for the earliest place-name evidence. The value of such names is most obvious in the post-Conquest period, when numerous new settlements were established and great swathes of land were cleared. There are literally hundreds of minor localities where the history of the by-name and the place-name are intimately interwoven, sometimes from as early as the twelfth century. Usually, the identification poses few problems and in many cases the surname can be seen to derive from a settlement of the same name. Butterworth and Hardcastle are typical examples, the former in Rochdale, the latter in Nidderdale. Occasionally, though, the spelling is different and it is difficult to be sure of the identification. The settlement from which the surname is derived may have disappeared: the Lancashire place-name Sharples, described by Ekwall as a long, narrow strip of land in the parish of Bolton-le-Moors, gave rise to by-names as early as 1250 and was a well-established surname by 1379, but there is no village or hamlet called Sharples, and the name was not even listed by Mills in his dictionary of Lancashire place-names. In other cases, the by-name appears to be the only record of a place that can no longer be traced on the map or located on the ground. Typical examples are Hemingway (Yorkshire), Lomax (Lancashire), and Sidebottom (Cheshire?) but scores of similar names from the Pennines could be quoted. The identification of these sites is a problem, and it is best dealt with by local historians.

Elsewhere, however, by-names have been used to throw new light on the antiquity of hamlets and farms that were once thought to date from the sixteenth century or even later. Examples in Holmfirth (Yorkshire) have demonstrated the connection between the descendants of Herbert of Butterley (1275–1349) and the hamlet of Ebson House in Fulstone. The key by-name is that of Richard, son of Hebbe, who is mentioned several times in the court rolls from 1307; that is over 260 years before the earliest mention of the farm in other sources. Smith mistakenly linked the place-name with George and William Hobson (1551), surmising that the spelling was incorrect. However, the two men lived in Stanley near Wakefield, a village fifteen miles to the north-east, and had no connection with Fulstone. A second example is the Shelley farm named Ozzings which has been successfully linked with a family bearing the surname Osan, overturning the suggestion that it meant Ox Ings. The progenitor of the family was almost certainly John, the son of Osanna, a lady who was referred to in a grant by Henry de Shelley in *c.*1250. The personal name derives from the word Hosanna and was probably given to a girl born on Palm Sunday. The accuracy of the dating in these two cases owes a great deal to the fact that both by-names, Osan and Ebson, were extinct by the mid-fourteenth century.

Two further examples can be quoted where the by-name itself is of interest. In the 1290s a tenant of Wakefield manor called Robert Chobard was living in or near Wakefield. His rare by-name has not been explained but he seems likely to be the same man as the Robert Chobard who acquired land in Holmfirth in 1313, if not his son. A new corn mill was being established in this upland part of Wakefield manor at that time and this coincided with extensive clearance, so perhaps Robert had moved there to take advantage of the situation. In 1316 Robert Chopard or Chobard of Holmfirth was guilty of several minor offences but was also named as the purchaser of eight acres of land in Wooldale, a hamlet division of Holmfirth. The by-name is not recorded after 1333 but it seems certain that the hamlet of Choppards in Wooldale owes its name to this family. Smith noted the place-name from 1647, but offered no comment on its meaning. The Wooldale evidence points to a much earlier date for the hamlet and opens up the debate about its meaning, via the by-name. A single mention in the same rolls of a man called Robert Chop may refer to the Wooldale tenant, given an abbreviated form of the name. If the two are identical it would clearly link 'chop' with one of the many meanings of that word, used pejoratively.

A contemporary of Robert Chopard in Wooldale was William Totty who paid 18d. in 1314 for 'a toft and nine acres', undertaking to keep the buildings in good repair. Totty was not a Holmfirth name, but as it occurred elsewhere in West Yorkshire it is likely that William had moved to Holmfirth for the same reasons as Robert. Almost certainly the hamlet called Totties commemorates his by-name, for he died in 1331 without heirs, and there is no later mention of the name in Holmfirth records. In all these cases, therefore, the unusual by-names and their short history in the district make it possible to date the settlements precisely. These are examples only, but the sum of evidence presents an accurate picture of a moorland landscape settled in the early fourteenth century.

By-names and personal names

Many of the by-names found in post-Conquest documents are simply personal names and not at all difficult to identify. Typical examples in a court roll of 1275 are John Issabell, German Philip, and Alexander Lucas, all immediately recognizable as names that are still in use. On the other hand, other personal names pose real problems for the researcher, either because they were survivors of naming practices that were no longer in common use or because they were part of a new tradition.

A relatively small number of north-country surnames can be traced directly to Old English or Old Scandinavian personal names, for these were falling out of use by the early thirteenth century. Typically, the most popular male names in a fourteenth-century tax list, drawn up when many surnames were becoming hereditary, were John, William, Thomas, Richard, Robert, and Henry; the women had names such as Alice, Agnes, Joan, Matilda, Isabel, and Margaret. All these, together with the less common personal names, had short or 'pet' forms and diminutives. Robert, for example, was abbreviated to 'Rob' and a common diminutive was Robin; Agnes was Annes or Annot. This is a well-known aspect of personal name study and a great deal has been written on the subject. The most authoritative articles are those written by Peter McClure, who rightly criticized the inadequate methodology found in many standard dictionaries of surnames. He proposed his own remedies: if a by-name or surname is said to derive from a personal name it is advisable to have examples that can be explained linguistically and to know that the personal name was actually in use at the time. Even then, the most important evidence is that which identifies variant forms of the first name all used of one person: these are actual or implied aliases, what McClure called 'prosoponymical' variants. It is a method that has produced new and more convincing ety-mologies for numerous by-names and surnames, including Malin and Mal-linson, Abb and Abson, Dawkes, Dakin and Dawson, Paw and Pawson. Nevertheless, there is still much to discover about the process, and about the pet forms which gave rise to by-names and surnames.

The circumstances in which Higson developed suggest that the customary explanation of its meaning might have to be abandoned. It is usually said that 'Higg' is a voiced form of 'Hick', a pet form of Richard, and that may be plausible enough as a theory. On the other hand, the distribution of the surname points to a localized origin in Lancashire, and it is there that import-ant evidence helps to identify the personal name. In 1881 no fewer than 82 per cent of the Higsons were still living in the county; the only other significant numbers were in neighbouring Cheshire and the West Riding of Yorkshire. The poll tax returns for Lancashire contain several scattered examples of the by-name in the period 1379–81 but the one that points to an alternative explan-ation for 'Higg' is recorded in Manchester in 1381. This list differs from most in that the name of the taxed individual was quite frequently repeated, with a slightly different spelling, for instance Thomas Graunt 2s. od., Thomas Grant, Alicia *ux' eius*; Henricus de Bethirton 2s. od., Henricus de Bethurton, Matilda *ux' eius*; and Johannes Higgson 2s. od., Johannes *filius Hugonis*, Alicia *ux' eius*. This last example is effectively an alias which indicates that 'Higson' meant 'son of Hugh'. As a piece of evidence it clearly has implications for a number of other surnames, such as Higgs, Higgins, and Higginson.

* * *

The large collections of by-names that appear in thirteenth- and fourteenth-century records have not yet been studied systematically for the light that they shed on the meaning and etymology of hereditary surnames. This rich body of material clearly provides guidelines for the study of naming practices in the long period when surnames became stable, and indeed for an understanding of the development of the English language. An awareness of how by-names were acquired and how they were used to distinguish one person from another is essential to an appreciation of the many and varied ways in which families eventually bequeathed a surname to their descendants.

ASHBURNER: distribution in 1881. Occupational surnames are amongst the most common in England, yet others are very rare and are largely confined to particular districts, thus raising the possibility that they are of single-family origin. Burning ashes to make potash was a fairly common practice but perhaps less commonly an occupation. That might explain why we have evidence for only one hereditary surname. The 422 Ashburners recorded in the 1881 census were found mostly in the neighbouring districts of Ulverston (143) and Barrow-in-Furness (46), which at that time were within the county of Lancashire. Three Lancashire men–two Adam Askbrenners and a Thomas Askbrenner–paid poll tax in north Lancashire in 1379. The surname is the only evidence for the term 'ash-burner'.

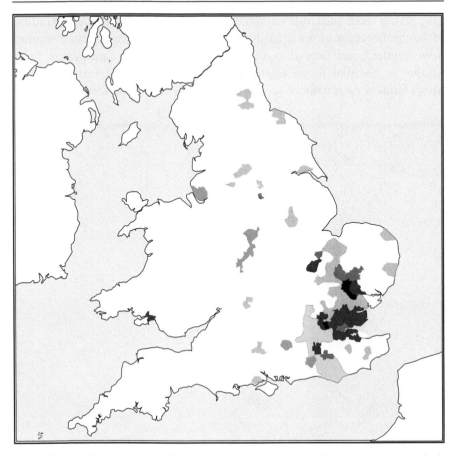

ARGENT: distribution in 1881. The census returns of 1881 recorded 1,418 Argents, including 434 in Essex, 143 in Suffolk, and 530 in or close to London. The registration district with the largest number was Halstead (102), about twenty miles to the west of Stutton. A Suffolk lay subsidy roll of 1327 names a John Argent in Stutton, on the northern bank of the River Stour, close to the boundary with Essex. This appears to be a nickname from the French 'argent', meaning silver, but we can only speculate about its meaning since the earliest examples of this word in the *OED* date from 1485.

2

Hereditary Surnames

Acquiring surnames

The term by-name is employed for those second names in earlier centuries that were not passed on from father to son. Such names have been shown to have value as lexical items but they are to be considered now as the sources which throw light on how and when surnames were inherited. Only when a person's second name can be shown to have been borne by later generations can we call it a surname and draw the distinction. In practice, though, it is very difficult to say exactly when and where any name was inherited, for the sources that throw light on names before 1350 are usually not detailed enough. The date 1350 is not a random choice for it marks the climax of the devastating plague known as the Black Death and is a watershed in the development of surnames as it is in other aspects of social history.

Some English counties have at least one taxation return in print for the period 1290–1334, known as a lay subsidy, but these are really lists of only the better-off inhabitants and they have limited genealogical value. Like many other documents of that period they seldom provide details about people at a lower social level, and that information has to be sought elsewhere. Without the help of additional documentation, such as contemporary manor court rolls, we cannot know whether the name of an individual taxpayer would be passed on to his descendants, nor whether it had already been inherited from a previous generation.

The lay subsidy for Ipswich in 1327 will illustrate those points. In it are numerous men with occupational names such as le Webbere, le Boteler, and le Barbour. Without more information we cannot know whether they were surnames: they have the appearance of by-names given to men who were practising those trades. In the same roll were Robert le Cuteler and Thomas le Coteler but again that information is not enough on its own to tell us whether the men were related. They may simply have followed the same occupation. Similarly, we can only speculate whether Richard and William le Smyth had a family connection and why two other smiths had their name recorded in Latin as Faber. It is even difficult to be sure that John, Peter, and Robert le Jay were related, although that seems likely. The place-name origins of de Burgh, de Hoo, and de Tunstall are clear but there is nothing in the roll to tell us whether they were, or became, hereditary surnames. The names Geldeneye and Gostalk were more obviously by-names and it is unlikely that either survived.

Other types of record confirm how unstable names were in the thirteenth and fourteenth centuries, even some of those that had apparently become hereditary. David Postles quotes an example from a deed of 1344, in which a cottage at Hanley in Warwickshire was in the possession of John *le Frenshe dictus Whitlokes* who was the son and heir of Richard *le Frenshe*. On this occasion, a seemingly hereditary surname was being replaced by a colloquial by-name, one which recorded the colour of the subject's hair.

Instability is similarly evident in the cartulary of Monk Bretton Priory in Yorkshire. Among the names of donors and witnesses is Siward Child, named in 1240 as the father of Robert Talun: shortly afterwards Robert Talun was said to be the son of Siwarde Neville. Another example is Thomas le Renderour called Cotyngham (1351), recorded later as Thomas de Cotyngham called Renderor (1373). A by-name had clearly not become a hereditary surname in 1250 when Richard de Hawile was described as the son of Robert Malet; nor in 1326 when Adam de Godeyare (sic) was named as the son of Adam de Swathe. Later, in 1389, Robert Pache was noted as the son of Richard Horcefent of Billingley. The deeds also contain examples of brothers with different names. In 1310 Thomas de Heselheved was said to be the brother of Baldwin del Hill, and in 1361 Thomas de Cudworth was recorded as the brother of John Taillour. Not only is it difficult to identify when a by-name became hereditary, it is unclear why a particular by-name was chosen, for men often had more than one.

Even when a surname derives from a distinctive place-name, it can still be very difficult to discover whether people with that name in the thirteenth century are the ancestors of those who bore it in later times. The Hallamshire name Staniforth is derived from a farm that stood by a stony ford, close to the present Meadow Hall shopping centre. A Robert de Stanford was recorded locally in 1239 and a Matilda de Staniforthe in 1297, but not until 1433, when John de Stannyford surrendered a farm in Stannyford to Richard de Stanny-ford, his son and heir, can we be sure that the name was hereditary. It is likely to have been so for some generations but firm evidence for that has not been discovered.

It is occasionally possible to establish just when a surname stabilized and to identify the progenitor. It has been shown, for example, that John Wilson of

Broomhead was the son in 1398 of William de Waldershelf, the first bearer of the surname in that part of Sheffield. There can be no doubt that Wilson is a surname with multiple origins but it should not be forgotten that these 'origins' relate to quite different families and they would be distinct within their own region. In such cases, DNA analysis might prove or disprove a relationship between families with the same common surname.

It is important to remember also that the inheriting of a name might take place over several generations, not at one particular time. David Postles recently quoted the case of a Derbyshire surname, which occurred as the by-name 'de Greves' in 1327 and could be linked genealogically with the surname Greaves by the second half of the fifteenth century. In the intervening period Thomas 'de le Greves', whose father was called Giles, was also known as Thomas Gylessone. The surname referred to the piece of land named 'Greves' which had been in the family's possession throughout that period and that seems likely to have been a stabilizing factor.

Regional studies

The English Surnames Survey, based at what is now the Centre for English Local History at the University of Leicester, has painstakingly established the broad chronological adoption of surnames by class and region in a number of different counties. This work provides very useful information for historians, but it may have less direct interest for family historians and genealogists.

The study of Oxfordshire surnames by Richard McKinley will serve as an example. He was formerly the Director of the Survey and in his volume on the county he was able to show that the first hereditary surnames there arose in the period immediately after the Conquest and that many of the tenants-in-chief at the time of Domesday Book bore names that were inherited by their descendants: during the twelfth century a number of families in the county who were of the baronial or knightly class also began to possess hereditary surnames. In his typically thorough way McKinley examined the records of both rural and urban communities and demonstrated how by-names became surnames right across the county. Moving carefully from one generation to another, he was able to throw light on that process at different social levels, producing examples among freeholders and serfs, landed families, and wealthy townsmen. Even so, there were some landed families in the county who did not have hereditary surnames as late as the fourteenth century, so the process was not uniform. Occasionally, a surname that appeared to have become established over two or three generations was altered for no clear reason.

Although McKinley found it more difficult to find evidence for the adoption of surnames lower down the social scale, he was able occasionally to identify the individual with whom a particular surname began, especially in cases where it derived from a rare personal name. A man named Passepaysius was first recorded at Sibford *c.*1190 where he held half a hide. His son Richard was no doubt the same person as the Richard Passepays who witnessed charters for Sibford at the start of the thirteenth century. Humphrey Passepays, who was recorded at Sibford at the end of the twelfth century, was almost certainly another son. This Humphrey had a son called Richard Passepays and a grandson with the same name, the third Richard Passepays.

Drew is another surname that can be traced back to the personal name of an individual. Dru of Easington, also called Drew or Dreu, was probably a small freeholder and the documents show that about 1230 he had a son called Roger: this man was sometimes called Roger son of Dru and sometimes more simply Roger Dru. He had at least two sons, John Drew and Hugh Dru, and they both held land at Easington during the late thirteenth century. Roger's wife was sometimes referred to as Joan Dru, but on other occasions as Joan Roke, for she was the daughter of Richard Roke. Hugh, who was Joan's son by Roger Dru, was sometimes styled Hugh Dru, sometimes Hugh son of Joan daughter of Richard le Rok. It may all sound confusing but it is evidence of the way in which a surname stabilized at this social level during the thirteenth century.

Surnames of other types can be shown to have become hereditary in that same class of freeholder. For example, a family named Justice held land at Ipsden and Stoke Marmion in the early part of the century. Robert le Justice, *dictus justiciarius*, probably a nickname, was recorded about 1237–50: he was succeeded by his son and grandson, both named John le Justice, and by a William Justice who held land at Ipsden in 1325 and later.

McKinley considered that about half the names listed in the Chadlington Hundred Rolls of 1279 became hereditary surnames, since he found them in the lay subsidy roll for the same hundred in 1327. It seems likely that much of the rural population of Oxfordshire acquired hereditary surnames in that period, when it was certainly rare to find anyone without a second name. Nevertheless, most of the poorer inhabitants of the borough of Oxford were still without names in the late fourteenth century, and even the wealthier burgesses generally acquired them at a later date than the landholding families of the county.

A few distinctive nicknames persisted in the county over many generations. The earliest is Lamprey, on record at Ascott-under-Wychwood from the thirteenth century; Startup and Tredwell were both recorded from the fourteenth century. The distinctive nickname Hauteyn derives from a word of French origin that meant proud or haughty, and it can be traced to the Banbury district in the thirteenth century. The spellings included Hauteyn, Hawtayne, Halthein, Halfthein, and even Aldeyn. The statistics from the census returns of 1881 show that it survived as Hawten in Chipping Norton and as Halten in Banbury.

It needs to be stressed that much of McKinley's material related to surnames that became extinct at a relatively early date. He dealt at some length with the names of important families such as Bolebec, St Valery, Choche, and Chevauchesul, accurately establishing the circumstances under which they became hereditary, but not one of these is represented in the English census returns of 1881. He traced the descent of the de Witefeld or de Wytefeld family through several generations but these names too are not found in 1881. At a lower social level he drew attention to le Byk, Carpi, Purpelot, and Wynegod. These were some of the names for the period 1279–1327, mentioned earlier, that he was confident became hereditary, but they were either extinct by 1881 or exceptionally rare. In any case, they were not recorded in Oxfordshire.

A closer look at some of McKinley's examples demonstrates how misleading those early surname sketches can be. He commented on Startup as a name which 'persisted in the county over centuries', using that evidence, in lieu of a connected pedigree, to prove that it must have been hereditary. That is an accepted method and he was doubtless right in his assumption, but no mention is made of the fact that the name subsequently disappeared from the county. In 1881 nobody called Startup was living in Oxfordshire and the distribution of the name places it firmly in Kent. If it could be shown that Startup had a single family origin, the name would have migrated to Kent from Oxfordshire, but that seems unlikely since examples of the by-name have been found in several different regions. It was noted by Reaney and Weekley, from 1190, in Warwickshire, Rutland, Norfolk, London, and Yorkshire. The meaning of Startup continues to be debated but Shakespeare used the word in the sense of 'opportunist' (our modern upstart) and the *OED* describes it as a kind of boot 'worn by rustics' (1517). The widespread use of the by-name suggests that the word was in much earlier use than these late references indicate.

In the same list as the above names was Welikempt and here McKinley was able to go far beyond establishing when and where it became hereditary. He found examples of the by-name, or one very similar to it, in several counties, including Essex, Sussex, Warwickshire, and Worcestershire. In the thirteenth and fourteenth centuries, even in Oxfordshire, it was not confined to one district and he came to the conclusion that more than one family must be involved. Nevertheless, he drew attention to individuals called Wellicomb or

Wellicond at Mixbury in 1665 and appeared confident that there was a link with the earlier name. At that time, he had no access to the data for 1881 that we now take for granted, for he would surely have commented on the rare names Wellicome and Wellicom in Buckinghamshire, or even Welcomb, Welcome, and Wellcome – all possible variants – in Surrey and Sussex. The fact that Sussex was one of the counties where Welikempt had been noted in the Middle Ages means that these could have had a different family origin. DNA evidence may eventually throw new light on the origins of both Startup and Welikempt.

It is clear that McKinley made his greatest contribution to family history when he was able to establish, or at least suggest, a link between a medieval by-name and a modern surname, and he increasingly saw opportunities to do that. For example, he followed Friday from its first reference in Sussex in 1200, probably as a by-name, to the Seaford area and to the east of the county in the sixteenth century. The surname was rare in Sussex in 1881 but relatively numerous in Kent and Surrey. He then threw new light on its possible origin and meaning by drawing attention to the fourteenth-century field name Fryday, recorded in a village not far from Seaford. Traditional explanations of the surname are that it was a nickname, given to a person born on a Friday or to someone who was as solemn and as gloomy as a Friday fast-day! These cannot be discounted, but McKinley believed it had a topographical origin in Sussex and was the name of a single family. It is too early to say that he was right, but the methods he employed and the examples he quoted demonstrate how important it is to examine all the circumstances in which a surname became hereditary.

It is difficult to reconcile the different ways McKinley dealt with Startup and Friday, and similar contradictions in *The Surnames of Sussex* are found where he commented in his final paragraphs on 'the character' of surnames in the county 'at the present time', that is 1988. For instance, he correctly identified Markwick as a prominent surname in Sussex, although it probably derives from a Surrey place-name. In 1881, 269 of the 440 Fridays lived in Sussex. The name has a long history there, for it was recorded in the Lewes area as early as the fifteenth century.

On the other hand, McKinley found Dimock in Sussex in 1332 and stated that it was 'still numerous in the county'. That seems most unlikely. In 1881 just 133 people in England had the surname and nobody called Dimock was listed in Sussex. The places where the name was moderately well established were Cambridgeshire (52), Middlesex (18), and Staffordshire (14). Even if the spelling Dimmock is taken into consideration, the statistics do not point to a Sussex connection. The total in this case was 1,097 and the main concentration was in Bedfordshire (165). Numbers over 100 were recorded in four other counties but just four people had the name in Sussex.

Two other names included in the same section were Evershead, a name that was 'already numerous' in Sussex in the sixteenth century, and Catchpole, 'now common in Sussex'. That is again misleading with regard to modern surnames, for Evershead had a total of just eight in the county in 1881 and Catchpole six. The latter was predominantly an East Anglian surname with significantly high counts in Suffolk (628) and Norfolk (422). Catchpole was not mentioned in McKinley's volume on Norfolk and Suffolk.

The work of Postles in Devon poses similar problems for family historians. Again there is a good deal of useful information on heredity, with carefully worked-out descents for names of different types. The Old English personal name Deorling is shown to have stabilized in the county in the twelfth and thirteenth centuries, with spellings that included Derling, Dirling and Durling, but these references may be irrelevant as far as the family historian is concerned. In 1881 these forms of the name were relatively uncommon and their 'home' was in Kent not Devon. Here, as sometimes with McKinley, no attempt was made to trace a connection between the medieval and modern surnames.

In a chapter devoted to what he called 'isonymy', Postles concentrated on the distinctive surnames that dominated a number of Devon communities at different periods in history, from 1524–25 to the nineteenth century. This is a topic of real interest to social historians and demographers but the fate of many of these 'core' names was not pursued. Two were apparently extinct by 1881 – that is Catrew and Winyeat (and the six variants indexed with it); Jedd had just one representative, in Nottinghamshire; Tomlin was quite numerous in several counties but rare in Devon, whilst the variants Thamlin and Thamlyn occurred just once each, neither of them in Devon. Such information would be of value to local and family historians.

The West Midlands

When the English Surnames Survey started it may have been intended to cover counties in every part of England, but that did not happen, and two important border regions were neglected; the West Midlands and the Northeast. Counties such as Shropshire and Herefordshire, because they were so near to Wales, were under the influence of quite different naming practices and these resulted in numerous additions to the stock of English surnames, some at a comparatively late date. The excellent sources for this region have been exploited by Welsh scholars, and one or two of their examples will show that some 'English' surnames may have late origins.

The Welsh Ieuan was the equivalent of John in England, and it was subject to a number of sound changes that complicated its spelling. Forms of the name noted in Shropshire registers include Thomas Jeuans (1564) and Owen Yeavens (1620). The addition of the 's' happened frequently in communities that were not Welsh-speaking and Jevons is essentially an English surname not a Welsh one, although the progenitor(s) would have been Welsh. In 1881, with a national count of 533, it was found principally in Staffordshire (268), Worcestershire (79), Warwickshire (58), and Lancashire (49). In Cheshire 19 people bore the name; Wales had just two. Jeavons (780) was more numerous, but the distribution pattern was much the same, except that Lancashire and Cheshire were less well represented. In Wales, only eight people shared the surname.

It is impossible as yet to say how many distinct family origins a name like Jevons might have, and that complicates the questions that relate to its heredity. It clearly has a Welsh origin but Ieuan would certainly have been the first name of more than one immigrant. The Welsh patronymic system lasted in many parts of the country into the eighteenth and nineteenth centuries, so the origins of Jevons or Jeavons have to be looked for over a very long period. Edgar Tooth notes that John Gevon was a taxpayer in Stafford in 1327.

Another Welsh first name that gave rise to English surnames was Einion or Ennion, formerly very popular. Prys Morgan found evidence in the Shropshire registers which proved that it could be responsible for Onion(s) and he quoted the case of Robert Inians who married Jane Smyth at High Ercall in 1599. When the children were christened the surname was Onions or Onians, both with a final 's', whereas Robert was buried as Robert Onion. In 1881 these were essentially English names in their distribution, and Onions, with a total of 1,666, was found over a wider area than Jevons. It also had a strong presence closer to the border: Staffordshire (534), Shropshire (285), Warwickshire (210), Worcestershire (115), and Leicestershire (105). There were 18 people in Wales with the surname. The history and distribution of both Jevons and Onions make it clear that traditional English explanations of their meanings should probably carry less weight than the Welsh meanings. Edgar Tooth noted that Onion was confused with the English Unwin in Ellenhall parish in the 1680s.

The poll tax return for Herefordshire in 1379 has direct evidence of early Welsh influence. In the short list of taxpayers for Bredwardine, for instance, are people named Yvan Day, Res Rossel, Gryffyt Taylour, and Ros ap Guylyn. In the bigger community at Lyonshall were John ap Hug(h), Houwel Glovere, Houwel Stretford, Jena Seyr, and two families with Madoc as a second name.

No fewer than six taxpayers had Houwel as a second name. Elsewhere, in Stretford Hundred alone, were scores of people with obvious Welsh connections. The proof lies in first names like Cadogan, Grenow, Heynon, Gryfyn, Madoc, and the very common Jena.

Little work has been done to determine the longer term impact of this on modern surnames but in 1881 Howell was prolific in many parts of England with a total of 12,632. Even though the surname had alternative origins, many of these Victorian families are likely to have had a connection with Wales, some quite recent and others dating from the fourteenth century. Howells (7,658) was predominantly a Welsh surname in 1881, with Glamorgan (2,577) and Carmarthen (1,016) at the heart of its distribution. The English counties with the highest totals were Shropshire (597), Staffordshire (276), Herefordshire (166), and Gloucestershire (163).

The North-east

No poll tax returns survive for Durham (1377–81) and only a few membranes exist for Northumberland, so there is less information available for this important region than we might expect. One useful source for the fourteenth century is published under the title *Durham Halmote Rolls 1296–1384* and it allows us to compare the county with others further south. Punshon is one example of a distinctive local surname with an early origin. The by-names filius Punzun or Puncon were noted by Reaney in Cumberland (1177) and Northamptonshire (1210). There is nothing to link either of these with the Durham village of Pittington, but one of the earliest entries in the rolls shows that the name was already hereditary there by 1296. In that year Robert Punchun became the tenant of a toft and land 'quondam Gilberti Punchun', paying two marks. The relationship is obvious if not explicit. There are gaps in the rolls in the early fourteenth century but frequent references to a John Punchoun or Ponchon between 1358 and 1378 indicate that the name survived the Black Death and from that time it can be picked up at intervals in a variety of published Durham sources. Examples from the Quarter Sessions Rolls are Edward Pounchon at Lumley in 1556 and William Punshon at Chester le Street in 1618. The surname was rare in 1881, with a total of 231, but the main concentrations were in Durham (163) and Northumberland (22). Variants such as Punshin, Punchon, and Punsheon had very small totals but were found predominantly in the same area.

Also in the roll for 1296 were Alan and Robert Pater Noster of East Rainton, and the same unusual name is recorded in the township a century later. A family connection seems likely, but there is no evidence for that in the rolls, and we are left to wonder what type of surname it might be. M.A. Lower, in *Patronymica Britannica* (1860), quoted the case of Alice Paternoster, a lady whose tenure of land in Berkshire obliged her to say the Lord's Prayer five times a day for the souls of King Edward I's ancestors. He noted similar tenancy agreements for other Paternosters in the county, and Reaney found the name there as early as 1197, so it is possible that it had been hereditary from the twelfth century. On the other hand, the sequence may simply reflect the conditions of the tenancy and, since the surname occurs in several counties over a long period, these were possibly less unusual than might be thought. Examples include: 1185 Roger Pater Noster (Lincolnshire); 1221 Robert Paternoster (Warwickshire); 1379 Nicholas Paternoster (Staffordshire). In 1881 the surname was rare, with a total of just 190, but these were families recorded in eight different counties, so it is likely that Paternoster had more than one origin.

It is sometimes said that most surnames were hereditary from about 1350 but that almost certainly overstates the case. In Durham, for example, the Halmote court rolls cover the period 1296 to 1384 and they include numerous examples of what were clearly late by-names, for example, Fair-John (1358), Roger Litilannotson (1370), Adam Jonson Tomson (1379), and Adam Carter, son of John Wilkynson (1379); among the women mentioned were Cecilia le Ponderswoman (1366), Alice Aneslaymayden (1370), and Agnes Felicedoughter (1371). That is not unusual: similar by-names occur in other counties in that period and even later.

We know from the English Surnames Survey that many surnames became hereditary before 1350 but less research has been devoted to establishing how late the process continued. It is by no means clear what percentage of the native population acquired a surname after 1400, nor what the impact on the English name stock was of aliens and of migrants from other parts of the British Isles. More attention needs to be paid to that later period, since a high percentage of our modern surnames were then in the process of stabilization. It is also important to remind ourselves that many of the early inherited names were already extinct by 1350, or became so soon afterwards.

Late development?

It is often said that surnames settled first in the south of England and were slower to stabilize in the northern counties and Lowland Scotland, and there is some truth in that. Nevertheless, the poll tax returns for communities away from the North clearly show that substantial groups of people elsewhere were still without a fixed name in 1377–81. Amongst the 50 taxpayers in the

Leicestershire village of Freeby in 1381 were four men, like William 'filio Hugonis', who were distinguished simply by their relationship to some other person, whilst another four were male or female servants, identified by the name of their master or mistress, for example John 'servo Ricardi Franceys'. Also in the list were Hugh 'bethe Watur' and Robert 'othe Grene', two men bearing what look suspiciously like by-names. The other taxpayers had second names but it is not clear how many were hereditary.

The Dorset town of Shaftsbury had 157 taxpayers in 1379, including 52 who were entered as male and female servants and who had no second name. Three servants of Robert Whytyng were identified simply by their first names: Edward, Henry and Mathew. Nevertheless, all four men each paid 4d. tax. The fact that Margery Upwode's servant was entered as Alice Skyle implies that some servants had second names. No fewer than 13 entries linked taxpayers to the person above them in the list, via 'filius eius' or 'filia eius': if these men and women had possessed surnames it would have been easier for the clerks to write one word rather than two. In all, more than one third of those who paid tax had no surname; they formed a significant proportion of the population.

We cannot, therefore, ignore those sources which continued to emphasize the high proportion of unstable names, particularly those derived from occupations. The fabric rolls of the great abbeys clearly demonstrate the enduring link between occupation and 'surname', in some cases well into the sixteenth century. It has been shown, for example, that skilled carvers in Ripon called Broomfleet had 'Carver' as a second name as late as 1537 and that in Methley parish, Carver was still an alias for Burton as late as the 1650s.

Aliases of this kind, which tell us that a person could have more than one surname, can provide a vital clue for family historians. Although *alias* was the word most commonly used by clerks, it was not the only one and similar terms include *aliter dictus* and *alias vocat'*, along with a variety of alternatives that had the sense of 'or', that is *sive, vel*, and *aut*. The use of *vulgariter* suggests that the alternative name was a colloquial pronunciation or a nickname: typical examples are 'John Squire vulgariter John Swyre' (1618) and 'George Sykes vulgo Thorp' (1709). With the increasing use of English in the post-medieval period, 'otherwise' and 'otherways' were also employed. Of course, these terms were not always a sign that a person had two surnames; sometimes they merely acknowledged a nickname or were a device of the clerks, especially when identifying married women.

Numerous aliases draw attention to alternative spellings of a surname, for example Brownhill and Brownell, Horsfield and Horsfall, or to abbreviated forms, for example Campinot and Campey, Wimpenny and Penny. They also point to confusion between similar names such as Mirfield and Murfin,

Stansfield and Stancliffe. The genealogist needs to know that such variations could survive independently, creating apparently new surnames. In other cases an alias could be documented over several generations: a family in the north Derbyshire parish of Norton, for instance, was recorded consistently in the parish register as Urton alias Steven. Of more concern is the fact that a clerk may have considered it unnecessary to record an alias because the associations were common knowledge. Examples of all these have been dealt with at greater length in *Surnames and Genealogy* (1997).

Genealogical work can sometimes identify an alias or explain what lay behind it. The vicar of Ecclesfield (Yorkshire) recorded the burial on 31 March 1599 of 'Maude Croftes (alias Mounteneye)', because he knew that Maude's first husband was John Mounteney and her second was Ralph Crofts. In the same parish, on 18 March 1591, Thomas Parkin, alias Cowper, of Hasle Clough, mason, made his will: three days later, the parish register recorded the burial of Thomas Cowper. The alias was passed on to his son, for on 9 August 1619 the baptism of Margaret, the daughter of Thomas Parkin alias Cowper was noted. On another occasion, on 21 November 1584, the Sheffield register recorded the burial of George Cook alias Hinchliffe alias Haldesworth. The explanation for these alternative names can be found a few months earlier in the record of 14 July 1584 when George, the son of Elizabeth Cooke alias Hinchliffe was baptized: the child's suspected father was Jacob Hauldsworthe. A similar case was recorded on 7 May 1583, when Richard Heppenstall, the son of Johanna Heppenstall alias Youll, was baptized and Henry Claxon was named as the suspected father. The following month, on 2 June 1583, the child's burial was registered as Richard Heppenstall alias Youle alias Claxon. In these cases the children did not survive, but the examples demonstrate how an alias might take hold. In fact, an illegitimate boy might retain two names right through his life and pass those alternatives on to his descendants.

Occasionally, a documented alias provides proof of a link between two surnames, or two forms of one surname that would otherwise be very difficult to establish. In an assize case of 1651, John Mannering said that he was 'sometyme called by the name of John Grosvenor, his mother being of that name', and in the same court Nicholas Postgate 'being demanded why he named himself att the first Watson' explained that he had 'sometimes been soe called, his grandmother on his father's side being soe called'.

Family historians should see the use of aliases as an advantage rather than a complication. When DNA samples point to what geneticists call 'a non-paternity event', meaning illegitimacy, adoption or a change of family name, an alias can help a genealogist solve the problem.

Surname heredity in Wales, Scotland, and Ireland

One of the biggest influences on English surnames has been immigration over the centuries from other parts of the British Isles, especially since naming customs in those countries, not to mention the languages and dialects, were quite different from those in England. John and Sheila Rowlands have shown how the earliest hereditary Welsh surnames in the English style were formed in areas of Anglo-Norman settlement, notably south Pembrokeshire, where names such as Arnold, Cole, Hay, Roblin, Scone, Trewent, and Wardlow have a continuous history from the thirteenth century to the present day. But the descendants of immigrants with non-Welsh names who were followers of the landed classes and who married native girls often changed to the Welsh system of naming within a generation or two. The fashion for English-style surnames was not widely adopted until after the Act of Union (1536). Even then, it spread very slowly down the social scale and into the remoter areas.

The traditional Welsh system of naming was based on the use of *mab* or *map*, a cognate of the Gaelic *mac*, meaning 'son'. The initial letter was dropped, so names took such forms as Hywel ab Owain or Gwilym ap Thomas. In general, *ab* was used before vowels and *ap* before consonants, but numerous exceptions to this rule can be found in the records. Welsh freemen were commonly able to recite six or seven generations of their pedigrees, each generation divided by an *ap*, so much so that 'as long as a Welsman's pedigree' became a common saying. When the English system of naming was eventually adopted, Welshmen used the name of their father, or that of their grandfather or an even earlier ancestor, so that Owain ab Evan might become Owen Bevan or Owen Evans: Dafydd ap Richard might give rise to David Richards or David Pritchard. The wealthier classes started the new trend, but as late as the eighteenth century, and sometimes the nineteenth, the traditional *ap* and *ab* system was still in use, even in parishes in upland Glamorgan and western Monmouthshire, not far from the border with England.

When the changeover to English-style surnames occurred, the number of personal names in use in Wales was rather limited, so only a small range of family names became established. The most common Welsh method of creating a surname was by adding -s to a father's personal name, in the fashion of the English counties just across the border, or simply by adopting a father's name without any suffix. Amongst the Welsh personal names in use in the sixteenth century, only Dafydd, Gruffydd, Hywel, Morgan, Owain, and Rhys, and to a lesser extent Llywelyn and Madog, produced large numbers of surnames. The English personal names John, William, Hugh, Thomas, Robert,

Richard, Henry, Edward, and Lewis became widely adopted and were used to form surnames. But not all the people with surnames such as Jones, Williams, Roberts, Thomas, and Hughes have Welsh ancestors, for these were ancient surnames also in parts of England.

Names derived from occupations, place-names, and topographical features are relatively rare in Wales, and pet forms of names, nicknames, and terms of endearment were used as Welsh surnames less commonly than in England, though Lloyd and Vaughan are well known and others, such as Beddoes and Gittins, have restricted distributions. Even some of the most common Welsh surnames are not spread evenly. For instance, Roberts is primarily a north Welsh name whereas Bevan is found overwhelmingly in the south of the country.

The sources for Scottish surnames in the Middle Ages are generally less full than for English ones. The process of name formation began with some major Lowland landowners in the late twelfth century, but the fashion took a long time to take hold and was not generally completed in the Scots-speaking regions until at least the sixteenth century. The surnames and by-names that were used were similar in character to those across the border in England, where the dialect and customs had much in common. In particular, the northern English fashion of adding -son to a father's name became common and it eventually affected even Gaelic surnames such as Ferguson.

Gaelic surnames or by-names were hardly known in the Scots-speaking regions, or indeed in England and Wales, until well after 1746 when Bonnie Prince Charlie was defeated at the battle of Culloden and the highland clan system declined. In the small, Gaelic-speaking communities of the Highlands and Islands the ordinary clansmen usually had patronymics with the prefix 'Mac', which denoted 'son of'. This was sometimes abridged to 'Mc' or 'M', which were indistinguishable in origin. As they spread south, some names were turned into forms that the lowland Scots and their southern neighbours could recognize but which were sometimes markedly different from the originals.

The Irish had adopted many hereditary surnames, which were mainly derived from the Gaelic language, well before the Anglo-Norman invasion of the twelfth century introduced a new stock of names, including some Welsh ones. These Gaelic surnames were normally formed with the prefix Ó (anglicized to O') attached to the name of a grandfather or earlier ancestor or with 'Mac' or 'Mc' before the name of a father. During the long period of tighter English rule, from the seventeenth century onwards, these prefixes were often dropped, but they were commonly re-introduced in the late nineteenth and twentieth centuries. By then, many Irish names had been altered, translated, or mistranslated into English forms. Those that the English could not pronounce were sometimes abbreviated or distorted beyond recognition, while some rare names were gradually absorbed by the commoner ones. The old surnames that were derived from the Gaelic language are the most difficult to trace back to their origins, but many of them are identified with particular parts of Ireland. For example, the Doyles are found mainly in Leinster, the McCarthys in Cork and Kerry, the Quinns in Tyrone, and the Quinlans in Tipperary.

Identifying origins

The circumstances in which a surname stabilized are matters of great interest to social and family historians and they have obvious implications for its meaning. It is an aspect of the subject which is attractive to genealogists on the one hand and raises the academic standing of surname studies on the other. The successful identification of a surname demands of the researcher that he or she establish conclusive links between the modern spelling and a medieval by-name. Once the circumstances of the name's heredity are known the way is open to a consideration of its origin and meaning.

Ogram is one of many distinctive surnames which offer the genealogist that possibility. It is not mentioned in any of our standard works, partly because it is so rare, although in that respect it is no different from thousands of other distinctive English names. Nevertheless, its history can be traced in a variety of published sources, starting with the census details of 1881 when the total nationally was just 117: all but seven of these people lived in Yorkshire, the majority in York and the East Riding. Parish registers for Holderness cover the period back to 1672 when just a few individuals were recorded in the hearth tax returns: Marmaduke and John Ogram were taxed that year in Ottringham. The modern spelling can be found in East Riding documents much earlier: a priest called Robert Ogram was living in Hull in 1500 and Richard Ograme died at Owthorne in Holderness in 1506. In that period the minor variations that occur, such as Oggram and Owgrem, pose no problems.

Changes in spelling make it more difficult to identify the name in earlier centuries, but because it was so rare and because the core of the family kept its association with the parishes on the north bank of the Ouse, it can be successfully identified in the fifteenth and fourteenth centuries. Key references in that period are William Ogrym of Hull (1465) and Adam Ougrim of Hessle (1366). In 1389 Richard Ougrym lived in Adlingfleet, higher upstream on the opposite bank of the river, and the fortunate survival of early deeds for that parish means that we can identify two early and evidently related bearers of the name in 1316–21, that is Richard and Thomas Augrim or Augryme.

This was probably soon after the surname had stabilized for there is evidence that 'Augrim' was a personal name in that part of Yorkshire in previous generations. Examples include Augrim, the son of Gocelin, who was selling land in Hedon in 1226 and Algrim de Frisemareis in 1195: 'Frisemareis' is an early spelling of Frismarsh, a settlement that was lost to the Humber in the years 1286 to 1310. The personal name from which Algrim derives, and its etymology, have been commented on at some length by Gillian Fellows Jensen in *Scandinavian Personal Names in Lincolnshire and Yorkshire* (1968).

Two other difficult names can be shown to derive from Matthew, via little-known pet forms, correcting entries in the most recent standard dictionaries. Moxon is the first of these names, traditionally interpreted as 'son of Mog', that is Margaret. It was suggested some years ago that the pet form may have been for Matthew not Margaret, but evidence for that was lacking. More recently, genealogist Steve Moxon found the proof that was needed in the Ronksley MSS at Sheffield Archives. In a sequence of early title deeds, dated 1333–36, one individual is recorded as Robertus *filius* Mathei or Robert Mokeson: 'Moke' was clearly a pet form of Matthew and it had a diminutive 'Mokoc', which had already been identified as Matthew.

Mawson is essentially a Wharfedale name that became numerous in and around Leeds. The traditional explanation is that it meant 'son of Maud', that is Matilda, or 'son of Maw', from an Old English name. These suggestions sound reasonable enough but do not fit the particular family circumstances. William Mawson was taxed in Burley in Wharfedale in 1379, in that part of the dale where the name later flourished. Previously, in 1357, John Mahewson was a Burley resident and his name clearly derived from the French form of Matthew. On its own that example would not be sufficient to prove that 'Maw' was a pet form of Matthew, although it certainly points in that direction. Fortunately, the essential 'alias' is found in documents for Fountains Abbey in the 1450s, when Matthew Knoll of Foxup is also described as Maw Knoll. It may be that both Moxon and Mawson are surnames with more than one family origin, but their expansion in the West Riding is at the heart of each name's distribution and both clearly derive there from Matthew.

The adoption of surnames

Much of this chapter has been devoted to the question of when and where surnames became hereditary, with emphasis on how long the process lasted.

The reasons why it happened are probably even more complex and little can be added to Richard McKinley's conclusions in *A History of British Surnames* (1990).

The change from an oral to a written culture at a local level may have played a part in the process. From the 1230s onwards, and especially from the 1260s, manorial courts across England began to record property transactions on rolls. About the same time, local deeds for the transfer of land became much more numerous. Peasants were as careful as were lords to secure their property and their privileges and pass them on to their children, so the spread of surnames that linked them to a piece of land or to an occupation is unlikely to have been coincidental. Patronymics or nicknames could just as easily link father and son and reinforce the claim to an inheritance. And yet the new written culture did not necessarily lead to rapid change. Manor court rolls and tax assessment lists long continued to record people merely by a personal name, sometimes with the addition of a by-name, and the system did not seem to cause undue problems.

Nor did manorial clerks have much, or any, role in the choice of the surname that was bestowed on a peasant. The use of nicknames, many of which were downright obscene, suggests that they were coined by neighbours rather than clerks. That was probably true also of surnames derived from diminutives and pet forms of personal names. These were rarely recorded in medieval administrative and legal documents, for the officers of the manor court, like the ministers and parish clerks of a later age, usually chose to give the Latin form of a person's name: these were preferred to Tom, Dick, and Harry. Most surnames began as by-names that were invented and used in local speech long before they were written down by clerks.

It may be, though, that a fundamental change in personal naming practices contributed to the general adoption of surnames. At the time of the Norman Conquest, the English were using names inherited from their Anglo-Saxon and Scandinavian ancestors, but few of these survived beyond the late thirteenth century and they were progressively replaced by Norman names and others from the Bible. It is not really known why this stock of names should then shrink dramatically but that is what happened, and by the mid-1300s relatively few personal names were in common use. Nationally, John and William accounted for 54 per cent of the male population and Thomas, Richard, and Robert formed another 25 per cent. There was a similar contraction in the stock of female names. This narrow range of personal names was insufficient on its own to distinguish the inhabitants of even small communities and by-names must have become increasingly important, taken from occupations, place-names, nicknames, and relationships. Even so, the lack of choice amongst first names does not tell us why so many by-names were passed from father to son in the form of hereditary surnames.

To each of these partial explanations we must add that of fashion. Surnames spread slowly down the social scale, perhaps conferring a status that was increasingly desirable – a label that everyone had to have. The poorest people in the remotest parts of the land were the last to follow the trend. Gradually, everyone came to accept that a surname was a normal requirement in society and it became rare for a person to be known by more than one by-name or surname.

Classifying surnames

William Camden, the eminent Elizabethan antiquary, became the first scholar to write about surnames when he devoted a chapter to the subject in his *Remains Concerning Britain* (1605). He showed how surnames could be arranged in various categories, derived from occupations or professions, from qualities and imperfections, colours, flowers, rivers, trees, fish, birds, and fruit, from Christian names, and from nicknames.

Neither was there any trade, craft, art, profession, or occupation never so mean, but had a name among us commonly ending in Er, and men accordingly denominated; but some are worn out of use, and therefore their significations are unknown, and others have been modified ridiculously by the bearers, lest they should seem vilified by them.

He noted also that that many old names had disappeared over time but that the stock of English surnames was being replenished by 'many new names dayly brought in by Aliens, as French, Scots, Irish, Welsh, Dutch, etc.'.

Since then, it has been traditional for writers to place surnames in one of four classes: personal names, nicknames, occupational terms, and geographic locations, with each major class subdivided into convenient categories. These appear to be useful aids for those involved in surname studies, but the classification of a name is often arbitrary, and not all surnames fit into the overall scheme. Even the numerous Wilsons may not all be descended from a progenitor called William, for a Swithland slate tombstone in the churchyard of Breedon-on-the-Hill (Leicestershire) informs us that Thomas Wilson, who died in 1773, was 'late of Wilson', an outlying settlement in the parish. Likewise, there are places called Benson (Oxfordshire), Sibson (Huntingdon-shire), and Thompson (Norfolk). Many other surnames remain difficult to classify simply because it has proved impossible as yet to say exactly what they mean. It now seems less important to attempt to classify names than to deal with them individually, concentrating on matters such as expansion and decline, distribution, migration, and linguistic development.

In conclusion, we need to remind ourselves that modern surnames form just a small percentage of those that were in use during the earliest centuries of the process. Most of them go back no earlier than the fourteenth century. The scholars in many disciplines who find that by-names and surnames are a potentially valuable tool need to be aware of the long drawn-out nature of the naming process and the genealogical complexities, while genealogists need to know more about how their ancestors' names developed and see their family history in a much wider, national context.

The nature of a name's origins is of particular interest where it is rare and largely confined to a particular locality. It poses the questions that DNA analysis might answer: do distinctive but rare names such as Cobbold, Daft, or Kerridge have a single origin, or two or three progenitors? And is there more to say about names such as Smith, Taylor, or Wright other than that they are common? Might it be possible to trace even a common name back to its local origins? Most surnames have something of interest in their history and each should be treated as a unique development. When that is done success-fully, its family history becomes an integral part of the nation's history.

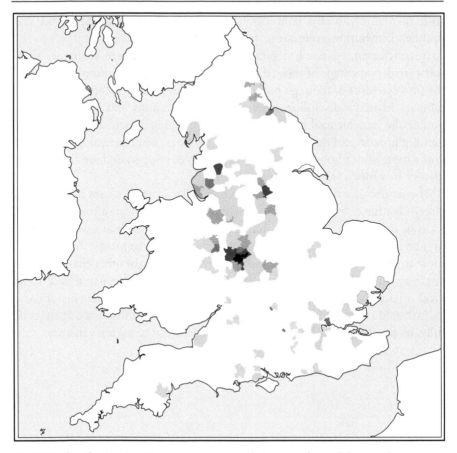

ROUND: **distribution in 1881.** Many surnames that were inherited from nicknames are distributed widely, but some have a marked local concentration. Reaney and Wilson suggest that Round was a nickname for a 'rotund, plump' man and quote early examples from Essex and Lancashire. They give no hint that the hereditary surname is remarkably concentrated in and around the Black Country. Of the 2,741 Rounds recorded in the national census of 1881, no fewer that 902 were living in Dudley, with large numbers in the neighbouring districts of West Bromwich (296), Stourbridge (247), King's Norton (104), Aston (89), Wolverhampton (81), and Birmingham (66). Edgar Tooth has quoted examples of the name in Leek in 1392 and Keele in 1414.

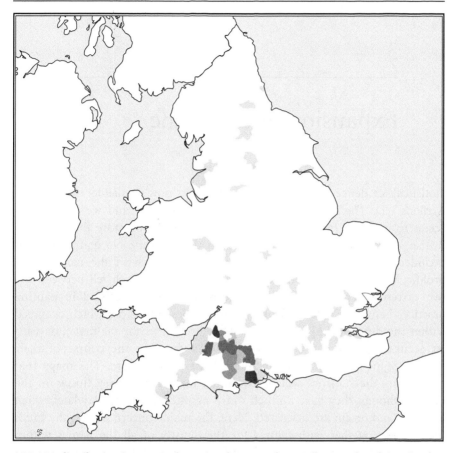

ADLAM: distribution in 1881. In the national census of 1881 Adlam was largely confined to south-west England. The significant totals then were in the neighbouring counties of Wiltshire (258), Somerset (130), and Gloucestershire (66), with a particular concentration in Warminster (121). The name provides earlier evidence for the word than that quoted in the *OED*. Reaney and Wilson derive it from an Old English personal name but that is pure speculation. The by-names they quote are not from that region and no examples are offered for the crucial period after *c.*1260. The origin of the hereditary surname needs to be looked for in the South-west.

3

Expansion and Decline

Statistical evidence from the 1881 census is now available on Stephen Archer's CD, *The British 19th Century Surname Atlas*, and we finally have access to accurate information about the frequency of more than 400,000 British surnames at an important date in their history. No name has been excluded from this list, and the data tells us which of the names were prolific, which were exceptionally uncommon, and which fell between the two extremes. These totals reflect the differences that existed in naming practices between England, Scotland, and Wales, and those which occurred within the different English regions. They present us for the first time with an accurate picture of how surnames had fared in the course of their history. Some had clearly done much better than others. The maps that accompany the statistics will be consulted for the light they throw on the totals, although they have a much more significant role to play later, when meaning and origin are discussed. Here, the main concern is with the totals themselves, together with figures for the density of all the names within their immediate regions. These provide vital information about each sur name's numerical success or failure, either at a county level or more accurately via the poor law unions, which acted as census enumerators' districts.

These related topics of expansion and decline have implications that go far beyond etymology and family history. They are themes that have been touched on over the years in the *English Surnames Series*, with supporting statistics from documents such as subsidy rolls and hearth tax returns, or from more recent sources such as electoral rolls and telephone directories, but there has never been a thorough investigation into the remarkable expansion of some names and the extinction or decline of others. The subject promises to reveal a great deal about the constitution of Britain's population and raises issues that are now coming under scientific scrutiny for the first time.

Problems with the data

It is important at the outset to say something about the data set itself, for there are ways in which it could be misleading. The very large number of names, that is 401,197, should certainly be treated with caution, for a significant percentage of those listed occurred once only, and many were clearly mis-spellings that are attributable to illiteracy or clerical error. Such entries cannot be considered as distinctive surnames and their later disappearance cannot be treated as extinction. That is not to say that all the names which appeared once only were errors, for some of the single entries in 1881 were undoubtedly for surnames with a long history, many of them on the point of extinction.

More importantly, scholars who wish to use the surname totals as evidence in other fields of research need to realize that they cannot take this statistical information at face value. Some initial detective work will usually be neces-sary. At its simplest this concerns names such as Clark and Clarke; Cooper and Cowper. These are not really separate surnames, for some families have used both spellings in the course of their history. Nevertheless, they are treated as distinct names in the lists presented on the CD, and that seems the right thing to do, even though the presentation masks the real frequency of the name. The difference could be considerable: Clark was the seventeenth most common name in 1881 and Clarke the fortieth; their respective totals were 90,201 and 60,675. If these were combined, only six British names would be more common.

The many names which have numerous variant spellings pose a much greater problem, for the variations are not always easy to identify, especially by non-linguists. The common surname Gledhill will illustrate the point at a basic level. In 1881 it was borne by 4,455 people, but this number does not include the totals of variant forms of the name, although they share its origin and history. It has been possible to identify at least fifteen such alternatives, none of them really unusual to a genealogist or from a linguistic point of view, but including Gleadhall, Gleadhill, Gleadle, Gledall, and Gledden. Where the CD presents surnames in alphabetical order, these are separated from each other, and from Gledhill. It is true that most of them are not very common, but their combined total comes to around 700, a significant enough number to place it higher than names such as Bridges, Child, and Hopkinson. The variants would be even more significant if Gledhill's distribution were being discussed. It is clearly very important to identify such variants and they must not be seen as surnames in their own right.

This is not a problem that affects all names. Smith and Carter, for example, have very few variants that are significant numerically because they were derived from occupational terms that are still in use and have an apparently transparent 'meaning'. In similar, but not identical, circumstances, the same principle seems to have helped a variety of names to preserve one conventional form. Obvious examples are nicknames such as Fairchild and Goodfellow, locative names derived from place-names such as Littlewood and Hardcastle, and surnames such as Williams and Johnson that are based on personal names. In these cases also, the elements are familiar lexical items and the surnames have few variants that are numerically significant: Ardcastle, Hardcassell, and Harcastle, for example, were all recorded in 1881 but together they add only twelve to the total of 2,656.

Son of Robert

Another difficult task for non-specialists is to discover what type of origin a name has and how it relates to similar names with much the same meaning. Some of the issues emerge in a study of three surnames that all mean 'son of Robert'.

Robinson, with a total of 95,495, is an excellent example of a multi-origin name, but it is characteristic only of the northern counties of England and is not generally popular. In 1881, even after centuries of internal migration, Robinson was still very uncommon in all the counties in south-west England and was rare in both Wales and Scotland, whereas in Yorkshire over 20,000 people bore this name. Of course, the totals for the biggest or most populous counties can be misleading, and this is where the relative concentration of the name comes into question. These statistics, which are also provided on the Archer CD, show how significant a name Robinson was in the smaller or largely rural counties, notably in Westmorland, Cumberland, and the North Riding of Yorkshire, and in Lincolnshire, which was virtually the southern limit of the surname.

Robertson has much the same meaning as Robinson but its history is totally different. In 1881 it was the 56th most frequent surname in Britain with a total of 50,256. Most Robertsons had their home in Scotland, where the name owes much of its importance to the Clan Donnachie, having been assumed as a family name by William, who became chief of Struan in 1509. Subsequently, it passed into general use among the members of the clan. It was still very prolific in Perthshire in 1881 with a total of 4,179, smaller than the total of 7,644 in Lanarkshire, but a much higher percentage of the population. Another high concentration was found in the Shetland Isles, where Robertson is likely to have had a quite different history. These figures can be contrasted with those for England, where Robertson was generally very uncommon. Understandably, it had a significant presence in counties such as Northumberland and Durham, and in one or two areas of high population, but in much of the southern half of England it was virtually unknown. In Huntingdonshire, for instance, just two people were called Robertson.

A third name to be considered alongside Robinson and Robertson is Robson, again meaning 'son of Robert'. In 1881 the Robsons numbered 19,730 and the name was 190th in order of popularity. In the sixteenth-century history of the Borders, the 'Debatable Lands' between England and Scotland, the Robsons were one of the four great clans or 'graynes' who dominated the North Tyne. The name is still markedly more popular there than anywhere else and in 1881 more than half of all the Robsons were still living in Northumberland and County Durham. Elsewhere, the name was not at all common and that is again particularly true of the South-west, for Cornwall had just two Robsons and Dorset only six.

Clearly, these three surnames have to be treated as distinctive and, because two of them are so closely linked with the clans and extended families of the North, questions remain unanswered about the nature of their origins. There is uncertainty too about the names Robison and Robeson, which were identified by Black as Scottish variants of Robertson. Theoretically, they might also be variants of Robinson and Robson but the numbers are in any case relatively small. The three surnames have multiple origins and they use -son as a suffix. This type of formation has been shown to be characteristic of the northern half of Britain and all three have their equivalents in other regions: Robins or Robbins, Robert and Roberts, Rob and Robb. This is not an exhaustive list but it illustrates the diverse ways in which 'son of Robert' could develop in different parts of the country. Such matters should be borne in mind when the popularity of a name is discussed, but they should not prevent those discussions taking place, for the statistical evidence can be used to great advantage by demographers, geneticists, and researchers in other fields. The benefits for local and family historians lie mostly in the information available about particular names, but the relative popularity of British surnames is of more general interest.

Prolific British surnames

In any discussion about the popularity of surnames it is useful to be able to employ the words 'common' and 'rare' and a range of qualifying terms. The availability of the 1881 census material might suggest that it should now be a relatively straightforward matter to classify names in order to do that, and yet, here again, problems arise. Many surnames, for example, have localized distributions, so that they are numerous in one area but not across the land. In 1881 almost 100 people in and around the small Wiltshire town of Pewsey bore the surname Flippence or Flippance, and it would certainly have been considered a common surname in that community. But the national total was only 118, which places it among the most uncommon names in Britain.

The striking fact is that most British surnames are not prolific. If a surname is borne by just one well-known person it becomes generally familiar and may be assumed to be more common than it is. Attenborough, Beeching, Dimbleby, Stobart, and Wogan are typical examples of such rare names; Cleese is a household name and yet just twelve people were so called in 1881. In 2009 the name of Robert Peston captured general attention in the media, but only seven people bore this surname in 1881. Nevertheless, a relatively small number of surnames are both numerous and widely distributed. The following list of the twelve most prolific names in Britain in 1881 makes it clear how dramatically the totals decline:

1. Smith 422,733
2. Jones 339,185
3. Williams 215,163
4. Brown 197,466
5. Taylor 191,485
6. Davies 152,406
7. Wilson 137,640
8. Evans 130,868
9. Thomas 123,599
10. Roberts 112,696
11. Johnson 100,632
12. Walker 100,295

The table confirms the pre-eminence of Smith. Although the position that this name occupies may fulfil our expectations, the failure of other well-known surnames to come close to it in numbers may cause some surprise. In 1881 these twelve were the only names which had totals in excess of 100,000, although a combined count for Clark(e) would place it between Davies and Wilson. Three names – Wilson, Johnson, and Walker – are more characteristic of the northern half of England than the southern, whilst six names testify to Welsh influence: Jones, Williams, Davies, Evans, Thomas, and Roberts. Some of these are not exclusively Welsh, but the list emphasizes how prolific the

Welsh patronymics are in comparison with most common English and Scottish surnames. Although this is a reflection of the quite different ways in which surnames in the three countries developed, it is worth noting that T.J. and Prys Morgan emphasized the 'Englishness' of Jones, Davies, Williams, and Evans, calling them 'by-products' of the Welsh patronymic system and its break-down. They stated further that none of these qualified 'to be considered Welsh in origin'. More genuinely Welsh products of that patronymic system were Rees, Owen, Llewellyn, and Bevan, names with much lower counts. Bevan, for example, had a total of just 7,331 in 1881.

The fact that only 583 surnames were more frequent than Bevan at that time shows how few surnames overall were really prolific, especially those of English origin. If a total of 10,000 is seen as the minimum number for a name in the prolific category, only 428 names qualify and this total includes a number of 'pairs' like Clark and Clarke or McDonald and MacDonald. More than 90 names in this category had their origins in either Scotland or Wales, with Campbell and Robertson the highest placed Scottish names at 55 and 56. That does not fairly reflect the Scottish influence, for names which were more highly placed in the lists, such as Brown, Wilson, Scott, Watson, Young, and Anderson, all had significant numbers from Scotland. With 10,000 used as the minimum number for a prolific surname, four additional categories can be identified:

Very common	7,000 to 10,000
Common	3,000 to 7,000
Uncommon	1,000 to 3,000
Rare	Under 1,000

The extinction of surnames

The lists drawn up by Stephen Archer are themselves a historical snapshot, providing evidence of name frequencies in Britain at the time the census was taken. Names which were missing in 1881 but had been recorded at regular intervals in earlier centuries must be considered to be either extinct by then or close to extinction. Indeed, it is to be expected that a considerable number of surnames from earlier centuries will have been lost. Family historians in particular are well aware of how many surnames disappear from the records and they are not surprised to find that some of their ancestors had names which have not survived. It is not difficult to understand why that happens. Because surnames are traditionally passed from father to son, down the generations, the failure to produce a male heir marks the end of the line, unless the name is preserved in some artificial way. In other cases, names have been lost to Britain through emigration, or apparently lost when the spelling has changed dramatically. Of course, in an expanding population the chances of survival are obviously greater, but even quite common names are perpetually at risk, more so in times of war or disease.

The poll tax returns of 1377–81 capture the population of England at a low ebb, only a generation or so after the Black Death. It is clear from the records that many surnames were already hereditary, whereas others were still stabilizing. Here again the data have to be used carefully, for a by-name that disappears is different from a surname that suffers the same fate. It should be accepted that many of the entries in the 1377–81 returns related to ephemeral by-names and that new names continued to develop and find their way into the records in the centuries that followed. There is much that is still not understood about the hereditary process in that period and what lies behind the decline of some surnames later in their history. The numbers that occur in the poll tax returns frequently create the wrong impression. In 1379, for example, seven taxpayers in Sussex had the name Dymhayt, six of them in Pagham; at least two were above average in status, for they paid a higher rate of tax. Nobody with that name was recorded in 1881 and its fate in the intervening period is not known. In the 1379 poll tax return for the West Riding of Yorkshire, two of the most numerous names with distinctive origins were Baildon (12) and Pudsey (14). In 1881 both these names were rare, even if the variants are counted: the Baildons and Beldons numbered 270 and the Pudseys 108. Yet in both cases moments arose during their history when the numbers might have increased rapidly. A stone slab at Bolton-by-Bowland which commemorates the death of Sir Ralph Pudsey in 1468 bears the figures of his three wives and their twenty-five children.

David Postles touched on this topic when he wrote of the Canon family of Werrington in Devon. He described them as one of the stable elements in the community throughout the later Middle Ages, a 'core' family, and yet their history demonstrates how vulnerable such a surname could be. In the second half of the fifteenth century, members of the family held a range of important manorial offices and they were numerous enough for each man's name to require some kind of defining affix. Those quoted by Postles were 'Richard Canon de Kylwere; Richard Canon de Panston; John Canon de Hamme; John Canon de Brasecote; John Canon myller; John Canon de Nytherbrygge'; as well as 'John Canon' and 'John Canon junior'. A rental of 1494 contained the names of seven Canons, and it would not be surprising if other families had the same name, since the by-name or surname is found in other counties in earlier centuries. Yet in 1881 there was no longer anybody in Devon called Canon and only 114 people with this name nationwide, mostly in London,

Scotland, and Lancashire. It should be said though that the alternative spelling Cannon was a common name generally, if rare in Devon.

When a name has more than one origin the national totals for 1881 can mask its disappearance in one region and raise questions about its history. In 1379 William Cokschute of Chithurst in Sussex was one of six local taxpayers with that name, yet there is no evidence that it ever expanded in that county. Indeed, in 1881 the surname was not found in Sussex, although it was well established in Lancashire. The most numerous of the variant forms of the name was Cockshott (548), the majority of whom lived in West Yorkshire parishes close to the Lancashire border. McKinley found the name in the fourteenth century at Ightenhill, a locality near Burnley.

The very large number of surnames that fall into the 'rare' category make it abundantly clear that many historically important surnames, which had formerly been quite numerous, were on the verge of extinction in Britain in 1881. Two persons called Markenfield, living in Lambeth, appear to have been the last representatives of a family once powerful in the Ripon area. Five Kellogs or Kelloggs, in locations as far apart as Liverpool and Holborn, were the only representatives of a name which had its origin in Essex in the thirteenth century. The sole Armatrading listed in the census was living in Birkenhead (Cheshire). This is a Lancashire surname which had not always been rare; indeed, McKinley commented on its frequency in and around Leyland in the seventeenth century. McKinley also wrote about the unusual name Straightbarrel, saying 'it ramified in Lancashire to some degree, but has never become as numerous as some other Lancashire surnames'. By 1881 it was unrecorded in Britain and may have been extinct for some time. Without statistical evidence, it can be difficult to say whether or not a surname is extinct. Strongbow is another name that was not recorded in 1881 and yet there is an entry for it in Wilson's revised edition of Reaney's dictionary (1997); examples are quoted from 1182 to 1395, after which date its history is obscure. This latest edition of the dictionary contains numerous surnames that are now extinct.

Surnames continued to decline even after the national population had begun to increase significantly. Many disappeared in the seventeenth century, as a few examples from northern England will demonstrate. The surname Slaidburn was never common: it derived from the place of that name near Clitheroe and occurred in neighbouring parishes as late as the seventeenth century. It had gone by 1881 and may have been extinct by then for over 200 years. Edward Sladeburne of Kildwick (1633) and Richard Slaidburne of Gargrave (1625) are both recorded towards the end of its history. Less easy to trace is the surname that derived from Flanshaw near Wakefield. Spellings include Flancell, Flanceld, Flansall, Flanshall, and Flansawe, all of which reflect the way the place-name developed. When Gilbert Flanson was buried in Rothwell in 1658, he may have been the last of the line. None of the above spellings featured in the 1881 census but they can be linked in earlier centuries by genealogical work. Without such evidence it might be thought that several different surnames had become extinct. The surname Mexborough, which seems certain to have been derived from the place of that name in South Yorkshire, has a complicated history. It was recorded at intervals in Birstall parish from the fourteenth century and then in the neighbourhood of Selby and Pontefract in the sixteenth century. Its last certain home was the parish of Snaith, where references occur from 1542 to 1655. Typical variations in spellings in that period included Mexbrowghe, Mexburgh, and Mexbur; less usual were Robert Mexper (1618) and Ann Mespah (1672), the latter possibly the last member of that family. However, in 1881 two people called Mexborough were both living in London and one called Mesber was a resident of Barnet. On the other hand, the name that was featured in the *Daily Telegraph* in 1964 seems to have been a naturalized version of Mecklenburg.

Many surnames were lost when families failed to produce male heirs, but there is obviously more to it than that. Some rare names, such as Kellogg, almost vanished from these shores but are now well known in the United States of America. Occasionally, names were deliberately discarded because they have proved embarrassing. William Smalbyhind of Bradfield, recorded in the West Riding poll tax returns of 1379, had descendants called Smallbehind otherwise Smallbent, and the latter form of the surname survived into the early eighteenth century, when Anna Smallbent married at Tankersley in 1712 and Sarah Smallbent married at Penistone in 1718. Perhaps the alias reflected a campaign by the family to give their name the appearance of a place-name, comparable with Broadbent, but by the time of the 1881 census no-one was called either Smallbehind or Smallbent. The decision to do away with an embarrassing name can be more abrupt, and recently published examples are Longbottom, which was replaced by Longley, and Trumper, which was discarded by one family for a quite unrelated surname, apparently after years of jokes at their expense. However, 248 Trumpers were enumerated in 1881, and the name survives alongside the even more uncommon Trumpeter, which has the same meaning as Trumper but has not found its way into the dictionaries, so perhaps it developed from an alternative spelling, preferred because it kept faith with the name's origin and thus stopped short of outright abandonment.

An alternative road to extinction was via assimilation to a better-known surname. Lickbarrow derives from a locality in Bowness and was well represented in the Westmorland hearth tax returns of 1674. However, only nine people bore this name in 1881, possibly because the abbreviated form Barrow was preferred; at least one prominent family had chosen this alias back in 1640. Abbreviations of that type were once commonplace and they have undoubtedly affected the totals of many names, especially those that might be considered long and unwieldy, such as Haythornthwaite, Barraclough, and Ormondroyd. More subtly, it is not unusual for a distinctive and inoffensive name to lose its identity through association with one that is simply more popular. The Lancashire Turnagh, which derived from a locality in Rochdale parish, was well established there as late as the seventeenth century, but it seems then to have given way to the more prolific Turner, helped by a similarity in pronunciation. Certainly no Turnaghs were listed in 1881.

Occasionally, where the evidence points to the probable extinction of a name, it may actually survive via an unusual variant spelling. The surname Threapland was recorded in a village near Bradford for over five centuries, from c.1200. In the eighteenth century, a branch of the family that lived in Calverley, just a mile or two away but closer to Leeds, then began to use the alias Threapleton, a spelling that had occurred infrequently throughout the name's earlier history. In 1881 Threapland was all but extinct, used by just one family in York, whereas almost all the 330 Threapletons, including the variants Thrippleton and Thrapleton, lived in the Leeds and Bradford area. Although the rare Scottish surname Thriepland has the same meaning, the two names are not otherwise connected.

In a recent article Ken Tucker of Carleton University, Ottawa sought to establish what percentage of the names in the 1881 census had survived, using the 1998 electoral roll as a source of comparison. He estimated that the total dropped in that relatively short period from 401,197 to 128,970, a shortfall of more than two-thirds. Having made allowances for 'mistakes' in the larger total, his conclusion was that roughly one third of the names recorded in 1881 had become extinct by 1998. Without some knowledge of the writer's familiarity with surname development in Britain, it is difficult to determine how accurate his calculation might be, but the way he arrived at that figure becomes much clearer if the names behind the statistics are looked at more closely.

One of the examples used by Tucker was Roxburgh, a Scottish surname derived from the town of that name in Roxburghshire. In the 1881 census return 924 people bore that name and most of them lived in Scotland or the northern counties of England. By 1998 that total had increased significantly. On the other hand, at least a dozen alternative spellings in 1881 added 130 names to the total. Most of the variant spellings were found in Northumberland, Durham, Lancashire, and the West Riding of Yorkshire, but Roxbury

(19) and Roxberry (15) were more common in the London area. By 1998 no fewer than six of the twelve names were apparently extinct, that is, Roxbery (4), Roxboro (2), Roxborrow (1), Roxbourough (1), Roxbry (1), and Roxburd (2). It is important to remember, though, that the spelling of many surnames did not stabilize until the nineteenth century, so the examples that were rare in the census may have been mistakes or temporary preferences rather than authentic variants. If that were so, it would be misleading to say that they became extinct. The fate of the six might be determined by genealogical research but the likelihood is that some at least were later given a more conventional spelling.

Nevertheless, the failure of families to produce sons, especially in a relatively stable population, is probably responsible for the biggest loss of surnames. Bryan Sykes was impressed by the way his own surname had ramified over the centuries and he gave a great deal of thought to the question of why some names proliferate while others decline. The name Sykes had, he wrote, 'increased way above theoretical expectations' and this caused him to speculate what might lie behind that expansion. In the process, he outlined how the majority of family names would naturally become extinct, over several generations in a stable population, and then went on to say how much more rapidly that would happen if the males in one of the families had a Y chromosome that somehow produced more sons. This offers a new perspective on the successful expansion of some distinctive surnames.

In some ways it may seem regrettable that surnames become extinct, especially if they have been the names of prominent or interesting families over several centuries, but there is no doubt that large numbers have been lost, even though no national figures are available. It is no surprise that many surnames disappeared as a result of the Black Death, for these were newly inherited names and they had not had time to ramify before the plague spread across the country. Names were clearly very vulnerable at that time. It is less clear why such large numbers of established surnames became extinct in later centuries, but the process has never ceased and names that have been important historically continue to be lost year by year.

The successful expansion of single origin surnames

On the whole, the names with the highest totals in 1881 are likely to have had multiple origins, no matter how they are classified. That is true of those which derive from common occupations, popular first names, uncompounded geographical locations, or even fairly unimaginative nicknames. It would certainly be true of Taylor, Turner, Walker, and Wright; Allen, Jones, McDonald, and Wilson; Ford, Hill, Lee, Shaw, and Wood; Brown, Grant, Reid, White, and Young. In all these cases, and many more, each name owes its popularity to the fact that it originated in a number of different places and in different circumstances. Such names may have identical spellings but there can be no presumption that they are in any way related, nor even that they have identical meanings.

In view of that, it is interesting to comment on the successful expansion of a surname such as Metcalfe, where the evidence for a single origin is over-whelming. In 1301 Adam Medecalf' was a taxpayer in Bainbridge, an isolated village in the parish of Aysgarth in the northern Pennines. No earlier example of the surname has been recorded and there is no evidence of an alternative source, although it is not possible at this stage to say whether Adam Medecalf' was the progenitor of the family. The ramification of Metcalfe has been the stuff of legends from an early date. When Sir Anthony Wagner speculated that all the Metcalfes might be 'of one stock' and he recalled Leland's comment on Sir James Metcalfe, who had 300 men of his 'knowen consanguinitie' when he died in 1589. Other stories testify how prolific the family was in Wensleydale, and a variety of records demonstrate the popularity of the name there from the early sixteenth century. In and around Bainbridge, the expansion was certainly remarkable; in the hearth tax returns of 1673, for example, no fewer than 70 Metcalfes were taxed in the township, with many more in neighbour-ing parishes. The total in the North Riding alone was over 170.

Metcalfe has long been the preferred spelling of the name. In 1881 the national total was 6,867, which means that only 617 British surnames were more popular. There can be no doubt that the majority of these common names had plural or multiple origins. The number of Metcalfes confirm how great the expansion of the name had been in the northern dales, for 523 were listed in Aysgarth and 245 in Skipton, while the much smaller communities of Reeth (Swaledale) and Settle (Ribblesdale) had 169 and 177 respectively. The surname was prolific too in the industrial areas of the West Riding, with 426 in Bradford and 264 in Leeds, and it had spread beyond Yorkshire, for over 3,000 Metcalfes were recorded elsewhere, especially in Lancashire (812) and Durham (717), though the name was rare in both Scotland and Wales. But these numbers do not tell the whole truth about how the name had expanded, for the many obvious variant spellings included some that were also numerous. In order of frequency they were: Metcalf 6,065, Medcalf 1,171, Medcalfe 123, Midcalf 102, Mitcalf 40, Mitcalfe 14, and Midcalfe 6. These raise the total number of 'Metcalfes' in 1881 to 14,388. If the spelling had not varied, fewer than 300 British surnames would have had higher totals. Surprisingly, no examples of the dialect spellings of the surname appear to have survived, although these feature regularly in earlier Yorkshire parish registers, for example Edward Mecka of Leeds (1605) and Sarah Meccah of Hartshead (1740).

A few other West Yorkshire surnames show that the spread of the Metcalfes was not all that unusual. The total for Sykes in 1881 was 14,383, almost identical with the conflated total for Metcalfe, and in this case DNA analysis has suggested that the surname might have had a single origin. A comparison can be made with Dyson, found in the same valley as Sykes. The progenitor can be identified as John Dyson of Linthwaite, a man on record in the court rolls of Wakefield manor from 1316: he was the son of Dyonisia of Linthwaite, also known as Dye of Linthwaite, a lady who stamped her personality on the Colne Valley in the late thirteenth century. It is true that Dyson occurs occasionally as a by-name in other localities but the single origin of the Yorkshire surname was confirmed some years ago when Bryan Sykes tested the DNA of 23 volunteers and found that nearly 90 per cent of them had the same or closely related Y chromosomes. Again, it is important to look at the number of people with the surname. In 1881 the total for Dyson in Britain was 9,712 and almost 80 per cent of these were living in Yorkshire and adjoining parts of Lancashire. An astonishing 2,260 still had their homes in Linthwaite and the surrounding district. Only 444 British surnames were more common than Dyson in 1881. In the same valley several names have similarly high totals.

The evidence shows quite clearly that whereas numerous hereditary surnames have become extinct, right across the country, others have proliferated to an extraordinary degree. Even more surprisingly, most of that proliferation appears to have taken place in a relatively circumscribed area in the Pennines. At its heart are the extensive parishes of Halifax and Rochdale. It is a phenomenon that was noted in early volumes of the *English Surnames Series* but at that time no national statistics were available and the findings aroused no comment. Now, that expansion needs to be seen in the context of surname popularity more generally.

A regional phenomenon

One or two points of real interest emerge if the prolific names in the 1881 census are examined more closely. Not surprisingly, the predominant 'English' surnames with a geographic origin are those with a single, common element, such as Wood (95,496), Hill (76,256), and Shaw (55,045), although the distribution of the latter in particular is quite regional in character. The localized distribution of Booth (29,570) is probably even more pronounced, with well over half the national total in Yorkshire and Lancashire. The highest compound names in this category are Burton (25,505), Bradley (24,047), and

Riley (23,724), all of which derive from relatively common place-names. On the other hand, a closer examination of the distribution maps reveals once again how significant such names are in certain regions. Over one third of all Rileys were living in Lancashire in 1881, with very high numbers in both Burnley and Haslingden, a part of the county where the surname has a long history. Very high numbers were also listed just across the county boundary, in Halifax and other parts of the Calder Valley. Riley is recorded in those adjoining areas from the thirteenth century at least.

The expansion of Booth and Riley in that part of the Pennines, the former textile areas of east Lancashire and West Yorkshire, is almost certainly part of the phenomenon mentioned above, although it seems unlikely that that these two names have single origins. In a score of other cases, though, we find totals in excess of 10,000 for distinctive surnames which had their origins in the tiny upland hamlets and farmsteads of that region. Two of these will serve to make the point. The Lancashire surname Butterworth (10,757), number 400 in the national list, derives from a township in Rochdale parish. The place-name is distinctive but not unique, for there is a Butterworth in Elland chapelry, just a few miles distant across the Yorkshire border. However, the evidence supports the view that the massive expansion of the surname took place in and around Rochdale, a proliferation that was commented on by the Lancashire historian Fishwick. It was noted also by McKinley who counted 37 males called Butterworth in Butterworth itself in the Protestation Returns for 1642, when another 79 were listed in neighbouring parts of Salford Hundred. The expansion of the name was largely confined within that same area as late as 1800.

The West Yorkshire surname Sutcliffe expanded in a similar way in and around Heptonstall, which was a chapelry of Halifax parish. The total in 1881, not including several significant variants such as Sutcliff and Sutliff, was 11,844, placing the name at number 364 in order of frequency. It had its origin in Hipperholme, lower down the Calder Valley, but the family was already settled in the Heptonstall area by 1379 and it ramified strongly in that part of the valley over the next 150 years or so. In the far from comprehensive subsidy roll of 1545 no fewer than 18 male Sutcliffes were taxed there. The ramification of Butterworth and Sutcliffe is remarkable, but they are not the most extreme examples, for Schofield (16,259) and Greenwood (23,256), the former from Rochdale and the latter from Heptonstall, were both substantially more numerous in 1881. There is no evidence of a similar expansion in any other English region, nor indeed in other parts of Lancashire and Yorkshire, although Metcalfe is testimony to the expansion of a single family from a part of the Pennines that was relatively untouched by industry. At the heart of this spectacular ramification was the Lancashire parish of Rochdale.

The surnames of Rochdale

More than a score of distinctive surnames had their origins in this extensive parish, and a significant number of them had ramified in a quite extraordinary way by 1881. After Butterworth and Schofield, the most 'successful' names were Buckley (16,309), Howarth (14,416), and Chadwick (13,098). A number of others expanded successfully, if not quite so dramatically, including Clegg (10,206), Hamer (5,607), Whitworth (5,013), and Redfern (4,174). Clearly, the ones that are most easily identified are those that derive from distinctive minor place-names, but the nickname Lord (13,813) was also prolific in Rochdale, as were less distinctive surnames such as Taylor, Hill, and Shepherd. It is also likely that Rochdale surnames contributed significantly to the totals for Ogden (8,488), Wardle (5,809), Healey (4,911), Stansfield (4,624), Shore (3,228), and Hollingworth (2,418). These derived from place-names that occur more than once in that part of the Pennines, some of them in West Yorkshire, and in each case it is possible that more than one origin is involved.

Distinctive Rochdale surnames that moved out of the parish at an early date into adjoining parts of Lancashire and the West Riding include Beardsell, Belfield, Dearnley, Lightowler, Sladdin, Wolstenholme, and Wordsworth, all of which have significant distributions but much lower totals. The history of Brierley is particularly interesting for the evidence suggests that it was derived from Brierley in South Yorkshire but ramified in Rochdale in much the same way as names that were formed locally. It had already settled on the fringe of the parish by 1379, and by 1881 it had a total of 5,334, not including the significant spelling variant Brearley (1,879).

When the search is extended to include all the distinctive surnames that we class as prolific or very common, the outlines of this Pennine district become much clearer. In the west it extended to Bury, Blackburn, Haslingden, and Burnley; in the east as far as the West Yorkshire towns of Bradford and Huddersfield. Within this wider area we find numerically significant names such as Ashworth, Brook, Firth, Haigh, Hargreaves, Hirst, Holden and Kershaw; names with dual origins, including Ashton, Marsden, and Whittaker; and some distinctive surnames with non-geographic origins such as Crowther, Hanson, and Stott. The census data point to a phenomenal expansion of a very large number of families whose origins were in east Lancashire and West Yorkshire, with Lancashire probably even more significant in this respect than its neighbour. It seems clear that a more detailed study would be of great interest to demographers and family historians. These surnames appear to have made a disproportionate contribution to the total population of England. Genetic evidence would reveal more about their precise origins.

The surnames of Cornwall

The story of Rochdale's surnames can be contrasted with that of the characteristic surnames of Cornwall. In the early fourteenth century almost half the by-names and surnames in this remote, south-western county came from place-names, most of them deeply rooted in the Celtic language. In this respect Cornwall had more in common with Brittany than with Wales, where personal names predominated, and this was enough to give a substantial proportion of Cornish surnames a very distinctive, almost 'foreign' quality. This separateness is further emphasized by the fact that in the Cornish language the first element is usually the generic, unlike English where the generic comes last. The Cornish 'tre' may be roughly equivalent in meaning to the English 'ton' but names such as Horton and Burton do not capture our attention in the same way as Trelawney and Trevelyan. Examples of similar names, drawn from the earliest Cornish sources, demonstrate their distinctive nature: they include Roger de Treredenek (1286), Matthew Trelesyc (1327), and Harvey Trefuswethen (1377). Because the generic 'tre' identifies such a distinctive corpus of surnames, they can be used as a group to throw light on how Cornish surnames ramified in earlier centuries.

The main source used to identify the surnames that are looked at in this exercise is G. Pawley White, *A Handbook of Cornish Surnames* (1972). The intention here is to examine the expansion, or the failure to expand, of characteristic Cornish surnames, not to comment on their origins and meanings, and the limitations of both the sources and the method should be recognized at the outset. Pawley White compiled his dictionary before many of the finding aids we now take for granted had come into use, so inevitably it does not contain a definitive list of 'tre' names. Nor can we assume that this single body of names is characteristic of Cornish surnames in general, although a wider, less targeted, search has not yet offered evidence to the contrary. Finally, no attempt has been made to consider the possible effects of emigration. This limited exercise is intended simply to test whether the materials now at our disposal can be used to identify topics of potential interest to demographers, family historians, and biologists.

In total, Pawley White's dictionary lists 121 names with 'tre' as a prefix. Some of these seem certain to be variants but they are treated here independently. No attempt has been made to include names which are not in the handbook but appear to be obvious variants. For example, Tremaine and Tremayne are listed and used, whereas Tremain is not. To take the study beyond this stage, all such variations would have to be identified. Even so, despite all these reservations, it is immediately obvious that several interesting conclusions can be drawn: notably the failure of Cornish surnames to ramify within the county or nationally, in the way that surnames in some other regions ramified. Not one name in the group had a count in 1881 in excess of 1,000 and a mere 32 totalled more than 100. All these would be categorized as rare, and they are listed below in order of frequency:

Surname	Total 1881	No. in Cornwall
Treloar	578	488
Trembath	531	439
Trebilcock	451	377
Tresise	451	411
Trewin	410	241
Trethewy	394	343
Tregoning	359	276
Tremayne	310	200
Treleaven	289	142
Treen	287	Nil
Trevorrow	282	250
Tresize	278	181
Trevena	268	178
Trevethan	244	175
Trewhellla	213	201
Trevithick	205	144
Tremaine	177	59
Tredinnick	172	112
Trethowan	162	140
Tregaskis	156	97
Tregenza	155	121
Trenerry	154	125
Treweek	152	98
Treverton	150	76
Trevarthen	148	124
Tregear	147	109
Trevaskis	135	112
Trengove	128	106
Trevelyan	126	7
Trelease	107	61
Treglown	107	94
Tregunna	105	88
Trestrail	100	75

At the other end of the Pawley White list are names which seem to have been extinct by 1881: Trebarthen, Tregagle, Trepress, Tresawne, and Treworgie. Close to extinction were Trevivian (7), Treais (5), Tremenheere (5), Trescothick (4), Tregloan (4), Trevain (1), Treveen (1), and Trewen (1). It is surprising to find that Trescothick was so rare, for the name has recently become familiar at a national level through the exploits of the England cricketer. In 1881 it had no fewer than seven alternative spellings, including Trescoreich and Trescothlick, but even so the total for all eight was only 44. Numerically, the most important was Trescowthick (20). Another prominent name in this category is Trelawney, widely known because of Edward John Trelawny, the author and adventurer, or even because of Stevenson's fictional Squire Trelawney. In 1881 just 24 individuals bore the surname.

The surnames of Sussex

Richard McKinley had a vast experience of surnames in Britain and he was certainly aware of the successful expansion of names in the Pennines. He detected a similar development in the Scots-speaking parts of Scotland and listed a number of names as examples. Actually, the totals for the names he quoted vary considerably, and those for Bathgate (697) and Cleghorn (822) represent only moderately successful expansion. More numerous were Drysdale (2,535), Dunlop (4,827), Moffatt (1,925), and Tulloch (1,987), but the only one of these that can be classed as generally common is Moffatt. A surprise omission is the name Crawford which totalled 14,684 and can therefore bear comparison with the Pennine names. At that time McKinley had no access to the census data that are now available, so it is likely that his comments were sometimes based on perception and not on statistical evidence.

He was less perceptive when he wrote of certain English surnames that 'proliferated within a given area, to become numerous there if not on quite the same scale as in Yorkshire and Lancashire'. The main examples that he quoted were Busby, Belchamber, Hoggesflesh, and Scarfield. It is true that Busby (3,155) ramified strongly in Oxfordshire and parts of adjoining counties, especially Northamptonshire and Warwickshire, but all the other names were rare. Only 65 people named Belchamber were enumerated in 1881, although the variants Belchambers, Bellchamber, and Bellchambers increase the total to 548. The majority of these families lived in Kent, Sussex, Surrey, and Middlesex, with smaller numbers in Hampshire and one or two more distant counties. It seems very likely therefore that all those who bore the name in 1881 owed it to a common progenitor, possibly the Richard Belechombre who was recorded at Slindon in *c*.1280. The expansion of Belchamber may have been modest but the continuity of the name in places such as Petworth and East Preston was remarkable. The two other names also had long histories in Sussex, but in 1881 they were so rare as to be in danger of extinction: just 99 people bore the name Hogsflesh, and just eleven were known as Scarfield.

It can be shown that Sussex has more in common with Cornwall in this respect than with east Lancashire and West Yorkshire. The distinctive names that are discussed here are drawn principally from two sources: the lists compiled by H.B. Guppy in *The Homes of Family Names* (1890), and those commented on by Richard McKinley in *The Surnames of Sussex* (1988). Numerous surnames are derived from Sussex place-names, but the majority of them had relatively small totals in 1881. It is true that not all the place-names are unique and one or two have origins that are difficult to determine, but the evidence for origins within the county of Sussex is convincing. One or two such names were very uncommon. Billingshurst had a total of just 18 but more typical examples are Balcombe (457), Bathurst (410), Eversfield (120), Farncombe (146), Gratwick (97), Grinstead (351), Lindfield (374), Nutley (434), Patching (628), and Strudwick (945). A few names which expanded more successfully were Chatfield (1,443), Crowhurst (1,404), and Tickner (1,296), but these numbers are not enough for any of them to be described as common generally. It is surely significant that two of the most popular Sussex names listed by McKinley were Singleton and Sedgewick, for there is no doubt that both of them owe their high numbers to the expansion of identical surnames in the north of England. Singleton is located near Blackpool and Sedgwick is in Westmorland: both surnames are far more common in Lancashire and Yorkshire than they are in Sussex.

The picture is much the same for distinctive Sussex names in other categories. The more successful were Boniface (1,075), Botting (1,121), Comber (1,008), Gander (839), Jupp (1,673), and Woolgar (1,069), all well established in the county in 1881, but still ranked as uncommon. Even the occupational name Cheesman which is likely to have had several distinct origins totalled only 1,535. McKinley described it as 'still very numerous in the county' but only 233 people bore the name in 1881. Some of the county's most characteristic names had even lower counts: Alfrey (60), Aylwin (193), Bourner (283), Comper (111), Dumbrell (227), Pentecost (304), Primmer (214), and Walder (705). Once again, it is worth noting that some of these rare names had been relatively numerous in 1379, where Aylwins were found in at least four villages and Woolgars in five; Comber was recorded in no fewer than seven different places and three taxpayers in the village of Patching shared the name.

* * *

How can we explain these striking differences between east Lancashire and West Yorkshire on the one hand and Cornwall and Sussex on the other? The parish of Rochdale was an unusually large one, covering 41,800 acres and four townships. It is not surprising therefore to find that most of the men found marriage partners within the parish. Richard McKinley's analysis of the surnames recorded in the marriage register for the parish in 1800 showed that only 21 per cent were not recorded in the Protestation return of 1642 and that many of the new ones had come from just beyond the parish boundary. The great rise of the population from well under 10,000 in 1642 to nearly 30,000 in 1800 had been achieved by long-resident families. This suggests that the booming textile industry was providing opportunities for earlier marriages and therefore more children. The same picture is generally true for the large parish of Halifax on the other side of the Pennines. We can see how surnames might proliferate in this situation, but it is not apparent why a relatively small number of names grew to such an astonishing extent. Other places with a thriving economy and the same topography, such as the Hallamshire cutlery district, have their characteristic surnames which expanded considerably though not so prolifically as in the Lancashire and Yorkshire textile districts. Clearly, this phenomenon needs much more investigation. In the case of Cornwall, the modest totals for its distinctive surnames in 1881 are partly explained by the collapse of the copper and tin industries and the emigration of thousands of families to the United States, where it has been estimated that there may well be seven or eight times as many people of Cornish name and descent than there are in Cornwall itself, yet these names had not multiplied in the same manner as the northern ones in earlier times when the local industries were thriving. Wider and more thorough analysis is needed to establish the differences between regions right across the country in order to explain these patterns of expansion and decline. Surname counts clearly have a role to play in population studies, and the wider use of DNA as a genealogical tool promises to open a new chapter in this aspect of surname research.

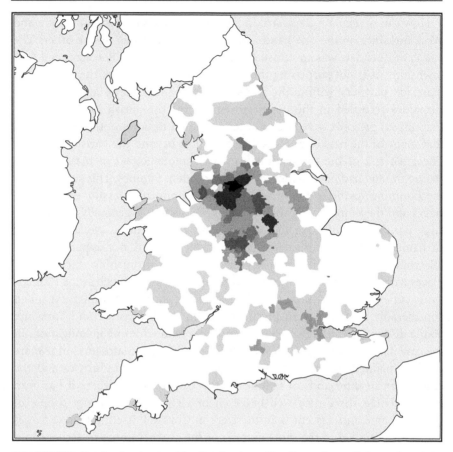

BRADBURY: distribution in 1881. The distribution of Bradbury throws light on the origin of this very common name, for it derives from Bredbury near Stockport. It ramified successfully in that area and both Lancashire and Yorkshire had high totals in 1881. On the other hand, the highest concentrations, linked with high totals, were in the north Midlands counties of Derbyshire, Cheshire, and Staffordshire. Although dictionaries link the surname with Bradbury in County Durham, which also gave rise to a surname, it was always uncommon there and can have contributed little to the national total.

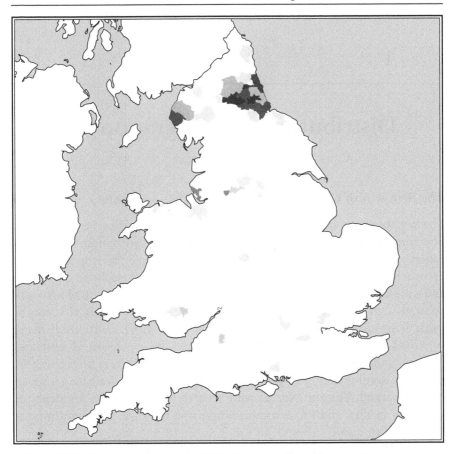

GOLIGHTLY: distribution in 1881. Golightly is an uncommon name, which Reaney and Wilson, quoting early English by-names, suggested was literally 'Go lightly', a nickname for a messenger. Only 665 with this name were enumerated in 1881. They were found chiefly in County Durham (377), Northumberland (78), Cumberland (41), and Scotland (43). The origin may actually be in Scotland for its history there also goes back to the thirteenth century. Typical spellings now are Gellatly and Galletly but Galychtly was recorded there in 1489 and this is very similar to examples of the name in Northumberland, e.g. 1574 James Galightly of Willimoteswick. The Golightlys were well established in the upper Wear Valley by 1666, for the County Durham hearth tax returns list four householders in Stanhope and two a little further down the valley at Wolsingham and Bishopley.

4

Distribution and Migration

The British 19th Century Surname Atlas: 1881 census data

The first volume in the *English Surnames Series*, published in 1973, emphasized how important it is to have information about the distribution and ramification of surnames in searching for their origins and development. This approach was demonstrated with counts of names from telephone directories and with hand-drawn distribution maps. It was difficult at that time to obtain accurate statistical information, but nevertheless those imperfect methods made it possible to demonstrate how regional in their distribution many surnames are. They also showed that the successful expansion of surnames was less random than might have been expected, with some regions being far more successful than others. The finding aids that are now available are much more advanced. They provide us with accurate data about the frequency of surnames in 1881, and the accompanying maps illustrate important aspects of their distribution.

Such aids are invaluable and they can be used to great advantage if the data are analysed in detail. Yet in some cases, total numbers per county can obscure a surname's real 'home', for over the centuries many families moved to neighbouring towns and villages and to busy commercial and industrial centres further afield, particularly to London, Lancashire, and the West Midlands. A clearer picture emerges from the statistics for the poor law unions, but even these figures cannot always be trusted: if they reveal small clusters in a thinly populated region, such as the Isle of Wight or Rutland, they can be misleading. However useful census material may prove to be, it will never be sufficient on its own to tell the full story and should be analysed in the context of each name's history.

Very many surnames, even some that are common, are still found mostly in one area. The distribution of Sharples, for example, places it firmly in Lancashire, where it was recorded in the mid-thirteenth century. In 1881 just over 90 per cent of the 5,245 people with that name lived in Lancashire. In many counties Sharples was not represented at all and even in neighbouring Yorkshire only 65 were recorded. The only other significant numbers were in Cheshire (152), Staffordshire (48), Middlesex (43), and Derbyshire (26). These totals are evidence of modest expansion into neighbouring counties and one or two major centres of population. The biggest concentration in Lancashire was in Blackburn (1,371) but a dozen miles to the south 447 were listed in Bolton, where the name was first recorded in the thirteenth century.

It is less surprising to find rare surnames that are concentrated in a particular area. All the 59 people with the Welsh surname Cunnick lived in the adjoining counties of Pembroke, Glamorgan, and Carmarthen. In Scotland, all but nine of the 189 people named Swankie lived in Angus. Garrie too was a Scottish name, borne only by 100 inhabitants, with small concentrations in Ayrshire and Midlothian. Emsden, Flathers, and Marsay, each with counts of just 100, were rare English surnames. The origin of Emsden may have been in Suffolk, for that county had 83 per cent of the total; the biggest concentration was in Bosmere (54), with a second cluster in Ipswich. By contrast, the Yorkshire name Flathers had a more scattered distribution and yet only one person with that name lived outside the West Riding – in neighbouring Derbyshire. The name Marsay was equally 'at home' in the North Riding which housed 98 per cent of the total, the majority of whom lived in Whitby and Guisborough. The two individuals who were not found there were recorded in York and just across the County Durham border at Hartlepool. Surnames such as these are quite likely to pose problems for the researcher, sometimes because they are unusual spellings of a more common name, at other times because they feature only rarely in the records.

More usually, even the most distinctive surnames had distribution patterns that were not so intense. Typically, a name that had its origin in Lancashire would be strongly represented in that county, with large numbers also in the neighbouring parts of West Yorkshire, Cheshire, and Staffordshire. In a few untypical cases the majority of the bearers of an uncommon name lived at a considerable distance from its origins. Redfern, which derives from a locality in the parish of Rochdale, serves as an example. McKinley's evidence suggests that its history was unlike that of many other Rochdale names for its expansion took place beyond its borders, notably in West Yorkshire and, less predictably, Nottinghamshire, where the name was recorded from an early date. At the time of the 1881 census only one quarter of the 4,174 Redferns lived in Lancashire. Even so, the distribution of the name was still markedly regional, with significant totals in Derbyshire (735), Cheshire (544), Staffordshire (473), and Yorkshire (408). The variant Redfearn (888) was mostly a West Riding surname.

Significant patterns of distribution can be discerned in most parts of the British Isles. Cornwall's characteristic surnames are readily identifiable by their prefixes. The distribution maps provide confirmation – if confirmation were needed – that Trelawney and Trewartha, Penhaligon and Pengelly, Polkinghorne and Polglaze are surnames that originated in the far South-west. Also distinctive are the names in the Isle of Man, where the prefix 'Mac' has been reduced to initial 'Qu', initial 'K', or initial 'C'. Typical examples are Quayle, Kermode, and Callister. Of course, some equally distinctive surnames on the island do not fall into these categories; the distributions of names such as Bridson, Mylchreest, and Teare accurately reflect their places of origin and the island's close ties with Lancashire and Cheshire, both historically and geographically. In almost every case, roughly 75 per cent of those who bore such distinctive names were still resident on the island in 1881, with a further 15 per cent or more living in Lancashire. This association is also marked by the presence on the Isle of Man of such Lancashire and Cheshire names as Radcliffe, Sayle, and Skillicorn.

The evidence for distinctive local names can be found in every parish churchyard in the country. In Kings Norton, a village just south of Birmingham, memorial stones and rolls of honour include the following names: Bolstridge, Clulee, Edkins, Farndon, Guise, Humpage, Jelfs, Pittaway, Raybould, Spilsbury, Tonks, and Warwood. Only one or two of these will be generally well known for most of them are still uncommon outside the West Midlands. The maps and statistics for 1881 reinforce the regional nature of such names, for they were rare in other parts of Britain. Raybould (903) and Humpage (357), for example, were most numerous in Staffordshire, Worcestershire, and Warwickshire, and were unheard of in counties such as Devon, Sussex, Norfolk, and Northumberland.

The maps draw our attention to similar regions, consisting of several adjoining counties. In Sussex, for example, it is common to find that a distinctive surname had expanded by 1881 into Surrey, Kent, and Middlesex, the three counties which together cover much of the Greater London area, and into neighbouring Hampshire, but that it was rarely recorded elsewhere. A typical example is provided by the 193 Aylwins, for 88 per cent of them lived in Sussex (100), Surrey (30), Hampshire (16), Kent (15), and Middlesex (9).

Welsh surnames

The surnames of the countries that make up the United Kingdom have their own national characteristics. Prolific Welsh names such as Jones, Williams, and Evans have already been mentioned but the origins of the names Price and Bowen are perhaps even more 'Welsh' since they preserve part of the prefix 'ap' or 'ab', which means 'son'. As we have seen, the patronymic system that gave rise to such names remained in use long after surnames had stabilized in England. Extracts from the records of the Caernarvonshire Quarter Sessions show how important the practice still was in the sixteenth century. In August 1542, when a case of assault was brought to the attention of the magistrates, the victim was named as Gruffydd ap Rhys ap Hywel ap Madog, a clear identity that linked him across the generations to his great-grandfather. Similar names among the gentry include Rhys ap David ap Hywel ap Gruffydd of Llanwanda, a 'gentleman' accused in that same year of illegally taking up a suit on behalf of John ap Harry ap Rhys ap Gruffydd ap Hwlcyn.

Some Welsh surnames had already become hereditary by that time and more would stabilize over the next 200 years but it was not until the early nineteenth century that some families finally acquired a surname that they passed on to their children. The great frequency of the patronymics Jones and Williams simply reflects the popularity of the first names John and William at the time when Welsh surnames were stabilizing, so it is not surprising that they are now common in many parts of Britain. Nevertheless, in 1881, even Jones was relatively uncommon in most of Scotland and down the eastern half of England. The lowest concentrations were in Lincolnshire, East Anglia, and the East Riding of Yorkshire; the highest were in Shropshire and Hereford-shire. The distribution of many common Welsh names followed a similar pattern, with numbers relatively high also in London and certain industrial areas, notably in Lancashire.

The distribution of Owens, with a total of 14,944 in 1881, is fairly typical. Over 60 per cent of those who bore the name were still resident in Wales, and a further 14.5 per cent lived in Lancashire. This figure is in marked contrast to the low total of 142 in the West Riding which amounted to less than 1 per cent. Other small but significant numbers were recorded in County Durham (372) and the border county of Shropshire (275). In many English counties the name was virtually unknown; nobody called Owens lived in Northampton-shire and very low totals were recorded in Leicestershire (1) and Norfolk (2). In Scotland Owens was well established only in Lanarkshire, no doubt a reflection of the importance there of the burgeoning city of Glasgow.

English names in Wales

Because so many Welsh surnames are among the most prolific in Britain the story of some of the less common names in Wales formerly received little attention. Fortunately, the valuable work of John and Sheila Rowlands has drawn attention to many of these, especially to a number of apparently 'English' surnames that have played their part in Welsh history. Some of these derive from personal names that came into use in Wales after the Reformation, such as Benjamin, David, Joseph, and Michael. These biblical names were not popular in England when surnames were stabilizing and all four surnames can be traced to Wales. David in particular has continued to be prominent in Glamorgan and that county accounted for two thirds of the national total in 1881. English writers have commented on all four names but have failed to recognize their importance in Wales.

The Welsh link is even more pronounced in the case of such uncommon surnames as Ephraim, Esau, and Jehu. Despite being very rare, Esau (71) was relatively widespread in 1881 whereas Ephraim (38) was found almost exclusively in Merioneth and may have had a single family origin there. It is claimed that Jehu (130), a name that is now dispersed around the world, originated with Jehu ap Richard, a carpenter from Montgomeryshire; if so, by English standards this was a late derivation, for he died in 1647 aged just over 70. These three names are not mentioned by Reaney and Wilson, and only David, of the seven discussed here, has an entry in T.J. Morgan and Prys Morgan, *Welsh Surnames* (1985).

The surname Harry is a particularly interesting case in this category, since it is mentioned in several works of reference without any comment on its distinctive distribution. The total in 1881 was 2,168, significantly smaller than that for Henry which shares the same personal name origin. In 1881 the majority of people called Harry lived either in Cornwall and Devon (649) or in Wales (960); the only other significant cluster was in London (199). It is not unusual for a name to be found in both Devon and South Wales for people moved between the two regions across the Bristol Channel, but the total in Cornwall (470) may point to an independent origin there. The spelling of Harry hints at a late derivation, for examples of the northern surname Harrison suggest that 'Herry' rather than 'Harry' was the usual English pronunciation well into the fifteenth century. Even as late as 1530 a York freeman was described as John Harryson the son of Richard Herryson. If it is true that the surname Harry's distribution points to its late development, the Cornish evidence is of particular interest.

John and Sheila Rowlands have drawn to our attention other names that have been treated by English scholars as English in origin, with no reference to their numerical superiority in Wales. The by-name Ace, for example, has been noted in numerous English counties and it certainly gave rise to a surname. A family called Ace lived in Holderness into the sixteenth century and the surname survives there as Acey, but otherwise the name appears to have no recent history in England. The national total in 1881 was 257 and most of these families lived in Glamorgan; only 22 Aces were recorded in widely scattered parts of England and Scotland, with a small cluster of six just across the Welsh border in Gloucester.

Among other names that have significant numbers in Wales but which have escaped the attention of English writers are Bufton, Benbow, Games, Hullin, and Peregrine. For example, Peregrine is usually linked with Pilgrim which is explained as a nickname meaning 'one who had made the pilgrimage to Rome or the Holy Land'. Pilgrim has many variations in spelling whose distribution points to a shared origin, probably in Essex, whereas Peregrine was a rare surname in 1881 that was found almost exclusively in the counties of Carmarthen, Glamorgan and Pembroke. In *The Surnames of Wales* the authors point to its occasional use there as a personal name but also link it to the Latinization of Perkin in the parish registers.

In most cases, the failure to identify names as Welsh in origin has not affected the explanation of their meaning, but some significant exceptions to this generalization can be found. Games is one of nine names which Reaney and Wilson derived from the word 'game' and they explained it as a nickname 'for one fond of or good at games'. In 1881 most of the 1,238 people with this surname lived in Breconshire and Monmouthshire; otherwise, the only significant English group was in London. In Wales the origin is the adjective 'gam' which means 'crooked', and the 'family of the famous Dafydd Gam of Breconshire' is regarded as a possible source. One interpretation of the meaning is that it referred to a person with a squint.

The distribution patterns of other surnames can sometimes oblige us to reconsider their meanings and origins. The suggestion that Lodwick derives from Ludwick Hall in Hertfordshire sounds reasonable enough but the numbers in Wales reflect the surname's long history there and they support the view of Welsh scholars that Lodwick is a form of the personal name Lewis. Worthing in Sussex may appear to be the most likely origin of the surname Worthing, and the by-name is on record from the thirteenth century, but the distribution suggests an alternative derivation. In 1881 just one person in Sussex had the name whereas it was well established in the counties of Radnor, Brecon, and Monmouth. The Shropshire parish of Worthen seems a more likely source.

John and Sheila Rowlands also provide evidence of migration from England into Wales. Among several lead-mining families who moved there from Derbyshire, some of them from as early as 1576, were those with the distinctive surnames Bamford, Bonsall, Hatfield, Sheldon, and Wigley. Brigstocke, derived from a Northamptonshire place-name, can be traced to John Brig-stocke who moved to Carmarthenshire in 1626. This spelling of the surname survives there, whereas Brigstock, without the final 'e', was still principally found in Leicestershire and Northamptonshire in 1881. Similarly, the distributions of Maybery and Mayberry reflect the move westwards of a Worces-tershire family: in 1753 Thomas Maybery acquired Brecon furnace and Pipton forge for his son John. In these and other cases, DNA might now confirm a link with English families.

Scottish surnames

The Gaelic prefix 'Mac', sometimes abbreviated to M' or Mc, is the equivalent of 'son' in English and it is hugely popular in Scotland and Ireland. George F. Black's monumental work *The Surnames of Scotland* (1946) has 125 pages devoted to surnames with this prefix and they range from the well-known MacDonald to the obscure McSporran, the latter found principally in Argyll-shire in 1881. Many other Gaelic names abound in Scotland, notably Cameron and Campbell, but it is names with the prefix 'Mac' that are traditionally associated with the Highlands by people in other parts of Britain. The data for 1881 testify to their northern origin.

If McLean, with a total of 20,479, is taken as an example, it can be seen that the name was still based principally in the Highlands and in Lanarkshire, the latter including the great city of Glasgow. Numbers in Lowland Scotland and the Borders were low, as the figures in the following counties indicate: Peebleshire (27), Selkirkshire (22), and Roxburghshire (39). In many English counties the totals were even smaller: Lincolnshire (2), Suffolk (5), and Nottinghamshire (6). Herefordshire and Huntingdonshire had nobody with the name. The picture is much the same for the common variant MacLean (3,723) and indeed for most Highland surnames. The names McDonald (48,170) and Macdonald (13,341) were among the most prolific in Britain in 1881 but they too were poorly represented in most English counties. No McDonalds lived in Huntingdonshire and only eight were listed in North-amptonshire.

In many northern English parish registers the names of highlanders were clearly unfamiliar to the ministers and clerks when they began to appear during the seventeenth century. The story of one Scotsman who settled in Skipton will illustrate the point. The John McFarland who was a shoemaker in the town in 1769 was probably the John, son of James, who was born there in 1735. James was a soldier and it seems likely that his wife Ann was a local girl for they had several children in the years up to 1752. By 1739 James was already being described as a labourer rather than a soldier. It seems unlikely that he was literate, so he would have been unable to advise the minister on the correct spelling of his surname. The entries in the register include the following variations: Mackfardnind, Mackfirnel, Mackferlin, McFarnell, Macfarnie, and Mackfarling. In the next generation the name stabilized in Skipton as McFarland and by 1881 most of the 339 bearers of this name lived either in England or the Lowlands, especially in Lancashire (125), Durham (31), and Lanarkshire (34). MacFarland (48) was also chiefly an English variant, whereas the characteristic Highland spellings were McFarlane (10,957) and MacFarlane (1,997).

A thorough survey would provide fascinating information on migration from the Highlands into England by 1881 but even without that it is possible to see that Lancashire was almost invariably the English county with the highest totals, and not just because it had such a large population. In the case of McDonald the statistics for some of the major counties were: Lancashire (3,314), Middlesex (1,439), County Durham (1,102), the West Riding (733), Surrey (416), and Staffordshire (233). The figures for some individual towns and cities are also of interest: Liverpool (640), Newcastle-upon-Tyne (251), Manchester (215), Leeds (109), Birmingham (72), Hull (38), Bristol (17), Nottingham (10), and Norwich (1).

Scottish surnames from the Lowlands and Border regions have more in common linguistically with English names; the population lists quoted by Black for the fourteenth century emphasize that point. The individuals named in 1357 as representatives of the royal burghs included Alexander Gylyot, John Goldsmyth, John Mercer, Robert Kyd, Thomas Johnson, Laurence Bell, and Simon Potter. Men with an obvious English background were Adam de Congleton and Andrew de Ponfret (Pontefract). Others took their names from Scottish place-names, for example Adam de Haddington and William de Leth, but overall the list is very similar to English lists for the same period. Nevertheless, numerous distinctive Scottish surnames arose in the Lowlands and Borders and some of them had become prolific by 1881.

Henderson (32,554) is etymologically 'the son of Henry' and can therefore be compared directly with several English surnames, especially Harrison (66,470). In 1881 it was still a very common name in the Lowlands, with high numbers in Lanarkshire and Midlothian, but it had also made a significant impact on all the northern English counties and the capital city. This was most evident in Durham (3,385) and Northumberland (2,601), but Lancashire (1,404) and Middlesex (1,408) also had high counts. The West Riding total of 569 was low by comparison, even when the relative concentrations are taken into account. Much lower still were the totals for Essex (77), Staffordshire (53), and Leicestershire (52). The statistics and maps for names such as Reid (31,517), Davidson (25,201), Paterson (20,417), and Kerr (16,356) are sufficiently like those for Henderson to indicate that they reflect a similar pattern of migration over the centuries.

English surnames in Scotland

A number of surnames that are essentially Scottish in terms of their history and distribution developed in the Anglo-Norman period and had their origins in England. Typical and well-known examples are Graham, Lindsay, and Ramsay, all found in Scotland from the twelfth century but traditionally linked to the English place-names Grantham, Lindsey, and Ramsey. Less well known is Congleton, a rare surname which probably derived from the Cheshire place-name. In Black's view, the barony of Congalton in East Lothian took its name from the family, who are on record in Scotland from *c.*1182. Black also commented on the name's decline but it was borne by 46 people in 1881 and small groups were recorded in Renfrewshire, Midlothian, and Fifeshire. Congalton (21) was principally a Lanarkshire surname; other variants included Conkleton (32), a Hexham name in 1881, and Congerton (23) and Conkerton (29), two spellings with Yorkshire connections. Several of these names were identical with variants of the Cheshire place-name.

Even less obviously English is the rare name Kinniburgh, found principally in Lanarkshire and Dunbartonshire in 1881. It had more than a dozen variant spellings, all of them rare, ranging from Kinnibrough to Kenburn and Kinnebaugh. They may appear to be characteristically Scottish but Black traced them back to Geoffrey de Coningesburgh who witnessed an important Scottish charter in 1164. The source of that name is the South Yorkshire place-name Conisbrough which was used as a by-name but not as a surname in its county of origin.

Lowland Scots is a dialect of English, and so many Lowland surnames have 'English' origins. These have not always been recognized by English writers as Scottish surnames, but the data for 1881 make it clear how Scottish they are in both origin and distribution. Reaney clearly considered Lorimer to be an essentially English surname and he noted by-names from the early twelfth century in various English counties. Nevertheless, most of the name's history was traced to different parts of Scotland by Black, whose examples date from the thirteenth century. In 1881 the total for the surname was 1,196, of whom 77 per cent were resident in Scotland, with significant concentrations in Dumfriesshire and Banffshire. The few English Lorimers were in scattered localities across the country and, as these included London, industrial

Lancashire and parts of Northumberland and Durham, some of these families, if not the majority, must have originated north of the border. The hereditary name may have an independent history in England, for it was recorded there from time to time, but if that is the case it never became popular.

Other occupational names in this category, which belong to Scotland more than they do to England, are Dorward, Hunter, Milne, Shearer, and Souter. Reaney recognized that both Durward and Dorward have a long history in Scotland but he gave the impression that they are also English surnames. Of course, the by-name was derived from an English term and it was recorded in the Middle Ages in places such as Norfolk and Hampshire, but the evidence suggests that the surnames are Scottish in origin and much of their history is certainly north of the border. More than 88 per cent of the people who bore either of the two names in 1881 lived in Scotland. Dorward was particularly common in Angus, whereas Durward was the more usual spelling in Aberdeen. The door-ward was literally the door-keeper and this became an official title under the early Scottish monarchy.

Sievewright is another rare occupational surname that is found principally in Scotland. Like Dorward and Durward it was especially well established in Aberdeen and Angus. It had several variants in 1881, among them Sievwright, Sivewright, and Seivewright. None of these was particularly frequent but together they came to a total of just over 600, with very few families in England. The only by-names quoted by Reaney were from sources in Yorkshire, with Simon le Siuewricht recorded as early as 1219. In a North Yorkshire subsidy roll of 1301 no fewer than four men had the name but there is no evidence that it ever became hereditary there. Curiously, the *OED* has no reference to the word 'sievewright', even though the craft was once practised in Edinburgh.

In other cases, it may be a particular spelling of the surname that belongs to Scotland rather than to England. Most dictionaries list Leaper, Leeper, and Leiper under a single heading, as though they share a common history and origin. Their meaning may be the same but the distribution pattern of Leiper shows that it cannot be treated as an English surname, for 97 per cent of the 688 bearers of this name in 1881 lived in Scotland, with a huge concentration in Kincardineshire; just 22 Leipers lived in England, half of them in Northumberland. In the early part of the name's history the spellings in England and Scotland were very similar but Black suggested that Leiper began to emerge as the preferred form in Scotland in the seventeenth century.

Other Scottish surnames that are found as by-names in England include Adam, Gibb, Orr, Pettigrew, Rankin, and Stark. The list must also include numerous patronymics such as Dickson, Thomson, Watson, and Wilson, all of which have high numbers in both countries. Reference to the distribution maps will reveal many more. It is clear that English writers have often failed to recognize some surnames as essentially Scottish, partly because they had no distribution maps and statistics of the kind that are now available and partly because the names were derived from English words rather than from Gaelic.

Irish surnames

The history of surnames in Ireland poses particular problems for all historians and it is impossible to ignore the difficulties. They are commented on by Edward MacLysaght, in his Introduction to *The Surnames of Ireland* (sixth edition, 1985) and looked at in the case of individual names from Northern Ireland by Robert Bell in *The Book of Ulster Surnames* (1988). The historian's principal concern is with the different ways in which Irish surnames were distorted under English influence, for the resulting forms threaten the interpretation of the distribution and ramification of surnames in Britain more generally.

For Ireland as a whole that distortion began when the English Crown attempted to forbid the use of Irish names in the fourteenth century, although Irish writers claim that this had little immediate effect. However, from the seventeenth century onwards, the unwillingness of the English to accept native forms resulted in widespread anglicization of almost all Irish names and the traditional prefixes Mac- and O' virtually disappeared. Their resumption in more recent years has not always been accurate and MacLysaght quotes the case of John Costelloe, the former Prime Minister ('Taoiseach') of Ireland, whose name was given the prefix O' in official Irish documents when it should have been Mac-. The resumption gathered pace in the twentieth century with the revival of national consciousness but many names of all types remained resistant to change and these are the ones that historians need to be aware of.

Many Irish surnames were simply translated into their English equivalent by clerks, a process that is perhaps best exemplified by the name MacGowan. In Gaelic this would apparently have been written Mac an Ghabhann, so that the form MacGowan already represents a partial anglicization. Because it means 'son of the smith' it was readily translated into Smith, although Smithson would have been more accurate. MacLysaght considered that it is impossible now to determine what proportion of English surnames in Ireland are really of English origin and that 'in and around Co. Cavan nearly all Smiths are MacGowans or O'Gowans in disguise'.

Mistranslation may have been very common. In Irish 'luain' was the word for Monday and so the surname Monday was used as the English version of

MacAloon, a variant of MacGloin. The change was influenced by the supposed similarity of 'luain' to the latter part of the name, even though there is no connection in meaning. MacAloon is itself a partial anglicization of Mac Giolla Eoin, for which an accurate translation would be 'devotee of St John'. The English surname Monday was rare in 1881 but was found in many counties, especially in and around London; the by-name is on record from the thirteenth century.

It is easy to understand that English officials would have experienced difficulty with the Gaelic spellings of Irish names and not surprising that they simplified and even abbreviated them. MacLysaght's own surname would have been written as Mac Giolla Iasachta but was regularly shortened to Lysaght, and it survives in America as Lysaught. It was only a short step from mistranslation and abbreviation to distortion based simply on a similarity in pronunciation. One example of this is Mucklebreed, a distortion of the Irish name Mac Giolla Bhrighde, which was usually anglicized as MacGilbride but was found also as MacBride, Gilbride, and Kilbride.

These developments are significant enough in the history of surnames in Ireland but emigration ensured that they became important issues for historians in every part of the British Isles. It is impossible to calculate the impact that Irish 'Smiths' will have had on the national total for Smith in 1881, but it has been reckoned that more than 400,000 native Irish were already resident in England, Scotland, and Wales in 1841, that is before the famine years of the later 1840s. Nor can it be safely assumed that only a very few prolific surnames such as Smith were affected, for a close study of the work done by Irish scholars throws new light on many supposedly English names. Typical examples include Buckley, which has a long history in England but was also the usual anglicized form of O'Buachalla, a surname found in Offaly, where it also has the variants Buhilly and Boughla. Buckley is said to occur mainly in the counties of Cork and Tipperary, but it is likely that some Buckley families moved across the Irish Sea. Many more examples could be quoted: Bradley was 'seldom of English origin' but a synonym of O'Brallaghan; Bingham, often linked with the Nottinghamshire place-name Bingham, is an Ulster name and is said by Bell to be a variant of the Scottish Bigham or Biggam. The evidence suggests that no English surname in Ireland should be taken at face value.

In an appendix to his dictionary MacLysaght listed common English and Scottish surnames that are now found in Ireland and have a count in excess of 4,000. They have all been in the country since 1659 at least and among them are Bell, Black, Clarke, Eccles, King, Russell, White, and Young. Some of them, he said, were 'as often as not Gaelic names in disguise'. By 1881 these would have found their way into most parts of the British Isles.

English names in Ireland

The English influence on surnames in Ireland is not confined to the anglicized spellings just discussed but goes right back to the Anglo-Norman period. Indeed, many names that are now regarded as essentially Irish were of Norman origin, such as Burke, Cusack, and Dillon. Genuinely English names followed soon afterwards: Sutton was prominent in the counties of Wexford and Kildare from the thirteenth century; Woodman was associated with County Louth from the fourteenth century, and Davenport occurred in Dublin in 1477. Skeffingtons have lived in Ireland since 1534, the year when Sir William Skeffington arrived, and the Irish Edgeworths claim descent from a family that settled in County Longford in 1583. In 1881 this name was very rare in England but a significant group remained in Gloucestershire where it is likely to have originated. Many more distinctive English names found their way into Ireland as a result of deliberate policies of colonization, especially during the seventeenth century: Hungerford moved there from Wiltshire and became quite numerous in County Cork; Penrose arrived in the country from Cornwall, via Yorkshire, and was prominent in the counties of Wicklow and Waterford. Other names from this period include Annesley, Beresford, Dawson, Proctor, Tarleton, and Tottenham.

Since many English surnames have such a long history in Ireland they are occasionally more common there than in or near their place of origin. Indeed, several have survived in Ireland which were on the verge of extinction in England by 1881. Mapother is one such name, associated with County Roscommon from as early as 1613 according to MacLysaght. It was originally Maypowder and is likely to derive from the Dorset place-name Mappowder. Early spellings of this place-name indicate that it was derived from the Old English 'mapuldor', an alternative word for the maple. In 1881 the surname was exceptionally uncommon in England, occurring once in Devon as Maypowder and eight times in other parts of the West Country as Mapowder. Six people named Mapother in Liverpool had the Irish form of the name and may have been recent immigrants. Also described by MacLysaght as a west of England surname was Thackaberry, established in County Wexford from the mid-seventeenth century. The name was unrecorded in England in 1881, although four rare variants occurred in London: Thackabury (1), Thackerbury (2), Thackenberry (1), and Thackburry (2). Tackaberry, which was as an alternative Irish spelling, was recorded just five times in England, three of these in the Liverpool parish of Toxteth Park, one in Chertsey in Surrey, and one in Newcastle-upon-Tyne; these too may have been immigrants from Ireland.

Irish names in England

By 1881 Irish surnames had found their way into many parts of the British Isles and in particular into the greatest cities. Murphy, the most common of them all, had a total of 23,881 in England, Scotland, and Wales, and only 140 names were more popular. In England it was particularly numerous in Lancashire (6,757) but significant counts were also recorded in County Durham, London, and the West Riding of Yorkshire. In Scotland, the biggest concentration was in Lanarkshire (2,247); in Wales the largest totals were in the southern industrial counties of Glamorgan (650) and Monmouthshire (280). Sullivan (12,692) may have been less popular but it was more common in London than Murphy, with a combined total in Middlesex and Surrey of 5,351. It was also more common than Murphy in Wales, with 1,260 in Glamorgan and 488 in Monmouthshire. By contrast, the numbers in Lanarkshire (172) and the West Riding (260) were low. In Lancashire (1,482) the total was high but numerically less significant than the total for Murphy.

A closer examination of these statistics reveals how unevenly the two Irish names were distributed. Sullivan, for example, totalled 70 in Redruth and Penzance but only 24 in Newcastle-upon-Tyne. The figure for Merthyr Tydfil (430) far exceeded the figures for Leeds (44) and Sheffield (26). In Jersey, Sullivan had a count of 44, whereas Suffolk had only 5, Bedfordshire 4, and Buckinghamshire 3. Even Murphy was uncommon in many places, as the following county totals indicate: Oxfordshire (8), Norfolk (9), Wiltshire (11); the name was absent from Rutland and had a very low count of 51 in Leicestershire. In the extreme north-west of England Cumberland had 460 Murphys but Westmorland had only two; the Cumberland families were established in Cockermouth (93) and Whitehaven (248).

Although Gaelic names were rarely found in England before the late eighteenth century, by the beginning of Queen Victoria's reign they were well established in the industrial centres. The earliest civil registration records for England and Wales, starting in 1837, provide a clear picture of migration from Ireland on the eve of the great famine. Lancashire and London were the favoured destinations for the Agnews, Keegans, Kavanaghs, Keoghs, Kearneys, and Rourkes, but the Keefs and Keefes of County Cork and other parts of Munster were less likely to arrive via Liverpool; 60 of the 108 who died during the five years ending on 31 December 1846 had lived in London, compared with 26 in Lancashire, and a few more in Bristol and south Wales.

London had always been a magnet for migrants, but now the industrial districts of northern England were accessible to the Irish and the Scots and they offered plenty of opportunities for unskilled workers. The deaths registered in England and Wales between 1842 and 1846 included those of 9,382 men, women, and children of Irish or Scottish Highland origins whose names began with the Gaelic Mc-. The various registration districts within London recorded 1,898 of these deaths, but the greatest concentration was in south Lancashire, from Liverpool (1,791) and neighbouring West Derby (338) to Manchester (850), Ashton-under-Lyne (183), Chorlton (179), and Salford (135). The northern part of the county was like most parts of rural England in having few immigrants but, altogether, Lancashire accounted for 3,988 or 42.5 per cent of the Mc- deaths that were recorded in England and Wales between 1842 and 1846. Other large numbers were found near these districts or close to the Scottish border: Newcastle-upon-Tyne (270), Berwick (178), Whitehaven (169), Greenwich (118), Medway (107), and Stockport (103). The industrial parts of the West Riding and the West Midlands were not yet major attractions for Scottish and Irish migrants, though Leeds and Birmingham each recorded about 100 deaths. Nor were the industrial valleys of south Wales, for only 92 deaths were registered in the whole of that country. Some other Mc- names were registered in and around southern ports – Plymouth, Portsmouth, Gravesend, and the Medway estuary – but few of these migrants had ventured far inland. The general distribution pattern of Irish and Highland names in the 1840s was much the same as it was a generation later, though by the time of the 1881 census the numbers had risen sharply.

Internal migration in the British Isles

The statistics for such prolific names as Murphy and Sullivan are of great interest but distinctive surnames with more modest totals can often be even more helpful to researchers, especially when those names have remained close to where they originated. However, it should not be assumed that a name will always be concentrated close to where it stabilized. An early migration, together with a period of successful expansion, can mean that it prospered far away from its roots. The surname Skillicorn illustrates that point to perfection for it is more numerous now in the Isle of Man, which is its adopted 'home', than in its native county of Lancashire.

Skillicorn is an uncommon surname with a difficult etymology and it has attracted a good deal of attention. Reaney correctly identified its Lancashire origin and noted its presence in the Isle of Man, a point made much earlier by Harrison in *Surnames of the United Kingdom* (1912–18). McKinley made the same observations and commented on the land-owning Skillicorn family of Preese in Amounderness. He had found the name in Lancashire from the early fourteenth century and said that it was quite common there in parishes such as Chipping and Whalley, even as late as the seventeenth century. He also made the point that one or two early examples were in the form 'de Skillicorne', which is usually an indication of a place-name origin, although he thought it unsafe to rely on the presence of the preposition when considering the surname's possible meaning. In 1881 only 384 people in Britain were called Skillicorn. Roughly two-thirds of these (251) lived in the Isle of Man and only 93 were resident in Lancashire. Most of the others lived in neighbouring counties, including two small clusters in Cumberland and the West Riding – the latter probably a single family in Dewsbury (16). The main concentrations in Lancashire were in the Liverpool area, notably in West Derby and Toxteth Park, and little evidence remained of the earlier expansion in Amounderness. It must be a possibility that some of the Liverpool families had moved back into Lancashire in more recent times. J.J. Kneen, in *The Personal Names of the Isle of Man* (1937), noted connections between the Skillicorns and the Christian family of Milntown and he stated that the Skillicorns of Kirk Lonan were direct descendants of emigrants from Lancashire.

This migration by the Skillicorns was not the only move to the Isle of Man by a Lancashire family; surnames such as Halsall and Radcliffe are numerous on the island. The unusual name Maddrell is thought to be a local variant of the Lancashire Mather, formerly Madderer. The connection between the two territories is not just one of geography. In 1403 the lordship of the island was granted to Sir John Stanley, whose family ruled as 'Kings of Mann' for 350 years. A Lancastrian was made Governor, and over the centuries a number of men from the county were appointed to important offices. These include individuals with such distinctive Lancashire and Cheshire names as Dutton, Fazakerley, Kirkham, and Greenhalgh, thus indicating how the distribution of surnames could be affected by great estate owners.

Tordoff is another distinctive and unusual surname that ramified away from its place of origin. It derives from a locality now known as Tordoff Point on the Scottish side of the Solway Firth. The John de Dordofe who was recorded in 1296 was one of those who signed the infamous Ragman's Roll in Berwick-on-Tweed and, according to Alasdair Steven, the surname survived in Dumfriesshire into the late fifteenth century. The next references place it in York between 1499 and 1524, where the family were pewterers, and then in and around Leeds and Bradford by 1572, where it ramified successfully in the village of Wibsey. More than 95 per cent of the 707 Tordoffs in 1881 lived in the West Riding, with Bradford (386) and Leeds (145) the major centres; the surname is still numerous in both places at the present day. The rare variant Tordiff (10) was found principally in Cumberland in 1881 and this family may never have moved far from the Solway Firth. One fascinating aspect of Tordoff's history is that some families in the Bradford area have clung to the belief that they originate from Scotland although the stories that are told in support of that belief attribute their arrival in Yorkshire to relatively late events in Anglo-Scottish history.

The migration and distribution of Hepworth, 1274–1881

The 1881 data has provided evidence of patterns of distribution which suggest that migration often took place along predictable routes, reflecting certain aspects of social and economic history. Nevertheless, each surname has its own distinct history, as the evidence for Skillicorn and Tordoff demonstrates. Sometimes, the effect of an early migration on a distribution pattern can be more subtle, as the history of the Yorkshire surname Hepworth will illustrate. This surname derives from a village of Hepworth, located six miles south of Huddersfield on the fringe of the moors. The climate there can be harsh and the acid soil is less suitable for arable than it is for pasture. For much of its history Hepworth was part of the extensive manor of Wakefield; it was a small community and had hamlet status in a territory called Holmfirth or the Graveship of Holme. In 1881 the Hepworths numbered 3,418, of whom 2,607 or 70 per cent lived in Yorkshire, mostly in the south-western part of the county. Another 421 lived in adjoining counties, including 236 in Lancashire. Smaller concentrations were found in and around London, which of course had long attracted migrants from all over the country, but it is possible that some of these, especially families in Essex, owed their name to Hepworth in Suffolk. That aspect of the name's history needs further research but the group is a relatively small percentage of the total and does not really affect the early history of the northern surname. The distribution map for Hepworth points to its successful expansion quite close to the place where it originated, but the influence that the Black Death had on that expansion can be appreciated only when the historical evidence is studied more closely.

The late thirteenth century saw an increase in the national population and great activity in the land market in Holmfirth, particularly in the eastern half of the graveship. Significant areas of former common land were cleared and numerous plots changed hands, some of them as large as ten acres. Individuals moved into the region from neighbouring territories, including several from South Yorkshire: William de Hallomschire was clearly from Hallamshire and Thomas de Billeclyf came from Belle Clive near Langsett. As a consequence, the area under cultivation increased considerably and some time before 1315 a new manorial corn mill was built down in the valley, by the stream where the small and aptly-named town of New Mill now lies. From the start, this mill was closely associated with Hepworth and the neighbouring hamlets of Fulstone and Wooldale.

It is difficult to decide how many of the surnames in Hepworth were hereditary at that time, for some were clearly in a transitional stage. In 1307, for example, the Thomas, son of Simon, who took 1½ acres from the waste in Hepworth, is likely to have been the Thomas, son of Simon de Heppeworth, who was recorded six years later. Throughout that early period, the name of the hamlet was a consistently popular by-name or surname. In 1274 no fewer than six male 'de Hepworths' can be identified in the rolls: Thomas, Warin, Adam, Henry, Jordan, and Simon. In the period 1348–50 at least five men bore the name: Roger, Nicholas, Simon, Richard, and William.

A significant percentage of the local population perished in the Black Death. The editor of the Wakefield court rolls for 1348–50 wrote of 'signs of an abnormally high mortality' and the roll of 14 July 1349 drew attention to the deaths of no fewer than 22 tenants. Nevertheless, as the poll tax returns of 1379 show, many families survived the disaster and continued to live in the graveship. They included people named Hinchliffe, Littlewood, Earnshaw, and Broadhead, surnames that had their origins in the longer-established western hamlets, not in the newly-exploited eastern territory. In contrast, nobody called Hepworth now lived in the graveship, though the surname was recorded in two neighbouring parishes: John de Hepworth was a smith in Dalton (Kirkheaton) and another John de Hepworth was taxed in Almondbury. These were both long-established townships, in a less hostile environment than much of the Graveship of Holme. Equally significant is the evidence that in 1379 several families called Hepworth were living further to the south or east, in Cawthorne, Greasbrough, Frickley, and Sprotbrough. The distance of these villages from Hepworth varied from eight to twenty-two miles. The surname is unrecorded in these places before 1379, so it seems that at least some of the families had found it either necessary or advantageous to leave the New Mill area after the plague, moving to districts where the land was less marginal.

The later distribution of the surname can be assessed at different times using subsidy rolls and hearth tax returns, which emphasize expansion in south-west Yorkshire, most notably in the parishes of Almondbury and Kirkheaton. In the hearth tax returns for the West Riding in 1672 none of the 40 taxpayers named Hepworth lived in the Graveship of Holme. Just one family was taxed in Huddersfield and another in Halifax, whereas significant expansion had taken the surname into parts of the Calder Valley lower downstream, into Birstall, Dewsbury, and Wakefield; other Hepworths lived in several South Yorkshire villages. This pattern of distribution, which had its origins in a migration that apparently took place before 1379, was emphasized in 1881, when Dewsbury, Wakefield, and Barnsley were at the heart of the surname's expansion.

* * *

In *The Midland Peasant,* his study of the Leicestershire open-field parish of Wigston Magna, W.G. Hoskins remarked on the 'great reshuffle' of the population caused by the Black Death, after which the peasantry gradually re-established roots, but little has been written about the impact that the plague may have had on the stability of the population in upland communities such as the one at New Mill, where new land had recently been brought under the plough. Surnames clearly provide one source of evidence. When we consider a number of other surnames that had their origins in the Graveship of Holme it soon becomes clear that each has an interesting pattern of distribution, one that can be attributed, in part at least, to a significant early migration. Examples include Earnshaw, Fulstone, Hogley and Ogley, Loukes, and Ramsden. As genealogy combines with genetics to produce ever more accurate histories of family names it seems inevitable that our analysis of their distribution patterns will open up a new role for surname studies, benefiting not only genealogy but the social and economic history of the country as a whole.

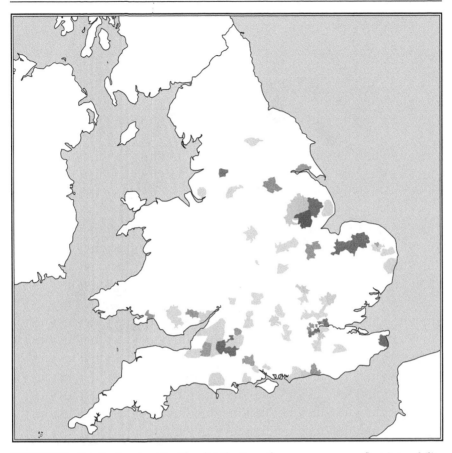

TROLLOPE: distribution in 1881. The distribution of a surname may reflect its mobility rather than its origin. That is true of Trollope, a rare but distinctive name which derives from Troughburn in Northumberland, formerly Trollop. Early examples are recorded in Scotland, Durham, and Yorkshire, and Robert Trollop was a saddler in York in 1424; by the 1500s Thomas Trollop was resident in Sussex and John Trollope in Norfolk. In 1881 the name was widely distributed, with significant numbers in Norfolk and Lincolnshire, Surrey and Sussex. Two larger groups were in Middlesex and the South-west, notably in Wiltshire (161) and Somerset (52). Northumberland had no Trollopes and only three Trollops. The novelist Anthony Trollope was born in London but his ancestors came from County Durham.

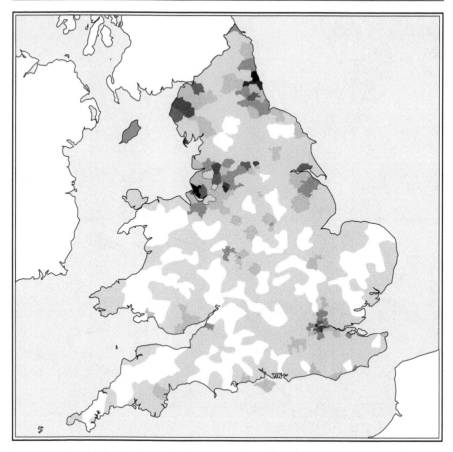

CAMPBELL: distribution in 1881. Numerous Scottish surnames were among the most frequent in Britain in 1881, but many of them cannot be separated from identical and prolific English names, e.g. Watson and Young. Two essentially Scottish names with huge totals were Campbell and McDonald (next map) and their expansion in England is of particular interest. The English counties with the highest concentrations were, in both cases, Northumberland, Cumberland, and Durham but their combined totals were substantially less than the totals in Lancashire. In other industrially developed regions, such as the West Riding, Staffordshire and Warwickshire, the numbers were much smaller than in Lancashire. The impact on London is less easy to estimate but even if Middlesex, Surrey, and Kent are treated as one region the numbers fall well short of those in Lancashire. It is a pattern typical of Scottish surname distribution generally.

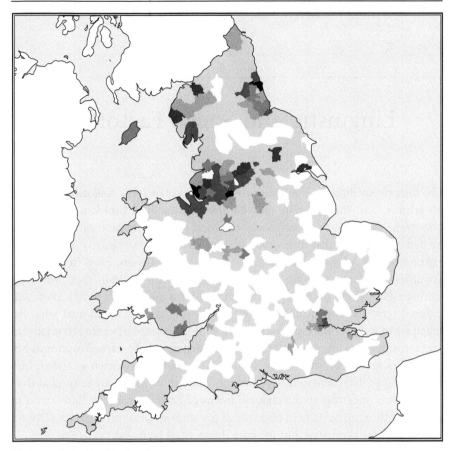

McDONALD: distribution in 1881.

5

Linguistic and Social Factors

The historic spellings of a surname are links in a chain that lead us back to the progenitor, and they present us with the etymological problem. This is an important aspect of every surname story and yet spelling as a topic is seldom treated in the depth that it deserves. It is true that writers regularly warn family historians that 'surnames are often spelt in various ways, even in the same document', but most advice does not go much further than that. Mark D. Herber rightly drew attention to the fact that Sims and Simms were sometimes indexed separately, with other names in between, and he mentioned what he called silent letters, offering Knott and Nott as an example: he also recorded the problems that he had experienced with the spellings of the name Voisey and his frustrating search for an ancestor whose name had been written as Heber, but more complicated variations were not touched on. When we are reminded that many of our ancestors spoke regional forms of English and were illiterate, it is as though they are being held responsible for variant spellings, since the clerk or 'scribe' had no alternative but to write down what he heard.

There is some truth in that, of course, but it may not be the whole truth. It is clear that some ministers in particular went one step further. Although Rodes was a common name in Yorkshire, usually pronounced as 'Roids', the variants Royd, Royde, Royds, and Roydes are all uncommon, and they are now found mostly in Lancashire where that pronunciation is not widespread. The dialect was evidently not a problem for most well-educated Yorkshire ministers who mentally corrected the name and then spelt it 'Rhodes', insert-ing the 'h', which quietly demonstrated their knowledge of Greek. Clerical interference could go much further, for some ministers were not above deliberately distorting surnames for their own amusement. Suspicions are aroused with spellings such as Tallowpot for Talbot, Gravestone for Grayson, and Shipyard for a Shepherd who was a 'navigator', but it is a Hull minister's spellings of the Halifax surname Gaukroger that confirm what was suspected. Initially this family's name was recorded as Cockroger, possibly a genuine error, but the subsequent change to Cockrobin is surely mischievous.

The reality is that for many genealogists their research is part of a learning process, as they move slowly backwards from one generation to another, gradually becoming familiar with the spelling variations that occur in the records. The danger is, of course, that vital information can be missed early in the search, for few surname dictionaries are allowed the space to catalogue historic spelling changes. Any scholar who seeks to use data involving surnames needs to know something about how they originated and how they developed linguistically. There are numerous instances where the linguistic evidence alters our perception of a surname and such information is crucially important. The subject has been dealt with in depth in George Redmonds's *Surnames and Genealogy* (1997), but the following paragraphs contain additional examples and the individual surname histories that follow will provide illustrative material.

Short forms of surnames

Surnames were often abbreviated or contracted, but the changes may go unnoticed unless our attention is drawn to them by an alias. The researcher's task is made more difficult when the abbreviated spelling is identical with an already established surname. In Leeds, in the period 1657–72, the John Manning who was usually referred to in the parish register as 'of Market Place' was almost certainly identical with John Manningham 'of Market Place', mentioned once only. Neither surname features in the hearth tax return of 1672 but a John Mangham of Leeds is listed and he is likely to be the same man: this spelling draws our attention to Elizabeth Mannum 'of Market Place' (1669). Manning, Manningham and Mangham, which can be three distinct surnames, are likely in this instance to refer to the same family and the fact that the place-name Manningham is occasionally spelt Mangham lends support to that identification. If no explicit alias draws attention to what was taking place, it can be difficult for researchers to establish the link between the short and long forms. One family historian whose search was for a family named McLoughlin finally located them in the 1891 census as Mack. A few explicit examples of shortened names demonstrate that almost any syllable could be affected:

1607	James Kilton alias Kilvington of Thornbrough.
1611	John Chester alias Lanchester of Graistock.
1611	John Lockey alias Lockwood of Scorton.
1757–58	George Dewse or Dewhirst of Horbury.

Surname confusion

A name that was well known in one region might have been strange and possibly outlandish in another: local pronunciations and naming practices made the names of strangers difficult to understand. So when a family moved into a new neighbourhood, it was relatively easy for their surname to be replaced by one that resembled it. Some editors who suspect that this was taking place are careful to draw attention to the possibility in the index. Louis Knafla, in *Kent at Law, 1602* (1994) linked the references to the names Holman, Holloway, and Hollywell, all mentioned in connection with the same village. In the index to *Sussex Coroners' Inquests, 1668–1603* (1996) the editor R.F. Hunnisett had an entry for Richard Sharvell and then put in brackets 'probably same as Richard Sherwood'. Aliases confirm that such confusion of names was common and demonstrate the ways in which surnames were subject to re-interpretation in their new localities – unaccented final elements being particularly subject to replacement:

1594   Thomas Robson alias Robinson of Rye.
1594   Thomas Harman alias Stope or Stooke of Lewes.
1628   John Garthwaite alias Garforth of Middleham.

Consonant and vowel change

In *The Surnames of Sussex* (1988), Richard McKinley commented on 'the tendency for the vowels used in any one surname to vary very greatly'. Among the examples he gave was Strudwick, derived from a local place-name: variations that he noted in the sixteenth and seventeenth centuries included Stradwick, Stridwicke, and Strodewyke. Similarly, an occupational name had the spellings Dender, Dinder, Dunder, Thonder, and Thunder. These last two provide evidence of how consonants were regularly interchanged. When that process affected the initial consonant it poses very difficult problems, not least the researchers' use of indexed material:

1546   Master Gressome or Gresope of York.
1605   Henry Creame alias Grime of Braithwell.
1640   Brian Bevers alias Vevers of Shipton.
1776   John Ridsdale alias Rudsdale of Richmond.

Popular etymology

A great number of surnames consist of one or more elements that are words in everyday vocabulary, or have the appearance of such words, and the meaning or apparent meaning helps to restrict the number of spelling variations. Typical single element names are Green, Hardy, Smith, and those with two such elements include Greathead, Hardcastle, Johnson, Littlewood, and Monkman. The spellings of Greenwood in the Halifax parish register include Gernwood, Girnewodde, Grynwod, and Grenword, forerunners of the few Grenwoods and Grinwoods who are listed in the census of 1881. These are not difficult forms to identify and they are unlikely to trouble the careful researcher. Similarly, when a name can be seen to have its origin in a well-known place-name the variations are likely to be fewer: Winchester would readily be associated with the city of Winchester over a much wider area than Hampshire; the names Kendal, Lincoln, Norfolk, and York would be easily recognized for the same reason. On the other hand, Cowperthwaite could have posed a problem: it might have been familiar to people living in Cumbria but it would sound unusual outside that area, especially when it was pronounced with a broad Cumbrian accent. The difficulty that strangers had with the name is obvious in the number of variant spellings it gave rise to, for more than thirty can be identified in the 1881 national census. These included Copperwheat in Bedfordshire, Copperwhite in Kent and Wales, and a solitary Copperwright in Sussex. Variants that have not survived are Copperworth and Copperfoot, the latter recorded in Skipton in 1630 as the name of 'a poor man which came out of the North'.

To a greater or lesser extent all these variants betray the influence of what is loosely called popular etymology. That is to say the spellings are those of educated people who were making the best sense they could of a baffling surname that was outside their experience. The listener's need to make sense of names has had a strong influence on their history, creating variants that are effectively 'new' surnames that do not conform to normal linguistic practice. Nor should the variants that did not survive be forgotten for they can provide the genealogist with vital information. The effects of popular etymology will be apparent in the surname histories that follow.

By-names and nicknames

There is a distinction between the nicknames with which we are all familiar and the by-names that characterized communities where just a few surnames predominated. In such communities an alternative naming system developed as an aid to identification, in some places from as early as the sixteenth century. Black drew attention to this in his piece on 'To-names' in the introduction to *The Surnames of Scotland*: there were, he said, 25 George Cowies in the small fishing town of Buckie in Banffshire in 1842, among them George Cowie, doodle, George Cowie, carrot, and George Cowie, neep. Similarly in east Lancashire, where Hartley was a particularly common name, one Roger Hartley was known as Litle Hoge whilst his neighbour was Roger by the wayter. In the Colne Valley, where the surname Bamforth was particularly numerous, an alternative patronymic system was in use until quite recently. The death notice for Harry Bamforth of Slaithwaite, aged 83, was announced in his local newspaper in 2004: it identified him as Harry o' Billys. Nicknames and by-names could both be inherited, and they are not just items of anecdotal interest: before civil registration, and occasionally thereafter, they might be used in records in preference to the family name and they could permanently replace that name in some circumstances. Once again, the clearest evidence is the explicit alias, used a great deal in parish registers, court rolls, and the records of quarter sessions. Some documents tell us more about the practice. The Taylor family was prolific in Meltham where each branch had a by-name: in 1787, the lawyer William Armytage wrote a letter to a friend about a tenant called George Taylor and felt obliged to add that he was talking about 'George of Dirtcars', using the by-name that identified this family's place of residence. In 1860 Jonas Bower of Thornton testified under cross examination that he knew Isaac Mortimer, who was 'generally called Ike o' Eltofts or Isaac Eltofts', a nickname or by-name that he owed to his mother's maiden name. Such names could even derive from a distinctive first name: Lancelot Trolisse of Swillington (1650) should really have been called Townend, but the more distinctive Trolisse commemorated his ancestor Troilus Townend. Some surnames were replaced by nicknames or by-names as late as the twentieth century.

Surname histories

In the case of the Sussex surname Verrall, the genealogist is helped by McKinley's research which shows that 'f' was the initial letter in earlier examples. This is implicit in the records of the county coroner, where Nicholas Verall, a juror at Cuckfield in 1588, can be identified as the juror Nicholas Ferall in 1592, also at Cuckfield. The identification is confirmed by the context in which the names appear, with at least three pieces of corroborative evidence: the man's function as juror, his first name, and the name of the locality where the inquest took place. The editor of the records lists no fewer than thirteen different spellings of the name in his index, ranging from Ferall and Ferold to Veroll and Virrall. It was McKinley's view that Thomas atte Fayrehale, a Sussex taxpayer in 1332, provides us with the earliest spelling.

This change from 'f' to 'v' was simply a reflection of the regional pronunciation, and other examples are listed in the same index. Similar substitutions occur in many parts of Britain and these inevitably complicate the researcher's use of published index material. An extreme case is Kirsop(p), a surname that in 1881 was found predominantly in the counties of Durham and Northumberland, where it has a long history. In 1598, for example, Ninian Kyrsop was a juror at the Durham quarter sessions. His surname derives from the Cumberland place-name Kershope which has a disputed etymology: the first element is Old English in origin although scholars are unsure from the early forms whether it was 'grass' or 'cress'. Typical examples are: Gressop (1200), Cressop (1332), Carsopp (1580), and Kirsop (1697), and the surname has a similar run of variant spellings. The historian who is using published source material is therefore obliged to search the indexes under the letters 'c', 'ch', 'g', and 'k', with the added difficulty posed by the interchange of 'i' and 'y', and such metathesized spellings as Grysehop, Cressop and Chrisop. In total, the surname might be looked for in over twenty different locations in an index, unless the editor has cross-referenced the entries.

Bewildering as these variations may appear they are nevertheless predictable to the linguist, given the history of the place-name. A variant that owes more to popular etymology is Grasshopper, which developed in the East Riding of Yorkshire in the seventeenth century. The earliest example noted is Stephen Grashopper of Withernsea, whose will was registered in 1620. Withernsea was in the parish of Hollym and the names Grysehop, Girshoper, and Grashoper were all listed there in the hearth tax return of 1672. The circumstances in which this took place are more easily understood when the regional pronunciation of the word 'grass' is taken into consideration. A 'gyrse garth' (1526) was a grass yard, and 'horsgrys' (1519) was grass for the horses. The fact that just one branch of the family in Withernsea was affected may suggest that Grasshopper was deliberately used in the first instance as a nickname.

Edgar Tooth's recent work on the surnames of north Staffordshire shows how an observant local historian can bring new light to bear on surnames, some of them apparently quite commonplace. Linguists may not always agree with the writer's interpretation of such names but his examples demonstrate great awareness of the ways in which surnames developed. Tellwright was linked with Telreight and Telrik from 1512, a development confirmed by the novelist Arnold Bennett, whose character Ephraim Tellwright was referred to as 'Mester Terrick'. The surname Hawthorne apparently had no early history in the county, and Tooth referred to it as a gatecrasher on the Staffordshire scene, quoting the example of Thomas Hordern of Norton-in-the-Moors who signed his name as Thomas Hawthorn in 1817. He found the name Wrixon in Walsall in 1666 and associated it with Rixon and Wrexham, speculating that all three were variants of Wrightson. The role of popular etymology is apparent in both these cases.

Many more examples are given in Tooth's study. For example, over a period of years, a family living in Seighford had their name entered in the registers as Swinshed, Swinswood, and Swingewood; Roger Swinshed was recorded as Roger Swineshutt in 1666. In 1881 these were all rare surnames but the main concentration of Swingwood, Swingswood, Swingewood, and Swinswood was in Staffordshire. Swinchatt was not recorded in the county but families with that name were living in Cheshire, Shropshire, and Worcestershire. Beardmore can also be identified in Staffordshire and its neighbouring counties. It had a national count of 1,371 in 1881 and its variant Beardsmore totalled 412. Tooth located examples 'around the Cheadle/Alton area from the Middle Ages up to the middle of the sixteenth century' and among those he quoted were Richard de Berdmor of Whiston (1311) and John Berdesmore of Froghall (1448). These clearly derive from a place-name and, although there is no immediately obvious source, they are tentatively linked with Broadmoor Wood in Hollington. In 1881 both names were more common in Staffordshire than in other counties; Beardmore with over 62 per cent of the total and Beardsmore with over 32 per cent. Beardmore was also well established in Derbyshire and Beardsmore had smaller clusters in Leicestershire and Nottinghamshire; both names had a significant presence in Warwickshire.

In South Yorkshire, towards the end of the thirteenth century, one branch of a family in Hickleton began to use the alias Campion, probably because it served initially to identify the junior of two John Campions. However, the alias survived and Campinot established itself principally in the Colne Valley, further to the north. The surname was recorded there over the centuries but it declined dramatically in Victorian times and had a count of only 13 in 1881. However, the name may have survived, much more healthily, in the abbreviated forms Campey (154) and Campy (55) both of which occur in that part of the county where Campinett alias Campie was recorded in 1611. All three surnames might be linked genetically, sharing the same progenitor in Hickleton.

In some instances the process of contraction has gone on over a very long period, with alterations to the spelling that make it difficult to identify the late medieval forms. Lomas and Lomax are the modern spellings of a surname that originated in the Lancashire parish of Bury, probably in the early fourteenth century, although the locality from which it was derived cannot now be identified. In his *Surnames of Lancashire* (1981), McKinley described it as more widely dispersed than many similar Lancashire names but probably having a single family origin. He included a few sample spellings but not

Henry de Lunhalgherus of Bury who is listed in the recently published poll tax return of 1379. It is a name that would be difficult to recognize in most contexts, but the following intermediate examples illustrate its development up to *c.*1600: Lunhalghus, Lumhalghs, Lummals, Loumals, Lumas. The suffix here is a plural of the element 'halh', a common element in Lancashire and one that has given rise to some of the most unusual variations in spelling.

The modern Wormald has a similar history of contraction. Elias de Wlfrunwelle owed his name to a locality in Rishworth near Elland which features in several charters for that township towards the end of the thirteenth century. These are the only references that identify the first element as the Old English 'Wulfrūn', a female personal name, for the 'f' was discarded soon afterwards. Sample spellings over the next four centuries illustrate how the name continued to be contracted. In 1286 the son of Nelle de Walronwalle was named in the court rolls as a burglar and it is worth noting that the suffix in this case has the word 'well' in its usual Mercian form. Over the next one hundred years or so the 'l' and the vowel 'o' of the following syllable also disappeared: in the poll tax returns of 1379, for example, Thomas de Wournewall was taxed in Rishworth at the standard rate of 4d. Through the fifteenth century, after the family had apparently moved into the neighbouring township of Barkisland, the typical spelling was Wormewall, and this became Wormall in the early sixteenth century, the form long preferred in Elland parish registers. The final 'd' was first recorded in the latter half of the seventeenth century, when Wormald became the most popular form of the surname. However, both Wormwell and Wormwood survive in the same area.

Some surnames developed a bewildering array of variants and aliases over the centuries. Ridehalgh is an extreme example, for at least eighty different spellings can be safely identified in the 1881 census returns. A summary of these serves to illustrate the points made earlier. Several predictable changes to the first element gave rise to Reddihalgh, Redihalgh, Redehalgh, Riddehalgh, Riddihalgh, and Ridihalgh. The major change to the suffix produced spellings such as Reddihough, Reddyhough, Riddihough, Ridehough, and Ridihough, whilst the loss of 'h' doubled the number, with Ridealgh, Riddehalgh, Reddiough, and Riddiough as examples. Further changes to both elements resulted in Readyhough, Readyhoff, Readyoff, Reddyhoff, and Redyoff. The 'gh' of the suffix experienced other changes, as when the aspiration was totally lost to give Rideal, Riddeal, and Riddial. Alternatively it became 'ck' in some parishes, just as Scottish 'loch' became 'lock'. This change lies behind the spelling of the rare variants Ridchick, Ridgoke, and Redchyk. Others did not survive but they paved the way for the curious variants Ridgwick and

Redgwick. The analogy here is with names such as Chiswick and Keswick, another clear case of popular etymology.

The national total for Ridehalgh in 1881, including all the variants identified, was 1,195, a modest ramification when compared with that of many other surnames from that part of the Pennines. The source of the name is Ridehalgh, a tiny hamlet in east Lancashire, very close to the boundary with Yorkshire, and just over 90 per cent of the name bearers were recorded in those two counties. On the whole 'halgh' remained unchanged in Lancashire, whereas most West Riding variants had the suffix 'hough'. Two clusters elsewhere are worth mentioning: Redihough (13) was recorded only in Derbyshire, and Rediough (6), Readyhoff (15), Readyhoof (5), and Riddea (2), were all found in Northamptonshire. The range of spellings suggests that the name may have a long history there, even though the total numbers were low. Finally, it should be noted that a branch of the family that lived in Lancashire near Colne had the alias Delves, which can be traced back to the by-name or nickname 'of Delvys' or 'of Stonne Delf' in 1514–30. It survived when members of the family moved across the Pennines into the Keighley area, occasionally as Delves. As this surname still occurs on both sides of the county boundary it would be an interesting subject for DNA testing.

Spelling variations and national totals

Research that is concerned with the distribution and frequency of surnames must obviously take account of variant spellings. The importance of this is highlighted in the following more detailed histories.

Wolstenholme

Readily available sources establish that this surname had its origin in Rochdale parish where the by-name 'de Wolstonholme' is on record from *c*.1180. As the place-name appears to be unique, the surname probably has a single point of origin, though it is possible that it was used from the outset by unrelated families. *The British 19th Century Surname Atlas* confirms that Wolstenholme was still a well-established surname in Lancashire in 1881, for no fewer than 79 per cent of the 2,392 people so called were still resident in the county. The only other significant total was in the neighbouring county of Yorkshire, with most of these families living in the old West Riding. If smaller totals in Cheshire and Derbyshire are taken into account it can be seen that 97 per cent of the people called Wolstenholme were still living within a relatively short distance of Rochdale. The surprising aspect of this distribution is the small number of Wolstenholmes in London and other major centres of population. However, that is not the whole of the story, for Wolstenholme had developed a large number of variants in the course of its history and, when these are identified, a clearer picture of the name's expansion and distribution emerges. The variations, many of which have survived, reflect the name's colloquial pronunciation over a wider area than the ancient parish of Rochdale.

Most of the variations are not difficult to identify in the 1881 census. They include Wolstanholme (53), Woolstenholme (59), Woolstenhulme (15), and two more uncommon Bury surnames: Woolstemholme (10) and Woolsten-ham (8). All these were still found principally in Lancashire, although a small group with the spelling Woolstenholmes (28) was concentrated in St Ives, in Huntingdonshire. The 'l' of the prefix was no longer in evidence in the (mostly) West Riding variants: Wostenholme (74), Wostenholm (37), Worstenholme (27), and Wostinholm (9), four surnames that were strongly represented in the Sheffield area. The Sheffield parish registers have examples of the surname from the 1590s, with Wosnam and Wostnam as two of the original spellings.

In 1881 the contracted spellings Woosnam (244) and Woosman (37) were well established in Wales but rare elsewhere: Montgomeryshire was at the heart of their distribution and according to John and Sheila Rowlands the name was already in Llanllwchaiarn by 1596. Historically, though, similar forms also occurred in some English parishes and, via the process known as metathesis, Worsnam gave rise to the Yorkshire variant Worsman (106). This name stabilized in Bradford (Yorkshire), alongside the more unpredictable Worsnop (629): the connection is explicit in the case of Jane Worsnop alias Worsman of Tong, noted in 1750. However, similar spellings are found over a wider area, so the pronunciation that gave rise to them was not idiosyncratic. Another important variant was Worsnip (143), of whom 50 were found in Saddleworth, a part of the West Riding that originally formed part of Rochdale parish, and which reverted to Lancashire in the boundary changes of 1974. The surname of a further 19 people was recorded as Worsnup.

In these revised statistics the total for the surname rises from 2,392 to 4,030. As a matter of interest, this places it just below the much more widely distributed surnames Major (4037), Spicer (4035), and Forrester (4031), which all seem likely to have several distinct origins. On the other hand, the revised total reduces the Lancashire proportion of the ramification from 79 per cent to 54 per cent, whereas in Yorkshire it rises from 13 per cent to 30 per cent. The surname still had a tightly-knit distribution in 1881, but the conflated total more closely reflects Wolstenholme's long history. The court rolls of Wakefield manor show that one branch of the family acquired land in the Yorkshire parish of Halifax as early as 1381.

Edgar Tooth notes that Wolstenholme was well established in Staffordshire as early as 1532, when three families were living in the villages of Horton, Colwich, and Cheddleton. What he calls 'bizarre distortions' occurred almost immediately and he cites three interesting spellings for the name in Cheddleton, that is: Wolsenholm, Wolsnam, and Wolstman (1531–41). Here, as in the West Riding, the final 'nam' was metathesized to -man: spellings for James Wolstonholme included Wolsnam in 1530 and the 'bizarre' Ulseman a year earlier. The loss of initial 'w' in this way may seem an unlikely development but similar changes have affected other surnames in the North and the north Midlands, as in Petternell Wobanck or Obancke of Selby (1682), or where Wolfenden readily became Ovenden. Because dialect speakers in these parts of the country pronounced 'home' as 'wom', Ulseman was deemed to be the correct spelling of 'Woolsman'. The variant noted by Tooth has survived in Staffordshire as Oulsnam, Oulsman, and Ousman, and the three names totalled 82 in all in 1881.

That is not the end of the surname's history in Staffordshire. Tooth makes the claim that Ousman became Housman or Houseman in the late seventeenth century and although his evidence is not absolutely conclusive it is certainly persuasive. His theory also puts the spotlight on Houseman more generally, for the early history of this name has always been unsatisfactory. There is no doubt that it occurred as a by-name in the Middle Ages, for Reaney has an example in Essex and another occurs in Airedale in 1377–79, but it has always proved difficult to establish a link between such by-names and later examples of the surname.

One important clue to the history of Houseman is its restricted distribution. The 1881 evidence points to just two major areas of expansion, one with Staffordshire as its focal point and the other in Yorkshire, with many families in and around Knaresborough and smaller groups in the York area. These are precisely the two regions where Houseman was recorded in the hearth tax returns of 1672, but the small numbers indicate that the expansion in Yorkshire was very late. Nothing points to the name having an early history in Knaresborough, but the register of St Mary, Castlegate, in York, records a family called Houseman who used the variants Howsman and Ousman between 1617 and 1673, and the rolls of the freemen of York record Houseman, Howsman, Owsman, and Owzeman. The first of the name appears to be John Howseman, a haberdasher, and it seems possible that he arrived in the city, directly or indirectly, from Staffordshire. If a link between Wolstenholme and Houseman can be proved genetically it would further alter the statistics for Wolstenholme and it would also emphasize how careful genealogists and surname historians need to be.

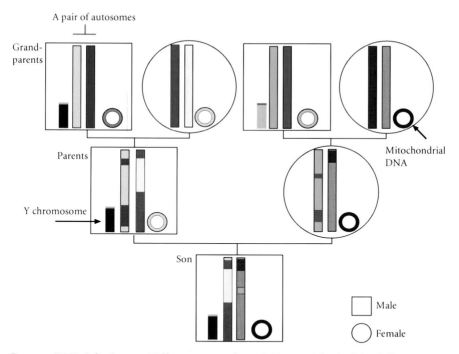

PLATE 1 **DNA inheritance.** Different parts of our DNA are inherited in different ways During the formation of gametes (egg or sperm) our pairs of autosomes undergo a process known as recombination which results in a shuffling of DNA within each chromosome pair. In males, the sex chromsomes (X and Y) exchange DNA only at the tips of the chromsomes and therefore the Y chromosome is passed down virtually unchanged from father to son. Our mitochondrial DNA also escapes recombination and is passed down only through our maternal line. While the autosomes that we inherit are a patchwork of those of our ancestors, both the Y chromosome and our mitochondrial DNA are unusual in that they are inherited largely unchanged, each down the single paternal or maternal line. Though only one pair of autosomes is shown, the same is true for all autosomes.

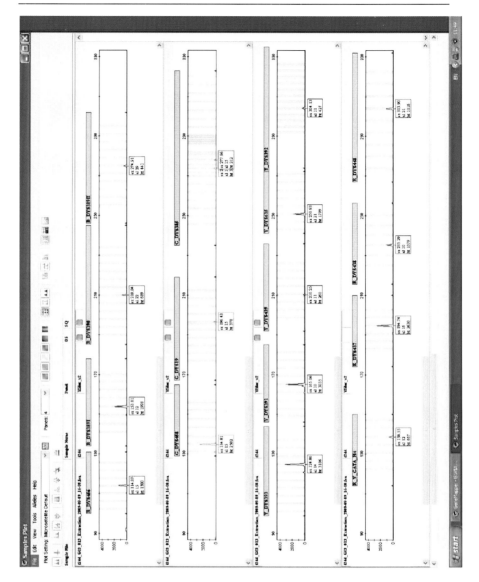

PLATE 2 An example of an electropherogram. The four colours are generated by four different flourescent primer dyes. The amplicons are separated by size: the further right on the electropherogram, the larger the amplicon. The assay is designed so that the amplicons of individual Y-STR markers fall into distinct size ranges and are linked to a particular dye colour. Within each Y-STR size range the amplicon sizes, affected by the number of repeats, fall into 'bins' (grey vertical lines) generated using the computer software. The software uses all this information to determine the allele that each individual carries for each Y-STR marker. For example, using this assay on this particular individual results in an amplicon which is 114.07 in size, carrying a blue dye. This translates to 15 repeats in the size range and colour for DYS456. Therefore DYS456 = 15.

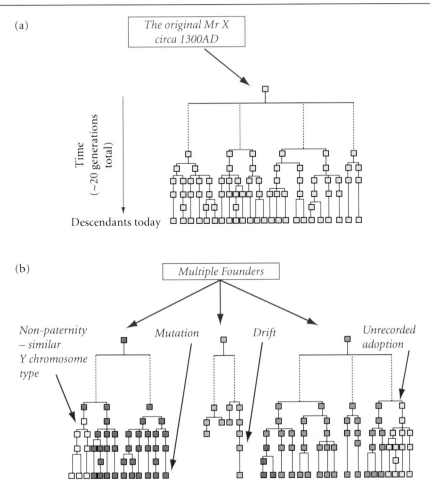

PLATE 3 Factors affecting the types of Y chromosome found in carriers of a particular surname. Different colours indicate different Y haplotypes. (a) The simplest scenario: an unbroken link between an individual surname and an individual Y chromosome type. (b) In reality the link between surname and Y chromosome type is far more complex.

Multiple founders will result in more than one Y chromosome type being associated with a single surname.

Non-patrilineal transmission of surname events (NPTs): events such as non-paternities (illegitimacy), adoption, and maternal transmission will all result in an individual carrying one man's surname but another man's Y chromosome. It is possible that one of these events could bring in a similar Y chromosome to that already associated with the surname.

Drift: the stochastic differences in the number of children (in this case boys) will act to cause some surnames to ramify whereas others will become less common or even go extinct.

Mutation on the Y will introduce differences in the Y chromosomes we see among men who share a common ancestor through their surname.

Sampling will affect the conclusions drawn about the number of founders for a surname. For example sampling men who suspect themselves to be related will bias the results. Sampling randomly will provide a more even sample but may over- or under- sample lineages purely by chance.

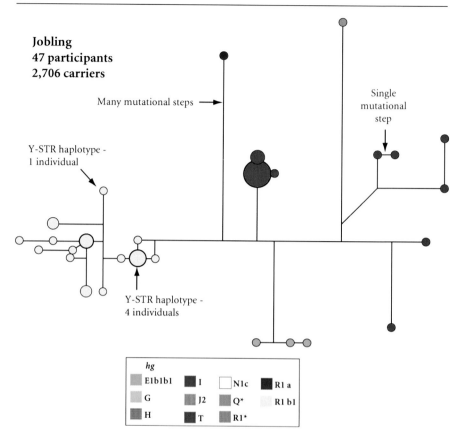

Jobling
47 participants
2,706 carriers

Many mutational steps ⟶

Single mutational step

Y-STR haplotype - 1 individual

Y-STR haplotype - 4 individuals

hg			
E1b1b1	I	N1c	R1 a
G	J2	Q*	R1 b1
H	T	R1*	

PLATE 4 **An example of a network**. Colours represent different haplogroups. Each individual Y chromosome haplotype is represented by a circle and, where two or more men share the same Y chromosome type, the area of the circle is proportional to the number of men who have that Y chromosome type within the set of men being examined.

A mutational difference between the haplotypes of two men is represented by a line which connects the circles of their Y haplo types. The length of the line corresponds to the number of mutational differences: the shorter the line, the fewer the mutational steps and the closer the relationship between the two Y chromosome types.

In what is known as a median joining network, the junctions (known as nodes) between the mutational steps need not be occupied by a haplotype: unoccupied nodes are considered to represent unsampled haplotypes and are not shown.

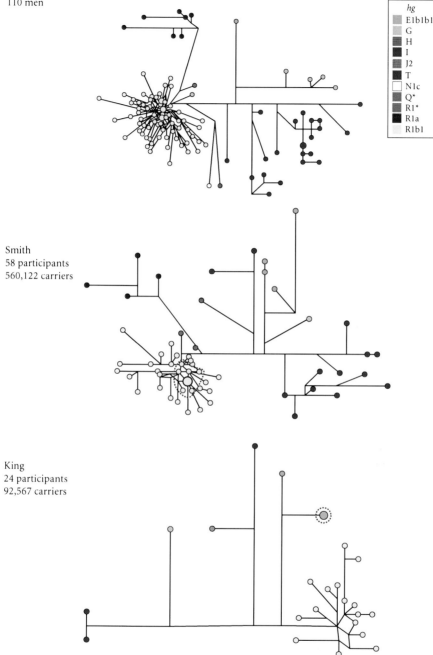

British controls - all
surnames different
110 men

hg	
	E1b1b1
	G
	H
	I
	J2
	T
	N1c
	Q*
	R1*
	R1a
	R1b1

Smith
58 participants
560,122 carriers

King
24 participants
92,567 carriers

PLATE 5 **The controls and the surname networks of the surnames Smith and King.** The control set is dominated by singletons with very little haplotype sharing: haplotype sharing is only found within the two most common haplogroups, R1b1 and I. A number of different haplogroups are represented. Descent clusters are circled in red.

The networks of surnames found at the highest frequencies in the population are statistically indistinguishable from the controls. The number of founders for these high-frequency names are thought to be so numerous that sampling men randomly with these names finds very few men sharing a common ancestor through their surname.

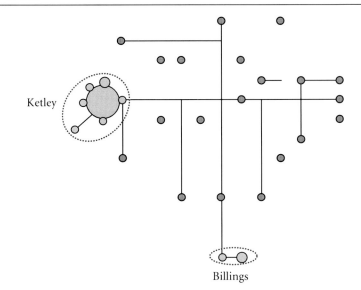

Billings

PLATE 6 **The relatedness of the Ketleys bearing J2 chromosomes set among all other J2 chromosomes from the study.** Examining the relatedness of haplotypes within rare lineages within surname groups allows us to determine a common set of characteristics regarding the number of mutational steps difference we might expect to see among a group of men who share a common ancestor through their surname. Carrying out this analysis within haplogroups that are rare in the general population makes it unlikely that one or more of these haplotypes will have become independently associated with the surname. The most plausible explanation is that all of these men share an ancestor through their surname and this therefore allows us to devise a set of rules in determining what constitutes a descent cluster (circled in red)

Even among all the J2-type Y chromosomes, the Ketleys form a distinct group. Another surname, Billings, also contained a small number of individuals with J2 chromosomes. They also form a unique group among the J2 chromosomes.

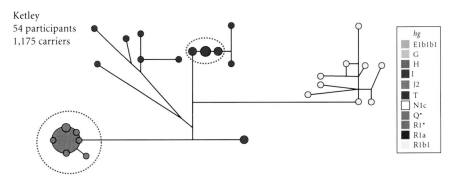

The Ketley surname network with descent clusters highlighted in red. This network also contains individuals with the spelling variant Kettley.

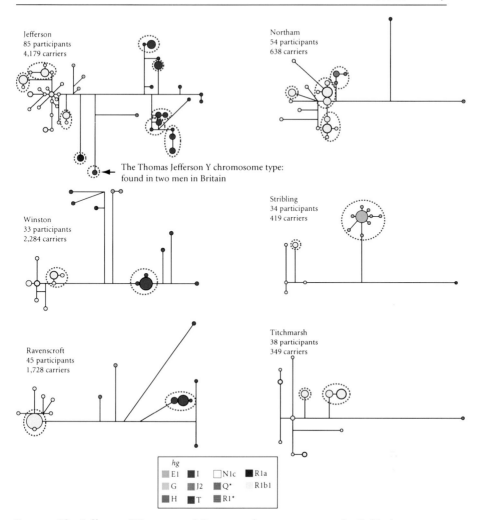

The Thomas Jefferson Y chromosome type: found in two men in Britain

Jefferson
85 participants
4,179 carriers

Northam
54 participants
638 carriers

Winston
33 participants
2,284 carriers

Stribling
34 participants
419 carriers

Ravenscroft
45 participants
1,728 carriers

Titchmarsh
38 participants
349 carriers

hg			
E1	I	N1c	R1a
G	J2	Q*	R1b1
H	T	R1*	

PLATE 7 **The Jefferson, Winston, and Ravenscroft surname networks** (left). As we move from common names down to middle-frequency names we begin to see clear descent clusters (outlined in red).

The Northam, Stribling, and Titchmersh surname networks (right). As we move info lower-frequency names, in general we begin to see a greater proportion of the haplotypes in descent clusters.

All of these networks, where applicable also contain individuals carryping spelling variants of the surname listed. The number of carriers listed also includes these spelling variants.

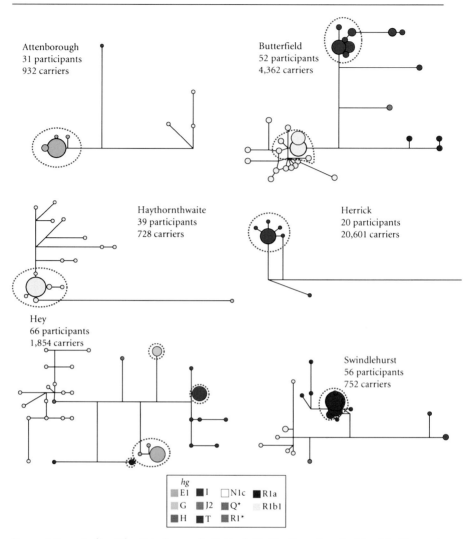

PLATE 8 **Case studies**. The Attenborough, Butterfield, Haythornthwaite, Herrick, Hey, and Swindlehurst networks. All of these networks, where applicable, also contain individuals carrying spelling variants of the surname listed. The number of carriers listed also includes these spelling variants.

Carruthers

Alasdair Steven said that Carruthers took him back to school stories that he had read as a boy and it is probably such tales that have helped English people to associate the surname with a public school background. Yet that perception is not supported by the name's history, which links it to 'the lands of Carruthers in the parish of Middlebie in Dumfriesshire', a locality with a Celtic name of disputed meaning. In the thirteenth century the family were the stewards of Annandale, under the Bruces, and Black quotes Thomas, the son of John de Carutherys (*c*.1320) as an early example of the surname. Among his other examples are several in which the 'th' is replaced by a 'd', one of them as early as 1468, i.e. 'Caruderis'. This reflects a local pronunciation of the place-name which approximates to 'Cridders', a spelling that has not survived as a surname. However, it is likely to have influenced some of the variants mentioned below.

In 1881 the number of people named Carruthers was 3,996: of these 42.5 per cent were resident in Scotland, and the largest concentrations were in Dumfriesshire (653) and Lanarkshire (383). That is clear evidence of the name's successful expansion in the area where it originated, and the pattern of distribution is further emphasized by the high number in Cumberland (936). Carruthers was particularly common in Carlisle and Longtown and its history there may go back to 1377 when Richard de Carruthires was taxed in Carlisle. These regions that straddle the border between the two countries accounted for two thirds of the total in 1881. The surname was not well represented in the Highlands and was absent from several English counties, while Shropshire, Somerset, and Warwickshire each had just one individual with the name. Carruthers was uncommon everywhere south of Lancashire and, even in the heavily populated areas of London and Yorkshire, the totals were small. The two variants Cruthers (113) and Crothers (168) were well established in Scotland but both also occurred in Lancashire and that may point to a relatively late migration. Less predictable were two more distant clusters of Crothers, one in Cornwall (51) and the other in Kent (12). Other variations were Carrothers (which was also found in Kent), Carothers, and Corruthers, but they were all rare and together totalled only 16.

A more detailed picture of the name's expansion and migration emerges once all the variants that have 'd' or 'dd' for 'th' are identified and counted. There are many of these, particularly in England, and they fall into several quite distinct categories. The most important group numerically is the one that includes Crudders, a spelling that is close to the place-name's colloquial pronunciation. However, this was a very rare name, as was Cruddors, found in Bridlington. Much more important numerically were Cruddas (123), Cruddass (21), and Cruddace (62). This group accounted for 322 individuals with 17 different spellings, most of them with only marginal differences: they were particularly well represented in both Durham and Northumberland where the surname has a long history. George Carruddes of Gateshead is referred to in a Durham quarter sessions roll of 1615 but much earlier examples could probably be discovered. Croudace (57) is an uncommon variant that bears a close resemblance to Cruddace and it is found in the same parts of north-eastern England. However, it has a much more scattered distribution generally, with a small but important cluster found in distant Monmouthshire. The other five spellings in the group are Croudice, Crouddace, Croudass, Croudess, and Crowdace, bringing the group total to 100 precisely.

The second highest total (245) has nine variations, including Carrodus (89) and Carradice (97). These names were found principally in and around Keighley, although the expansion reached the industrial cities of Bradford and Leeds and a string of towns and villages from Skipton in Yorkshire to Kendal in Westmorland. These places were sited on a traditional route into the West Riding from Scotland, and history tells of raiding parties into the district rather than peaceful settlement. Nevertheless, examples of Carruthers are recorded in the area from well before the Act of Union: William Carruders and his descendants were named in the parish registers of Kildwick from 1577, and John Carridus was a Keighley resident when the hearth tax was collected in 1672. John Tiplady Carrodus was an eminent Keighley violinist in the nineteenth century.

Another variant found in that part of Yorkshire was Cardus (158), although it was even more numerous in Lancashire, especially in Bolton and Haslingden. Five variant spellings included the Leeds name Cardis (30) but the others were all uncommon and the total was just 194. It is not clear whether Cardus is connected historically with the migration into Airedale or whether it has a quite distinct history. It is best known of course from Sir Neville Cardus, the cricket and music writer who was born in Lancashire.

It should be said that David Dorward, in *Scottish Surnames* (1995), expressed the opinion that names such as Carradice, Cruddas, and Cardus have no connection with Carruthers but derive from other place-names. He did not say what these place-names were and the evidence that is available supports the view that they are English forms of Carruthers, preserving the medial 'd'. In the parish register of Penrith, for example, in the period 1556–65, the name of Nicholas Carruddas was also recorded as Carruds and Carrddes. These might be attributed to errors by the transcriber but similar spellings occur in other northern English counties. One other name that should be mentioned is Carruth or Caruth which MacLysaght considered to be an Ulster variant of Carruthers, from the seventeenth century. Dorward and other Scottish writers say that it had a quite distinct history and link it with the lands of Carruth in the parish of Kilmalcolm.

The regional distribution of these variants, mostly in northern districts, seems to reflect different strands of early migration, and the fact that so few of them are found in Scotland emphasizes the wider dispersal of the surname. However, much of that story remains to be told, with important roles for both genealogists and geneticists. What can be said is that once the variants are taken into consideration, the total for Carruthers rises from 3,996 to 4,962, whereas the percentage based in Scotland is reduced to 36.6 per cent. Even so, it remained essentially a northern surname.

Cadwallader

This rare surname derives from the Welsh personal name Cadwaladr, which meant 'battle-leader', and the etymology is said to explain why it was given to the sons of kings. It is associated with heroic figures in Welsh history, and yet the surname is actually more common in England than in Wales, with a major concentration in Shropshire and a smaller group in Staffordshire. In the sixteenth century, when the patronymic system was still in operation in Wales, migrants into the border counties of England were no doubt required to adopt surnames simply because they were already usual among their new English neighbours. The English clerks are likely to have influenced the process and this may explain why Cadwallader is still so well established in Shropshire. Johannes ap Thomas Cadwalder (1572) is an early example in Shipton.

In the 1881 census 600 people were recorded with this surname, 61 per cent of them in the two adjoining counties of Shropshire and Staffordshire. Fewer than 16 per cent were living in Wales and two small groups accounted for a further 10 per cent in Lancashire (29) and London (31). The remainder were in locations scattered right across England. Not surprisingly, given that English clerks would have found the name difficult to spell, the parish registers of the border counties, particularly those of Shropshire, contain scores of variants. Prys Morgan identified many of them and drew attention to forms such as Cattwoalliter, Cuttwallet, and Cutwaller, none of which seem to have survived. He also found evidence of several abbreviations. In Clunbury, in the period 1668–85, Hugh Chadwallader was also recorded as Hugh Cad, whilst in Sheinton, in 1804–06, William and Sarah Cadwaleter had their name shortened to Walliter. John and Sheila Rowlands make the point that this variant would have been easily assimilated to Walter. Other spellings of this second type were Welliter, Wallider, and Wallardor. In the registers of St Chad's, Prys Morgan also found Catwallit and Wallet. The 1881 census lists more than 40 variants of the surname, although nearly half of these occurred once only. Those with a count in excess of 20 were Cadwalader (59), Cadwallender (52), Cadwaladr (41), and Cadwalleder (28). Examples of the abbreviated variants included Wallender (19), Wallador (8), Wallader, (5) and Walliter (4).

Cad occurred 22 times in 1881 and, as some of these were living in Shropshire and Warwickshire, it seems possible that they were surviving variants of the type found by Prys Morgan. A total of 71 people who had the surname Wallet included a significant number in Shropshire and Stafford-shire, 25 in all, so these too may be variants of Cadwallader. If Cad and Wallet can be shown to be alternatives of Cadwallader, they raise the overall total for the surname to nearly 1,000, and they throw into doubt the meanings traditionally suggested for them.

Surnames from Continental Europe

English clerks had even more difficulty in interpreting a wide range of foreign surnames. It is rarely possible to discover the circumstances behind entries in the records but just occasionally genealogists can work out what happened and provide us with an insight into the topic. One lady recently discovered that the William McKain she was looking for was actually the son of Daniel Mesquene of Guernsey: William had married the daughter of a Glasgow innkeeper! When migration took a name away from where it originated, the move increased the probability that it would come under different linguistic influences and there is no doubt that many apparently characteristic British names conceal a foreign origin. Unfortunately, the problems cannot always be solved by the historians of the countries or regions involved.

On the whole, it is usual for writers to comment on the large number of aliens who settled in Britain at different times whilst stressing the relatively small influence that their surnames had on the British surname stock. No nationwide survey has ever been carried out into the subject but the topic has been touched on by a number of writers, and important contributions include Sir Anthony Wagner's chapter on 'Strangers' in *English Genealogy* (1960); Richard McKinley's comments on the 'Names of Aliens' in *The Surnames of Sussex* (1988); and George Redmonds's notes on 'Names from Abroad' in *Christian Names in Local and Family History* (2004). The latter work stresses how important the combination of first name and surname can be in making such identifications. Many other publications contain significant paragraphs or individual surname histories of real genealogical and linguistic value.

Foreigners are numerous in modern Britain and are often easily identified by their surnames, but that cannot be said about earlier immigrants. Many of them came from countries with no tradition of hereditary surnames and so were probably given a name for the convenience of the clerks. Such a name might link them with a place or a trade, or more often with their father, in the tradition of the patronymic system. The first name John, or its equivalent, was very popular throughout Europe and the foreign versions would probably have been readily understood by the clerks when they needed to record a name. The evidence suggests that they gave the surname Johnson to numerous immigrants and the practice must have influenced the statistics nationally.

In 1424, for instance, Diryk Johnson was a York goldsmith, identified as an immigrant from the Low Countries by his first name; Ingare Johnson (1469) was a baker in the same city '*et non fuit Anglicus natus*'; Godmondr Johnson (1473) was an 'Iselandman'; and Gilbert Johnson (*c*.1528) 'a Ducheman'. In a West Riding subsidy roll for Wakefield in 1545 George Johnson was 'an aliant', and a neighbour in Crigglestone was simply listed as 'Johnson a heigh alman'. The same process was going on in many other parts of the country. David Postles noted that Johnson was the name of several aliens in Devon between 1402 and 1522 and Richard McKinley found enough examples in Sussex to convince him that it probably 'led to an increase in Sussex of surnames of that type'. Some Welshmen may also have finished up as Johnson rather than Jones, for Prys Morgan quotes the example of John ap John alias Johnson of London (1553). Similar names are found as late as the seventeenth century in North America: in 1687 Clause Johnson and Derick Johnson were the plaintiffs in a case of assault that was heard at Burlington court in West New Jersey.

Johnson may have been one of the commonest names given to immigrants but the publications in the *English Surnames Series* prove that the practice influenced names in many categories. Postles found Gilleson and Peterson as the names of immigrants in Devon and McKinley quoted Clark, Knight, Nicholas, Exeter, and Corner as the names of Sussex aliens. In other cases, of course, the immigrant's name was simply anglicized or translated. Typical examples are Henry Churchyard alias Kirkhoff (1484) and James Fundam alias Vandamme (1604). Churchyard occurs as a by-name from the thirteenth century and the surname is now found principally in Suffolk, whereas Fundam appears to have no precedent. No doubt it sounded English. It is clear that both genealogy and genetics will have a role to play in determining the origins of names in this category.

Sir Anthony Wagner wrote of England as a country that attracted refugees and also immigrants with special skills, adding that the two motives were often linked. He speculated on the possible Dutch or Flemish origins of the Gloucestershire surname Clutterbuck and noted that the descendants of Robert Derrick, a German armourer who came from Aachen, adopted the Derbyshire surname Dethick. This is unlikely to have been a random choice, for the Mappin family of Sheffield were also from the Continent and they sometimes used Dedick or Dedwick as an alias as this closely resembled the first name Derrick. Otho, the son of Derricke Mappin was baptized in 1594.

Some foreign names survived virtually unchanged and others were anglicized more gradually. This aspect of family history demands considerable expertise on the part of the genealogist and a measure of good luck too. Particular use was made in Redmonds's *Surnames and Genealogy* of what might be termed the traditional genealogical sources, but since then additional material has become available, including major new publications and a variety of Internet sources of varying quality. John Titford is one genealogist who has demonstrated how that might be done, successfully tracing the history of a number of foreign names. In his essays on the rare surname Behagg he draws attention to its numerous variants, its origins in mainland Europe, and the more problematical issue of its precise meaning. He also makes the case for a possible link with Beharrell. He is able to show that Behagg has a French Protestant origin and he takes its history back to the seventeenth century in the fenlands of Cambridgeshire and Huntingdonshire. Two 'Beehague' marriages were registered at Whittlesey in 1655 and Pierre Beehague had several daughters baptized in the French Huguenot church in Thorney soon afterwards. By the 1680s Behagges were settled in Doddington and the surname was later prominent in Benwick in the same parish. An individual with the name Behaguel had the author looking for a possible link with Beharrel and its variants. This is also a Protestant surname which is on record from 1642 in the register of Sandtoft in Lincolnshire. A man called Jan Behagel had his daughter Elizabeth baptized at the Walloon or Strangers Church in Canterbury as early as 1582. Titford pursued the possibility of a direct connection between these two surnames and also considered a less obvious link with such names as Beagle and Barrell. No examples were quoted but a search of the parish registers supports the suggestion. There seems no doubt, for example, that Francis Barrel and Francis Beharell, who are referred to in the register of Drypool near Hull in 1811, are the same man.

In 1881 neither surname was common but the variants of Behagg located the name in a number of adjoining counties. One or two families still lived in Cambridgeshire, including Behaggs (2) and Behagge (1), whereas Behagg was found principally in Huntingdonshire: Beehag and Behag were Essex surnames. Behague was also found in Huntingdonshire but a larger group lived in Staffordshire (10). Two people called Behagen were recorded in Northampton- shire and Beague and Beheague were confined to single references in Warwick- shire and Kent respectively. Beharrell had a wider distribution, with significant clusters in Cambridge and Huntingdonshire and slightly more numerous groups in Yorkshire and Lancashire. There are historic links in this case with the East Riding parishes of Beverley and Howden and this evidence points to Sandtoft as the likely source. Less common variants were found in both regions: these include Beharrel in Yorkshire and Cambridgeshire and Beharell in Essex. The value of John Titford's research lies in the impressively wide range of genealogical sources that he consulted. Among them are 'loving memory cards', websites, published works on the history of the fenlands, and a variety of registers that provide information about foreign communities in England. They are all carefully listed at the end of his article and they illustrate how speculation can go hand in hand with meticulously detailed research.

Similarly, in *Searching for Surnames* (2002) Titford was able to show how Stonehold and its variants, all of them very rare, are anglicized versions of Van Steenkolen, the name of a seventeenth-century immigrant from the Nether- lands. More recently he traced the ancestors of the playwright Alan Ayck- bourn to Germany where the family was called Eichbaum. Frederick Ayckbowm or Eichbaum was born in 1793 in Dublin where his father was a glass-maker, a skilled craft that brought other foreign families to these shores. When Denis Ashurst told the story of 'The Silkstone Glasshouses', in *Old West Riding* (1992) he traced the descendants of a Frenchman called Pilmay who worked near Salisbury in the late sixteenth century. In following their craft the Pilmays moved in the course of several generations to Shropshire, Manches- ter, and the West Riding of Yorkshire. The alternative spellings of their name included Pilme, Piline, Pilaye, Pillnay and, possibly, Bullney. It is uncertain whether or not the name survives but in 1881 Pilneys were recorded in Sussex.

John and Sheila Rowlands traced the arrival of one foreign surname to south Wales in c.1568. The immigrant was a specialist smith who had been brought over from Westphalia to help in the production of iron wire. He worked for the company of Schütz and Humphrey who had a licence for that purpose from the Queen. The first spelling of the workman's name in Wales was Corslett and this version continued in use into the nineteenth century, although it may now be extinct. Nevertheless, several variants survive. In 1881 the most numerous were Coslett (136) and Cosslett (85), which occurred most commonly in Glamorgan and Monmouthshire along with the less common spellings Coslet, Cosslet, Costlet, Costlett, and Cosstlett. The combined total came to 272 and it seems likely that they all owe their names to the original German immigrant.

Corslett was not a real problem for the clerks, so it was easily assimilated into the name stock. Many other immigrant names had a similar range of variants. A group of French ironworkers, mostly from Lorraine, who came to work in the Weald of Kent and Sussex in the sixteenth century included a 'Perygo', who was recorded without a first name in the Rape of Pevensey in 1543. He presumably came from Périgueux. The surname remained uncommon but its distribution in 1881 reflects the family's movements to other parts of England, for by then groups were found in ten scattered counties, including the West Riding of Yorkshire, Herefordshire, Warwickshire, Worcestershire, and Durham. The main spellings were Perigo and Perrigo, but Perigoe was almost exclusively a Sussex surname, along with the variants Perigol and Perigor. Periego survived in Bromyard in Herefordshire.

Between 1540 and 1600 over 50,000 people crossed the Channel or the North Sea to settle in England. French Huguenots came to escape religious persecution and Dutch, Flemish, and Walloon refugees fled from Spanish oppression. They settled mostly in London or in the towns of East Anglia and the Southeast: Norwich, Colchester, Canterbury, Sandwich, Maidstone, and Southampton. Immigration continued in the seventeenth century with small groups of German miners and Dutch drainers and a fresh wave of Huguenots in the 1680s. Some of their distinctive surnames can still be recognized but numerous others were changed out of recognition or adapted to English forms.

* * *

In the late nineteenth and twentieth centuries fresh waves of immigrants introduced large numbers of new surnames into Britain. From 1881 onwards Jewish families that fled from Poland, Lithuania, and other parts of the Russian Empire to escape the pogroms settled particularly in the East End of London, Leeds, Manchester, and Glasgow; other Jewish refugees escaped from Hitler's Germany in the 1930s. Many of them changed their names to English ones, such as Harris and Moss, that sounded similar but did not have the same etymology. After the Second World War Ukrainians, Poles, and (later) Hungarians fled from Russian occupation. Then, during the 1950s families from Commonwealth countries in the West Indies, Africa, and Asia began to enter Britain in large numbers. Those from the Caribbean often possessed surnames handed down from English slave-owners, but immigrants from India and Pakistan brought new names, some of which, notably Patel, are now amongst the most common surnames in the country. In the early twenty-first century Britain is a much more cosmopolitan society than ever before.

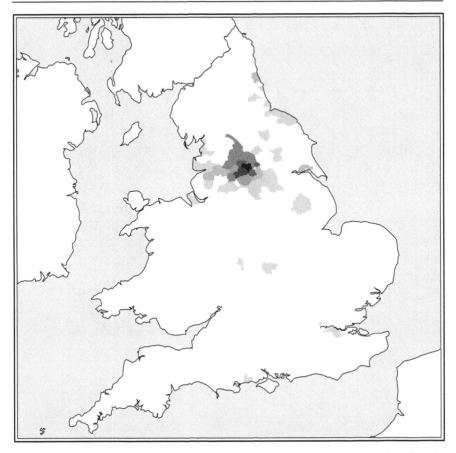

BOOCOCK: distribution in 1881. The distribution of Boocock in 1881 accurately reflects its history and casts doubt on traditional explanations of its origin. The main concentration (94.5 per cent) was in the West Riding and Lancashire, but the Archer maps based on poor law unions show it was more precisely between Rochdale in the west and Leeds in the east. The first examples are recorded from *c.*1600 and the linguistic evidence shows that Boocock is a variant spelling of Bulcock, via Bowcock. This name can be traced to Colne in 1425, on the border between the two counties. Typically, a family living at Knotts in Bowland spelt the name Bulcock/Bowcocke/Boocock in the period 1608–30. The variation is explicit in the case of Edward Bowcock alias Bulcock of Howgill (1677). Dictionaries link Boocock incorrectly with a variety of names, including Baud, Balding, Bawcutt and Boulting. Possible links with Balcock and Bawcock have still to be proved.

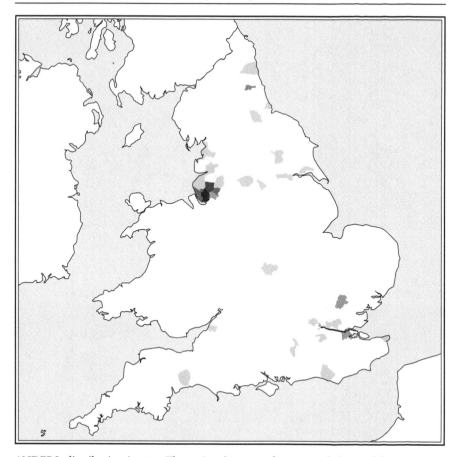

ANDERS: distribution in 1881. The national census of 1881 recorded 430 of the 543 people who bore this surname as living in Lancashire. No fewer than 269 of them were enumerated in Prescot, together with 69 in Wigan and 39 in West Derby. The rarity of the name and its tight concentration suggest the possibility that it had a single-family origin. The distribution confirms that it should not be linked with names such as Andrus or Andress which have their own distinctive histories. If early examples cannot be found it would be worth investigating the possibility that it is an abbreviated spelling of Anderson. Ralph Androwson was also called Ralph Androwse in 1446–58.

6

Meaning and Method

Very many British surnames have a straightforward meaning. The medieval forms of common names such as Thomas or Wilson, Fox, or Wright, are similar to the modern ones and present no difficulties in their interpretation. But as we have seen, it is dangerous to guess the meaning of names just from the present spelling, without linking them by genealogical methods. There are many pitfalls to be avoided.

By-names

By-names that were derived from words in common use in Middle English can be of great help in solving the meaning of a surname. The poll tax returns of 1377–81 provide clear evidence of how transparent the meaning of many by-names could be, for in many cases the by-name and the given occupation were identical. The 1379 list for Derby includes Nicholas Cotyler, cotyler; Gilbert Sadeler, sadeler; Hugh Sherman, sherman; and William Plummer, plummer. Equally transparent in meaning are those by-names where the occupation was entered in clerical Latin rather than in English: John Pyper, *ministrallo*; William Glasier, *vitario* (sic); Gilbert Fyssher, *piscenar*, and Peter Peyntor, *pictore*. In a few cases the Latin actually clarifies the meaning of names that are perhaps less obvious: William Leche, *medico*, and John Wayte, *vigilo ville predicte*. In the same roll Walter Ferrour, John Smyth, and Thomas Marchall each had *fabro* written against his name; they were all workers in iron but perhaps had different roles.

The origins of names in other categories were also clear, if not the meaning. It is safe to assume that John de Berde and Henry de Shardelowe owed their names to the Derbyshire villages of Beard and Shardlow, and that Edward Walischemon was indeed a Welshman. The entry for William Brekefart presents us with a typically derogatory nickname, but it is probably safe to assume that it did not become hereditary. It would be unwise to quote examples such as these as evidence for the interpretation of any modern surname unless it could be shown that there is a definite family connection.

Two of the names mentioned above illustrate aspects of the problem. Beard was a very common surname in 1881, with a count of 7,877 and a distribution that makes a single origin most unlikely; it was well represented in the north Midlands so the Derbyshire village is certainly one potential source, but it was also very common in Gloucestershire and the South-east, where it is most unlikely to have had any link with Derbyshire. Clearly, alternative origins should be sought for Beard in those regions, and the frequency there of the by-names *cum barba* and *a la barbe* make a nickname derivation from a man's beard a real possibility. Leach was even more prolific in 1881, with a national total of 12,358. It is impossible to say how many of these families can consider that 'leech' in the sense of physician is the source of their name for the word was used in the northern half of the country for 'a marshy stream' and used commonly as a by-name, over a long period: Adam dil Lach of Tarbock in Lancashire (1381) and John del Lech of Yeadon in Yorkshire (1434) are just two examples. Leitch is said by Black to be a Scottish version of the name and he favoured 'physician' as the origin. However, among the names that he listed was William de Leche (1362), though he dismissed the 'de' as an error for 'le'.

Mistakes have occurred when the connection between a by-name and a modern surname has been too readily assumed. 'Bonsire', the French for 'good sir', has several times been given as the source of Bonser and the well-documented surname Bellamy supports that origin in principle. Nevertheless, the more likely explanation is that Bonser is a variant of the name of the Derbyshire village of Bonsall, for the spelling reflects the colloquial pronunciation of the place-name and the distribution supports that origin. Similarly, the Cheshire surname Bramhall became Brammall and Brammer.

Good documentation can throw further light on the variant forms of by-names at the time when they were stabilizing. Reaney established that the by-name Porter referred to a gatekeeper, quoting William Portarius, janitor (1183), and Miles Portarius (1086) who did porter-service at the jail or castle of Winchester. John Porter of Wadworth (1322) was also a door-keeper and his name is found in a sequence of title deeds covering the years 1322–26. It occurred there also as *ad portam* and *Atteyate*, giving us the French, Latin, and English alternatives of his occupation. If he had descendants who inherited the office they might therefore be called Porter, Port, or Yates. Of course, Porter was also the name given to workers whose task it was to carry goods from one place to another, so this is clearly an alternative derivation for the surname. Porters were highly organized groups in medieval towns and cities, charged with carrying burdens at fixed rates over considerable distances. In York, in 1495, it was ordained 'that every porter observe and kepe theyr ordinauncez in every poynt and article', or risk a heavy fine. Without accurate genealogical evidence and an explicit context for the progenitors' names, it is impossible to distinguish this surname from that of Porter meaning 'door-keeper'.

Many by-names were written in Latin and some writers have stated that the Latin forms gave rise to British occupational surnames, such as Pester (baker) or Sutor (shoemaker), but it is difficult to understand how a Latin term written down by a clerk could become a spoken surname. Why would an English speaker whose father was a smith and had Smith as a by-name, accept being called Faber? Close study of this group of names suggests that he did not. *Sutor* is certainly the Latin word used by clerks to translate 'shoemaker' but it also has an Old English origin and derives ultimately from a word that meant to sew or stitch. At the time when surnames were stabilizing, *c.*1386, Chaucer had the line 'And of a souter a shipman or a leche' in the Reeve's Prologue. The surname now has several different spellings and occurs in different parts of the country but Souter is essentially Scottish, particularly well established in the Aberdeen and Moray areas. Suter is found along the south coast of England, whereas Sowter is more widely distributed but had good numbers in Derbyshire in 1881. Only 70 Sutors were recorded and almost half that number was in the Aberdeen and Moray region.

Pester is essentially a West Country surname, found most commonly in Somerset, Devon, and Dorset in 1881, with another cluster across the Bristol Channel in Monmouthshire. It is true that the Latin word *pistor* was used regularly enough for 'baker' in early documents but so was the French word *pestour* and this is a more plausible source of the surname. Robert de la Pesterye was recorded in Somerset in 1280. In France, where both Pesteur and Pestour occur, there is no suggestion that they derive immediately from the Latin word.

There are also doubts about Faber. Abraham Fawbar married Elizabeth Iles in Leeds in 1579, but when he a witnessed his father-in-law's will seven years later he was recorded as Abraham Faber, and when his wife was buried in 1588 he was referred to as Abraham Fawbert, a spelling that eventually became the usual form of the surname. A direct connection between this man and a tallow chandler called Abraham Fawber, who was enrolled as a freeman of York in 1596, seems likely. When this second Abraham held the office of chamberlain in 1619, he was entered in the rolls as Abraham Faber, chandler. In 1645 another Abraham Faber, tallow chandler, also featured in the rolls. By the time of the hearth tax returns of 1672 the family had achieved minor gentry status and a Mr Faber was taxed on six hearths in the York parish of St John the Evangelist.

Ralph Faber of Heaning, a hamlet in Newton in Bowland, was also a 'gentleman' and he featured regularly in the records of Slaidburn parish in the seventeenth century. We can be confident that he was the same person as Ralph Fawber of Heaning whose children were baptized at the parish church in the 1630s. 'Fawber' is the clue to an earlier spelling, for a 'w' often replaced 'l' and this was the usual form of the surname in previous generations. Earlier members of the family included Ralph Falber, who witnessed a Slaidburn will in 1594, and the widow of Ralph Falber who was taxed in Newton in Bolland in 1545. This rare surname is difficult to trace in the period before parish registers, but several spellings guide us towards its origin; for example, in 1422 John Falbergh was a juryman in Skipton. The source of this surname is the tiny settlement of Fawber, in Horton-in-Ribblesdale, and the spelling 'de Falbergh' is recorded in 1338 and 1375.

Many of the by-names in early records were derived from the pet forms and diminutives of first names that were in common use at the time. This area of research is a minefield for the unwary and in some works of reference the surnames derived from them are dealt with quite badly. Recent research has thrown new light on the meaning of names such as Dawson, Gemson, Mallinson, Pawson, and Abson, and the work of Peter McClure in particular demonstrates the methods that should be employed if the pet forms are to be accurately identified. In most cases the meaning of surnames of this kind can only be determined if two references to one person are found, one using the full name and a second using the pet form or diminutive. Fortunately, sequences in court rolls and title deeds sometimes make that possible.

Typical of these is a collection of deeds that relates to land in Tickhill where a certain John Cutson is mentioned from 1352. In 1353–54 he was named as John, son of Custance and the first deed in the series, which is undated, identifies Custance via her relationship to William, the son of John. Clearly she had no surname but her son's name became hereditary in Tickhill and the likelihood is that a later John Cutson (1430) was the grandson of Custance. Although this identification is not absolutely watertight and the surname may not have survived very long, it appears to confirm that 'Cut' was a pet form of Custance. This was itself a colloquial version of the feminine name Constance and it suggests a new interpretation for the surnames Cutt and Cutts. These have always been said to derive from Cuthbert although the distribution of the names was often in parts of the country where Cuthbert was rarely used. It remains a possibility that 'Cut' was also a pet form of Cuthbert but that must now be proved. Black has shown that Cuthbert was shortened to Cuttie in Scotland but his examples date only from the end of the sixteenth century.

The poll tax returns of 1377–81 can offer the researcher a similar opportunity for they occasionally list a person twice, thus providing us with two versions of the same surname, and making us look again at some traditional etymologies. One sequence in Manchester in 1381 lists Thomas Graunt or Grant, Richard Bybbe or Bibbe, Henry Thighul or Thughul, and John Higgson or *filius Hugonis*. The traditional explanation of 'Higg' is that it is a voiced form of Hick and therefore a pet form of Richard. That may be true in some instances but it would need to be proved, whereas this by-name tells us that Higg was undoubtedly a pet form of Hugh. That assumes more significance when the meaning of the surname Higson is discussed, for 82 per cent of the 1,565 people who bore the name in 1881 were resident in Lancashire; the percentage rises to over 95 per cent if Higsons in the neighbouring counties of Cheshire and Yorkshire are included. This may not be a surname with a single family origin but it is certainly very local in its distribution and the by-name evidence of 1381 seems relevant. If Higg is indeed just as likely to derive from Hugh as from Richard, it also raises questions about several other names, for example Higgs, Higgitt, Higgins, and Higginson. The interchange between the vowels 'i' and 'u', explicit in Thighul/Thughul above, emphasizes the possible linguistic connection between Higgins and Huggins. In most dictionaries Higson is dealt with briefly and no early examples are quoted. Many similar pet forms await clarification.

The compilers of surname dictionaries simply do not have the space in a single volume to enter each surname individually and provide adequate evidence of the meaning and origin, with the result that large numbers of them depend on little more than guesswork. Some writers seek a way round this problem by including as many names as possible under a single heading, but this is a dangerous practice and can create an enormous problem for all those who wish to use surname data. The Lancashire surname Sagar will make this point for, even in the most recent works of reference, it is linked with names such as Seagar. Indeed, Reaney and Wilson have it as the first example of twelve surnames that are said to derive from an unrecorded Old English personal name Segar. The half a dozen references offered in evidence are exclusively by-names for the period 1066–1275 and they are all drawn from sources in the South-west or East Anglia.

Non-linguists can be intimidated by such entries. Richard McKinley identified Sagar as a Lancashire surname and even noted the use of 'le' in the case of Roger le Sagher in Hindley (1379), yet he wrote that he considered it 'doubtful if the presence of the definite article can be relied upon in interpreting the name'. In other documents the Latin equivalent of 'le Sagher' was 'sarrator', a clear reference to a sawyer. The occupational term 'sager' was used by dialect speakers until quite recently and may not yet be extinct. Sawn wood was 'sagen wood' in 1693 and the Halifax historian John Watson gave 'saghe' as the local term for a saw; the 'reets and sagers' referred to in the *Leeds Mercury* in 1896 were wrights and sawyers. In 1881 the surname Sagar belonged almost exclusively to an area that linked Burnley and Bradford, a telling reflection of the migrations that have taken place since the late sixteenth century. The national total was 1,217 and of these 93 per cent lived in Lancashire and Yorkshire.

The problem is more complex where Ely is concerned. This is listed by Reaney along with Ealey, Eeley, Eley, Hely, and Heley and two origins are suggested, one from the place-name Ely in Cambridgeshire and the other from the Old French personal name Elie, itself a form of Elijah. By-names such as Huna de Ely, recorded in Cambridgeshire in 1086, and Philippus *filius* Helie, recorded in Somerset in 1213, confirm that such origins are possible. Similar explanations of Ely are found in other published works, although some writers are content to link the surname only with the place-name.

In Yorkshire the by-name 'de Ely' occurs several times in the fourteenth century, and examples in York seem likely to derive from the Cambridgeshire place-name, for example Adam de Ely, *piscarius* (1322). It is at least a possibility that one or other of these became hereditary but, if so, the surname does not appear to have survived. Ely has not been noted in the county from 1500 to 1675 and it is missing from major published indexes for that period, including wills, fines, and tax lists. If the name's more recent history in Yorkshire is examined, using only genealogical evidence, a quite different picture emerges, for the search places Ely in the parishes that lie to the south and south-east of Huddersfield, with several families of that name established in the townships of Honley and Lepton from *c*.1700. It is a variant there of the surname Heeley or Healey which derives from the local place-name Healey and is always pronounced without the initial 'h'. Parish registers, deeds, wills, directories, and the like confirm the origin. For example, Abraham Heeley or Ely was the explicit alias of a man living in Kirkburton parish in 1690 and data from Honley records illustrate the wide range of variant spellings from the same period. In the following examples, distinctive first names have been chosen with the aim of confirming the identifications: Caleb Heeley/Eeley of Thurstin, Honley (1689–98); Matthew Hely/Hilley/Eley/Illey of Honley (1763–78). This is not to say, or imply, that Healey is the source of all the names listed by Reaney, but its late change to Ely emphasizes the role of family history in surname studies and the danger of grouping surnames under one heading when suggesting how they might have originated. The 1881 totals for the listed names in order of frequency are Eley (1,853), Ely (1,576), Heley

(312), Ealey (243), Hely (43), and Eeley (33). Hidden within these statistics are many fascinating local concentrations, including Eley in Derbyshire and Essex, Ealey in Wiltshire and Northamptonshire, Eeley in Oxfordshire, Hely in London, and Heley in Bedfordshire and Buckinghamshire.

Surname histories

Cinnamon/Sinnamon

Spelling variations of the kind seen in the history of Ely are often compounded by popular etymology. Cinnamon is one of several very rare but related surnames that were found principally in Lanarkshire in 1881, with four main variant spellings: Cinnamond (15), Cinnamon (10), Cinamont (1), and Sinnamon (4). Cinnamon was found in Liverpool, the Isle of Man, Whitehaven (5), and King's Norton (3). In Black's *The Surnames of Scotland* (1946) Cinnamond is said to be a variant of Kinninmonth, which has a territorial origin in Fife and is also a very uncommon name. Unfortunately, there is no proof of a connection in the examples that Black quotes, so he may simply have been speculating. The same author made no mention of either Cinnamon or Sinnamon although both occurred in Lanarkshire alongside Cinnamond: the spelling and pronunciation of Sinnamon in particular may cast some doubt on Black's explanation.

He is not the only scholar to have had a theory about the names. Cinnamond and Sinnamon were additions to Reaney's dictionary in 1997, placed there by Wilson who claimed that they were derived from the French placename Saint-Amand. Three by-names are quoted in support of the theory, the latest being Aimery de Sancto Amando, noted in Somerset in 1280. Almost certainly, Wilson was influenced by the history of Sinclair, for which a derivation from Saint Clair has been satisfactorily demonstrated. Unfortunately, no evidence is given that links Sinnamon to Sancto Amando, and the suggested origin is unconvincing to say the least.

In theory there is no reason why Cinnamon should not derive from the spice cinnamon, for it was already familiar to the English at the beginning of the fourteenth century. The accounts for Bolton Priory record the purchase of two pounds of cinnamon in 1306–07 and the word was familiar enough to have been used by Chaucer later that century, as a term of endearment. In the Miller's Tale Absolon addressed his lady love as 'My faire brid, my swete cinamome'. Similar words such as 'leman' became hereditary surnames, but no early examples of 'cinnamon' as a by-name have yet been noted.

An account of possible alternative origins will illustrate the sort of spelling changes that affected some surnames from the sixteenth century onwards and demonstrate how those changes can be identified. The enquiry starts with the name Francis Cinamon, entered in the published index of the Act Books in York. This man was said to be of Leeds and the administration act was dated 13 October 1684, confirming that he died during that year. Although this spelling is not in the printed registers for Leeds, a family called Sinamon was living in Briggate about that time and several entries for James Sinamon or Sinemond occur in the 1680s. Partial confirmation that Francis belonged to this family can be found in a manuscript that was formerly in the possession of the Leeds antiquary, Ralph Thoresby. This has details of a damaged tombstone bearing the names of Francis Sinemond, his wife Elizabeth, and their son James who died in 1702. Unfortunately the details for Francis were already partly illegible, but he had been buried in August, in a year for which only '16 –' survives. The Yorkshire hearth tax return for 1672 lists Francis Sinnimond, who was then living on The Headrow in Leeds, and this was the only record of the surname in the West Riding.

Francis Sinnimond or Sinemond is reasonably well documented, since he served as the deputy constable for Leeds until his death. His election to that post is recorded for the years 1681 and 1682, when his name was spelt Siniment. The administration act and the tombstone together point to the death of Francis some time in August 1684. The registers of that period have no reference to a person with that surname, but a Francis Silleman was buried there on 22 August 1684, and further evidence from the registers establishes that this was an alternative spelling of the surname. The Silliman family of Briggate can be traced back another hundred years at least, with confirmation that Francis Silliman, the son of James Silliman of Briggate, was baptized in 1629. An earlier Francis Silliman was baptized in 1597 and Bryan Silyman of Briggate was baptized in 1579. The earliest surviving register for Leeds dates only from 1572 but from other sources such as wills and tax lists it is possible to take the history of the surname in Leeds back further. In 1539, for example, the name of Bryan Selyman was listed in a Leeds muster roll and his first name was so uncommon at that time that a family connection with the Bryan Silyman who was baptized in 1579 seems certain. Other examples of this same surname occur in other parts of the county back to 1306.

The interchange of 'l' and 'n' is a well-documented phenomenon in surname studies. It gave rise to variant spellings that could then be 'legitimized' by popular association. Sinnemond may have been a genuine linguistic variation that was preferred to Silliman because the latter was becoming open to ridicule, but that is speculation. This account of a family in the

Leeds area demonstrates how the spellings of one surname varied in the period 1539–1702, but genealogists should be wary of linking the examples quoted with present-day bearers of surnames such as Silliman and Sinnamon. Any such link would need to be demonstrated genealogically or via DNA.

That point is emphasized by evidence from the parish register of Mirfield. In May 1649, Godfrey Synamon was married there and his sons Joshua and Robert were born soon afterwards. These are the only indexed references to Synamon in the published register, but a careful search shows that the name had several variants, including Semanit, Simonet, Simmolit, and Surmolit, all rare entries for individuals called Godfrey or Joshua. A Quarter Sessions document in 1687 mentions Joshua Seminot of Mirfield. These may all be versions of another Yorkshire name, Simmonite, but even if that is not the case it seems clear that Synamon in Mirfield had nothing to do with Sinamon in Leeds, only a few miles away.

Pankhurst

Pankhurst is a surname that offers further evidence of the influence that association played in spelling. It was an uncommon name in 1881, with a national total of 1,041 when the distribution was characteristic of the south-eastern counties: it was particularly well established in Kent (42 per cent) and Sussex (24 per cent) and numbers were high also in Middlesex and Surrey, a group that accounted for a further 21 per cent. The several obvious variant spellings were all rare: Pinkhurst (2), Penkhirst (5), Panckhurst (1), and Pankerst (1). The traditional etymology of the surname linked it with Pentecost, used as a personal name in the Middle Ages, possibly for a child born at Pentecost. Reaney has examples of individuals named Pentecost in the period 1187–1230 and he also recorded the by-name Christina *filia* Pentecuste (1250), which shows how the surname might have developed. In 1881 Pentecost was rare (304) but there was a significant small group in Devon and Cornwall and a slightly bigger group in Sussex and the neighbouring counties of Surrey and Kent. The view that Pankhurst derived from Pentecost appears to have been based partly on the similarity in sound between the two words and partly on two aliases. In 1605, for example, the Surrey place-name Pankhurst was referred to as Pentecost alias Panchurst, and in 1770 a Sussex man was named as Richard Pankhurst alias Penticost. These are proof that Pentecost and Pankhurst were assumed by some to share a common origin but they do not prove that origin.

Richard McKinley, who was not a linguist, challenged what had become an apparently traditional explanation of Pankhurst when he attributed the aliases to mistaken popular etymology. He accepted that there was some confusion between the names, certainly after 1600, but found no evidence that they were linked in origin. He was confident that Pankhurst derived from a place-name in that part of England and mentioned one or two possibilities, quoting the by-names 'de Pynkhurst' and 'de Pynkherst', which he found in West Sussex in the thirteenth and fourteenth centuries. The more recent publication of the Sussex poll tax returns has John and William Pynkhurst at Clapham in West Sussex in 1379. Crucially, McKinley traced the history of this surname in detail, not with strict genealogical evidence it is true, but over many generations, and his sense of evidence as a historian obliged him to differ with the experts. The problem of which place-name was the actual source may have to be decided by local and family historians but the nature of the origin is not in doubt. Almost in passing, McKinley noted other variant spellings of the surname Pankhurst, with particular reference to Dunstan Pankherste who lived in north Sussex in the reign of Elizabeth I. One of the variants was Pancost, which illustrates how easy it may have been in that period to confuse Pankhurst with Pentecost. The unusual first name gives the identification great credibility, as does the status of this man in the local community. In a recent publication the same Dunstan is recorded as serving on several occasions as a juror on inquests of the Sussex coroners and other spellings of his distinctive surname include Penkeherste (1572) and Pancrasse (1577). The influence in the second of these was St Pancras, the name of two early martyrs.

Over-interpretation

Oliver Rackham once famously accused scholars of reading more into place-names than they actually tell us. The same criticism can often be made of surname specialists who feel they have to elaborate on earlier etymologies.

Lillicrop

Lillicrop, a Devonshire surname which has attracted unwarranted elaboration, had numerous variants in 1881 but a relatively low national total (440). The most popular spellings then were Lillicrap (266), Lillicrapp (33), Lillycrap (29), Lillicrop (21), and Lillycrapp (18). Just over half the name-bearers lived in Devonshire, mostly in Plymouth or places close by, but small numbers resided in London, South Wales, and the neighbouring counties of Cornwall and Somerset. Most current surname dictionaries do not mention the name but it is sufficiently unusual to have attracted the attention of some historians and David Postles contributed useful information on its early history in *The Surnames of Devon* (1995). His evidence points to an origin in the neighbourhood of Sourton where Lillicrop was recorded in 1332 and again in 1545. On the second occasion it was quite numerous and accounted for 20 per cent of the taxpayers.

The later spelling quoted by Postles was 'Lyllyecroppe' which he stated was 'a nickname reflecting a white head'. The question here is whether the linguistic evidence supports the etymology and justifies the interpretation, for the *OED* has one reference only to 'lily-crop', which was a word used by the poet Gower in 1390 when he described Tarquin striking off the 'lilie croppes' in the garden; that is the heads of the lilies. The traditional interpretation of the by-name presumes that it was given to a person with hair that was coloured like the lily. This may be a plausible theory but writers present it as a fact and not as a possibility. Who is to say that the progenitor of the Lillicrops had a head of blond hair? If the circumstances in which the name was coined are not explicit it seems better to simply make suggestions that are clearly labelled as 'possibilities'.

Murgatroyd

Basing an etymology on a single example is in any case unwise, as a closer look at the Halifax surname Murgatroyd makes clear. This has usually been said to mean 'Margaret's clearing', on the strength of one, uncharacteristic, spelling, that is 'Mergretrode'. 'Royd' was a common element in minor place-names around Halifax and it identified assarts or clearings that often had a first name as a prefix: this seemed to support the traditional interpretation of 'Meergre-trode' and the derivation went unchallenged. Now, more spellings have been located and they point to a quite different meaning: typical examples for the period 1371–1499 are Moregaterode, Moregateroid, and Morgetroide, the first of these occurring numerous times. They indicate that the prefix was not 'Margaret' but 'moor-gate', a term which is found in many early documents although it has no entry in the *OED*. The earliest use is in a deed dated 1323 in which land was said to abut on 'le Moregate' and this could have referred to a way leading to the moor. In Beverley, for example, 'Minstermoorgate' was a street name judged to have that meaning. However, the word may have referred to a gate in the fence that divided the moor from the cultivated fields and there is support for that in contexts where the spelling 'mooryate' clearly points to a gate. On one occasion tenants were actually instructed not to leave the moor gate open.

Cherriman

In the case of the Sussex name Cherriman it is the consistent modern spelling that is responsible for a dubious etymology. Its distribution pattern is typical of a single-origin surname in the South-east: it had a count of just 96 in 1881 and most of those so called lived in Sussex. Even less common were the Sussex variants Cherryman (73), Cheryman (10), Cheriman (7), and Cherman (15) which may share the same family origin. The main centres of distribution were Brighton, Lewes, Steyning, Horsham, and Cuckfield. The traditional explanation is that Cherriman has an occupational origin, denoting a person who bought or sold cherries. A number of writers have given it this meaning, from Lower to Reaney, without any supporting evidence and despite the fact that there is no entry for 'cherryman' in the *OED*. Richard McKinley first raised doubts about the derivation, saying that he had found no examples of the name in Sussex before 1571 when Thomas Cheryman was a native of Horsham. In the parish register for Horsham, earlier spellings of this man's name were Chyryam and Chyriam. In Pulborough, a similar sequence had Cherian as the forerunner of Cheryman from 1570. These examples were sufficiently different from Cherriman for McKinley to describe the origin as uncertain.

The parish register of Howden, in the old East Riding, may hold the key to the problem, for the names Cheriam, Cheriom, and Cherion all occurred there in the 1580s, in a village called Barmby-on-the-Marsh. In 1560 a Thomas Cherome had purchased land in Drax just across the river and it is in that parish that earlier examples of the surname have been recorded. Typical spellings include Cheriholme (1559), Chereholme (1495), and Chereholme (1410). In Eggborough and Kellington, just upstream from Drax, John Chyrholme and William de Teriholme (sic) were taxed in 1379. The origin seems likely to have been a minor place-name but unfortunately that cannot now be traced. However, the surname Cherryholme is still found in South Yorkshire.

The linguistic evidence points therefore to a connection between Cherriman and Cherryholme, but this would imply migration from the East Riding to Sussex in the mid-sixteenth century and there is no proof that such a move took place. It was certainly possible, for McKinley noted the presence of Yorkshire surnames in Sussex from the fourteenth century: Bonwick was one example and the gentry family called Dawtry had land in both counties. It may be relevant that all the parishes associated with this family in the early period were close to the river Ouse and its affluents the Aire and Derwent. Perhaps the Cherryholmes were seamen, like the Edward Cherryholme who arrived in New England late in the seventeenth century? Speculation of that kind may be tempting to the family historian but the absence of genealogical evidence means that only DNA tests could demonstrate a clear relationship between the two surnames.

Blacker

It was the late suffix 'man' that obscured Cherriman's origin and assumptions of that kind have led to other mistakes. Some of these have to do with surnames which end in -er and are mistakenly thought to have occupational origins. Information that is now available for Blaker and Blacker make the point. These names were placed under one heading by Reaney and two of the by-names that he quoted clearly point to an occupation, that is 'le Blaker' (1291) and 'le Blackere' (1312). The meaning of these by-names is not at all straightforward, since the Middle English word 'blake' meant 'pale' or 'white', and it is difficult to distinguish from early spellings of 'black' in some contexts, but Reaney, like several of his predecessors, thought the terms referred to 'bleachers'. An occupational origin for the Sussex surname has become generally accepted, but we need to be wary, for McKinley noted that Blaber, which has a quite different origin, was also found in Sussex and he suspected that it was frequently confused with Blaker from the sixteenth century. There is no phonetic explanation for that confusion but it is not unknown for written versions of a surname to defy the rules. Alternatively, transcribers may simply have mistaken the letters 'b' and 'k'.

More importantly, no proof of a direct connection between Blacker and Blaker has been put forward. The distributions of these names in 1881 show that Blaker clearly 'belonged' to the South-east whereas most of the Blackers lived in the West Riding, with a smaller but still significant group of Blackers in Somerset. We may be dealing with two or perhaps three distinct names. It is possible that the Blacker families in Somerset and Gloucestershire are linked with either Sussex or Yorkshire, and DNA might solve that problem. Equally, they might have had an independent origin, in which case it is worth noting that Blatcher, a very rare surname in 1881, was found in exactly the same region as Blaker. Once again, Reaney's by-names are of value, for the examples that he quoted under the heading Blatcher include Robert le Blacchere of Somerset (1305). More importantly, he was able to show that 'le Blakkere' and 'le Blecchere' were alternative versions of the same by-name in 1313. More genealogical work may establish whether the West Country surname Blacker also means 'bleacher'.

The West Riding Blackers have a quite different origin. An article published in the *Yorkshire Archaeological Journal* in 1943 establishes a clear geographical origin for the surname, since most of the early forms were 'de Blakker'. Several minor localities in the region are named Blacker, one of which in Crigglestone in the parish of Sandal near Wakefield is where the Blacker family lived until the middle years of the seventeenth century. It is named as 'Blackerre' in a court roll of 1306 and Matthew de Blacker of Sandal is mentioned soon afterwards; when Robert Blakker died in 1458, an inquisition found that he 'held divers lands called Blakker in Crigglestone'. The different spellings of Matthew's surname include Blakeker (1338) and this helps to confirm the meaning as 'black carr'.

Harker

Similarly, Reaney interpreted Harker as 'eavesdropper', that is one who 'harks', on the strength of the by-name 'Robert le Herkere', recorded in Somerset in 1280. He derived it from the Middle English word that is still used in the sense of 'listen or give ear to'. His only other example under that heading was Ralph Harka of York (1479). Here again, the distribution of the surname is of vital importance for in 1881 Harker was a common north-country surname (3,157), found mostly in the adjoining counties of Durham, Lancashire, and Yorkshire, where it has a quite different origin. Although it is rare to find Harker in any north-country record before 1600, it was common in and around Swaledale in the seventeenth century: in the hearth tax returns of 1673, for example, more than thirty examples of the name were recorded, principally in the parish of Grinton. In the sixteenth century Herkay or Harkay were more typical: these are the spellings for Swaledale in the rentals for Rievaulx Abbey in 1539 and in a published series of Swaledale wills for the years 1522–1600. In 1366 Thomas Herkay paid 6s. 8d. for the agistment of twenty cattle in a remote part of Swaledale. Arkay was a variant without initial 'h'. The first example there of the spelling Harker was in 1599.

The meaning of the name remains a problem although the origin seems clear. There are localities named Harker in Cumberland but the evidence for them is late and they are unlikely to be the source of the surname. 'Herkey' was a locality in Swaledale first recorded in twelfth-century charters but omitted from A.H. Smith's *The Place-Names of the North Riding of Yorkshire* (1928, reissued 1969). Other spellings from that period include Hercay and Herchai and all these are likely to be early forms of Harkerside in Grinton, especially if Herkasyde (1549) is taken into consideration. Swaledale is in a part of the northern Pennines, close to County Durham and Cumbria and this is reflected in the name's 1881 distribution.

This history of Harker throws light on the rare surnames Harke, Harkey, and Arkey, all recorded in 1881. The fact that they are found in localities away from Swaledale may explain the survival of what are really archaic spellings, and for that to have happened the move away from Swaledale must have been early. The by-name 'le Herkere' is of interest in its own right but it can have nothing to do with the north-country surname Harker. On the other hand the spelling of the Reaney reference of 1479 identifies the named individual as a member of the Swaledale family. The history of names such as Cherriman and Harker testifies to significant spelling changes in the sixteenth century, just when the population was increasing and parish registers came into use. It is a major watershed in surname development.

Knewstubb

Knewstubb is another rare surname with an interesting variation in spelling that has obscured its origin. The best clue to that origin is the distribution in 1881, when just 46 people bore the name. The only variants noted at that time were both rare: Knewstub (1) and Newstubb (2). A significant percentage of those listed lived in Westmorland, in what was called the East Ward, where Knewstubb occurs as a surname over several centuries. The spellings vary considerably but are at least recognizable. Examples in the hearth tax returns of 1674 were Knustub and Knutsupp, whilst a generation earlier, in the protestation returns of 1642, they were Knewstubb, Knewstuppe, and Knewstopp.

The recently published poll tax returns of 1379 identify the family home and throw some light on the probable meaning. William Knokstub was a married man paying tax in Waitby and this spelling identifies the first element as a word of Irish origin, brought into the North-west by Scandinavians. A 'knock' was a small hill or perhaps more often a heap of stones, and 'stob' probably referred to a place where trees had been 'stubbed', that is taken out by the roots. No settlement with that name is known but 'Knowstubb' survived as the name of a field in Soulby into the seventeenth century. Soulby and Waitby are near neighbours so perhaps Knokstob was a locality close to the boundary between the two. These later spelling developments are a reflection of local pronunciations and they can pose a bigger problem if they are linked with migration.

Camplejohn

Another example is the rare Camplejohn, which has never been satisfactorily explained, though Weekley suggested that it might mean 'wry-mouthed John, from the Celtic word that has given Campbell'. This was a guess, based on the modern form of the name, and he made no attempt to trace its earlier history. Reaney omitted Camplejohn from his dictionary but it was included in the revised edition by Wilson who interpreted it as 'fighting John'. He compared it with Campleman, another rare Yorkshire surname, but it is doubtful if Camplejohn has anything at all to do with the popular first name John and

Campleman is actually a variant of Cappleman. In 1881 a mere 32 people bore the name, all of them resident in Yorkshire, although they lived in different parts of the county, with just two concentrations around Barnsley and Selby and a smaller group in York, where the name arrived late in Elizabeth's reign. Thomas Camplechon, tailor and freeman in 1588, was also called Thomas Campleion; later spellings of his name included Campleshon. These variants suggest that the 'i' in the final element of Campleion was pronounced something like 'y' and this would help to explain how it later became 'john'. Variants of this name can be found in a variety of Yorkshire sources back to 1466, when a certain John Campilyon of Norton made his will. It is not clear which of the several places called Norton this refers to, though by the mid-sixteenth century families of Campilyons were living in the parishes of Wilberfoss, Seamer, and Whitby, in the eastern half of the county. The spellings were much the same as those found in York, but no earlier examples of the name have yet been discovered there, so it either developed later than most other names or it had its origins elsewhere.

There is good reason to suppose that it came from Norfolk, where an identical name was relatively common at the time of the poll tax returns in 1377–81. Typical examples are Campilion (Buckenham), Caumplion (Great Dunham, Caston and Griston), and Camplyn (Strumpshaw). Earlier by-names found in Norfolk are William Campelin (1275), mentioned in the Hundred Rolls, and Stephen Camelin (1230). The migration north to Yorkshire would not have been unusual, for the records of both counties show that the sea was already a great highway between the two regions in the Middle Ages. Even so, the meaning of the surname remains a problem. Reaney and Wilson did not connect this name with Camplejohn but offered the plausible suggestion that it derived from the Middle English word 'camelin', apparently a kind of material that is supposed to have been made from camel hair. If this is the origin, the surnames predate the *OED* evidence by 170 years. The one unsatisfactory aspect of the theory is the absence of early forms with 'ion' as the final element. Perhaps there was some influence from 'chameleon', a word certainly known to our ancestors in the fourteenth century.

That is not quite the end of the story. It is likely, for example, that the influence of Camplion/Camplejohn was responsible for the equally rare Campleman, and both names are found almost exclusively in Yorkshire. In North Yorkshire Camplion, Camplin, and the quite separate Campion were frequently confused. In the parishes of Danby and Lythe, for example, the confusion goes back at least to the sixteenth century and was well enough known for one local historian to write: 'Camplin is still the common, almost conventional, corruption or pronunciation of the name Campion in all this district'. The conclusion must be that some Yorkshire Campions are likely to share the same family origins as Camplins and Camplejohns – another challenge for geneticists!

Unsolved names

Brownsword

Even the most careful and methodical research does not always lead to a successful conclusion and the meaning of many surnames is still in doubt. Brownsword is one that has still not been explained. Professor Wilson was of the opinion that it was derived from the Cheshire place-name Brownswolds, a locality in Congleton; Kenneth Cameron who edited *The Place-Names of Cheshire* (1967–68) had no evidence for this place-name earlier than 1595 and said that it was named after a local man called Thomas Brownsworth. Cameron's opinion is the more convincing. For Richard McKinley, who found examples of Brownsword in the neighbourhood of Manchester, around 1540, it was a surname that 'originated in south Lancashire at a relatively late period'. He found no earlier instances outside the county and no obvious place-name connection. He thought it possible that it had developed from Brounson, a name also found in that part of Lancashire from the fourteenth century, but expressed his doubt about such an origin.

In 1881 just 211 people called Brownsword were recorded in the national census, the majority of them in Staffordshire, with smaller numbers in Lancashire (31), Derbyshire (29), and Cheshire (10). The eight or nine fairly obvious variants found in much the same area include Brownsworth (24), Brownswood (80), and Brownsord (19). Edgar Tooth is confident that Brownsword is a Staffordshire surname, and he derives it from Brownsett, a locality mentioned frequently in Leek parish registers from the 1600s. The place-name spellings that he quotes include Brownsford, Brownsort, and Brownsword. Unfortunately, he has no early examples of the place-name and no references to the surname that predate those quoted by other writers. He notes that John Brownsword was the headmaster of Macclesfield Grammar School in 1561 and comments on Ralph or Randal Brownsword of Stoke-on-Trent whose name was also spelt Brownsord and Bromsford in the period 1633–75. Bardsley's examples, which he found in Cheshire, date from roughly the same period and have similar spellings to those noted in Lancashire and Staffordshire but they are all too late for the origin to be clear cut. Without earlier evidence for the Lancashire surname or the Staffordshire place-name the problem remains unsolved but it is at least worth noting that the distribution pattern of

Brownson in 1881, except for one cluster in Devon, closely resembles that of Brownsword and its variants.

Pennyman

Pennyman was near to extinction in 1881. It was prominent enough in the past to attract the attention of several writers and it provides us with a good example of how divided the opinions of experts can be when it comes to the question of meaning. For Reaney it meant the servant of a person called Penny, an explanation that was approved of later by Richard McKinley. Neither of these scholars had any examples to support that etymology but it is formally possible, and they both felt that Pennyman could safely be compared with names such as Matthewman or Priestman. David Postles, on the other hand, found the name alongside Hardepeny in a Lincolnshire subsidy roll and classed both of them as nicknames, given to individuals whose acquisitiveness 'transgressed locally expected conventions of charity', possibly another example of over-interpretation. Pennyman may be a surname where the two elements are apparently transparent in meaning, but in combination they have proved very difficult to interpret.

Unfortunately, the surname was so rare in 1881 that we have no distribution pattern to help us understand its history, and the by-names provide most of the early evidence. These have been noted from the 1200s in counties as far apart as Somerset, Cambridgeshire, and Lincolnshire, which may imply that 'pennyman' was a widely used term, with no particular local or regional significance. Just where and when it became a surname has not yet been established but examples occur in Yorkshire from 1472, when John Pennyman, a 'litster' or dyer, was granted freeman status in the city. It is there also that we have plausible evidence of a possible explanation. In 1589 the ancient ordinances of the city's butchers were amended and it was agreed that 'the penny-men' should have the right to dress 'anie manner of fleshe' away from the butchers' premises, but might not 'kill or putte to saile by retaile any fleshe'; two major restrictions that drew a distinction between common butchers and pennymen. In Doncaster, in 1610, a similar order made it clear that 'a penny-man' was a butcher, but that he operated under different regulations.

Of course, that is not to say that this little-known occupational term was responsible for the surname, or that the scattered by-names necessarily share a common linguistic origin. The word 'pennyman' may have a number of additional meanings that are as yet unknown to us, but the Yorkshire evidence does offer a plausible alternative to those mentioned above. Family historians should always be encouraged to examine the types of documentary material that are illustrative of customary practices and the English that was being spoken when by-names were in use.

Identifying a progenitor

Many genealogists work towards a goal that may be unattainable but occasionally the evidence falls into place and the researcher is put in touch directly with the person responsible for his surname. That is occasionally possible if it has distinctive qualities and is found in one particular region over a long period. In the case of Tillotson, which has a continuous history in the Airedale parish of Kildwick back to 1379, the evidence points to Tillot de Northwod as the source of the name. She was taxed there alongside John and William Tillotson and was probably their mother. The precise genealogical evidence may be lacking but there seems to be no doubt about the origin. These three individuals and John de Northwod are all listed together towards the end of the roll, catching a family group at the very time when their surname was stabilizing. The meaning is also quite clear since Tillot was a popular diminutive of Matilda, via the pet form Till.

The researcher who seeks to discover the meaning of a surname faces numerous problems and yet the method to be employed can be expressed quite simply. The starting point must be an awareness that each surname goes back to a single person and originates in unique circumstances. Ideally, there should be a chain of genealogical evidence that links the modern bearer of a name to his or her distant ancestor, bridging several hundred years and innumerable generations. Once the name-giver has been identified the question of meaning can be considered.

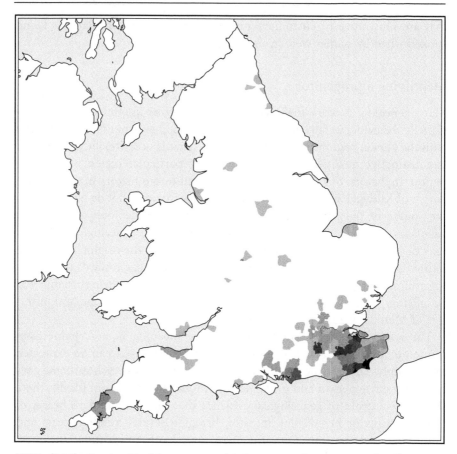

APPS: distribution in 1881. Many topographical names such as Green and Hill are very common but others have a pronounced regional distribution. Reaney and Wilson explain Apps as 'dweller by the aspen tree' and quote early examples from Surrey and Sussex, including Roger atte Apse in 1327. South-east England is indeed the home of this surname. The 1,346 people named Apps in the 1881 census included 498 in Kent, 332 in Sussex, and 302 in or close to London. It is worth noting that Reaney gave the same meaning to the Sussex by-name 'atte Hepse' (1327), for Epps is predominantly a Kent surname. It was particularly evident in Ashford and Faversham in 1881.

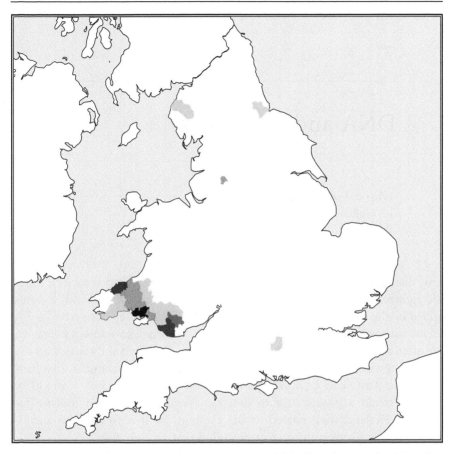

PEREGRINE: distribution in 1881. Dictionaries invariably link Peregrine with Pilgrim, but provide no evidence for that origin, relying completely on early examples of the by-name. Its distribution in 1881 placed it firmly in south Wales where John and Sheila Rowlands noted that it was a latinization of Perkin. The 1881 maps show that Pilgrim and its many variants, e.g. Pagram, Peagram, and Pigram, had expanded in Essex and neighbouring counties.

7

DNA and Surnames

'What did you say your name was?'
'It's Holland, ma'am.'
'What? Not those frightful Whigs?'
'No, ma'am. I'm not related to Lord Holland.'

This dialogue is from Rose Melikan's recent book *The Blackstone Key*, set in the eighteenth century. In this passage our hero, Captain Holland, is being grilled by the rather grand Mrs Tipton as to his possible relations based solely on his surname. The notion of 'one's relations' through surname is pervasive. We often refer to a family by their surname ('the Joblings') and the notion of a surname giving an indication of possible relatedness is found in literature from Jane Austen to P.G. Wodehouse. These days, of course, it would be possible to do a genetic test to determine which other men bearing the surname Holland were related to the Captain. So it is to genetics and its uses in family history and surnames studies that we now turn.

People researching their surname and family histories have a perennial problem: what to do when the paper trail runs out? How do we find whether or not the Nottinghamshire Hollands are related to the Hollands who live in Bedfordshire when there are no documentary records to link the two? This is where recent advances in genetics have been found to be invaluable in the perhaps unexpected fields of surnames and family history.

Surnames have long been an inherent part of our understanding of what signifies a family. Indeed, another term for surname is 'family name'. When our ancestors began to apply labels to themselves in the form of hereditary surnames, they created a system of cultural markers of common ancestry among people. Surnames soon became a shorthand for a biological relationship signifying family groups, such as the Jacksons and the Osmonds, or dynasties, ranging from the Tudors to the Kennedys. The fact that people who are more closely related to one another will share more of their genetic material than people who are more distantly related forms the crux of the marriage between the fields of genetics, genealogy, and surname history. Each of these fields is able to augment the others and together build a fuller picture of individual and collective histories. But before we explore how genetics, in particular the Y chromosome, can be useful to family and surname historians, let us start with a genetic primer. What is DNA? What parts of our DNA are we interested in? And why?

Fortunately, people who have never taken a biology class already have a basic knowledge of genetics. As visitors to the Genetics Department at the University of Leicester are often told, we are all geneticists. We notice that siblings all look similar to one another and to their parents and that family traits can be passed down through the generations. While the molecular basis of inheritance has been deciphered only in the last hundred years, a basic knowledge of genetics has been with us for thousands of years. We humans noticed that such traits were not just confined to our species and, with the advent of agriculture and the domestication of plants and animals, this knowledge was used to our advantage, for practical purposes, from breeding more docile cattle or sheep with paler wool for dyeing, to selecting particular types of wheat. This knowledge was also applied to more pleasurable purposes: for example in the breeding of new types of roses. This has been possible because all the cells of each organism carry information, in the form of DNA, which provides the instructions needed for the organism to be constructed, to grow, survive and go on to have offspring, as well as determining what characteristics the organism will have.

A common but apt analogy is to liken our DNA to a molecular instruction manual which is passed down from parents to their children. The fact that we all inherited our DNA from our parents, who inherited it from their parents, and so on, means that our DNA carries information about our ancestors as well as our contemporary relatives. So what is DNA?

The structure of DNA

DNA, or deoxyribonucleic acid to give it its long name, is a made up of a number of similar building blocks that are bonded together. The four different building blocks of DNA are known, in genetic jargon, as nucleotides. If we look at these building blocks in more detail we see that they are themselves made up of three parts. Two of these parts, a molecule of sugar and a phosphate molecule, always remain the same regardless of which building block they belong to. The third part is known as a base and comes in four different types: adenine (A), thymine (T), guanine (G), and cytosine (C). Geneticists tend to refer to these in a shortened form using the first letter of each base: A, T, G, and C. In essence, our entire instruction manual can be thought of as being written with just four letters.

These nucleotides are linked together in a chain and they can be ordered in any sequence. A molecule of DNA is made up of two of these chains and looks like a ladder; some geneticists prefer the analogy of a zip. The sugar and phosphate molecules form the sides of the ladder and the DNA bases pair up (as 'base pairs') with one another to form the rungs. Adenine always pairs with thymine, and cytosine always pairs with guanine. So if the sequence of one half of the ladder is known, then it is possible to deduce the sequence

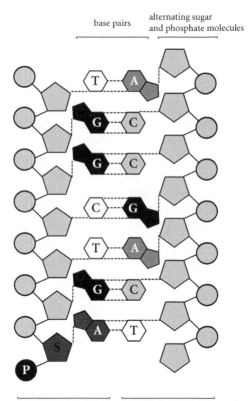

FIGURE 1 **DNA Structure.** The structure of DNA is often likened to a ladder (or zip) with the sugar and phosphate molecules forming the sides of the ladder and the bases (A,C,T, and G) pairing together to form the rungs. Because A always pairs with T and G always pairs with C, by knowing the sequence of one strand, it is possible to determine the sequence of the other strand. S=sugar molecule, P=phosphate molecule, A=adenine, C=cytosine, G=guanine, T=thymine.

of the complementary strand that forms the other half. The ladder has a little twist, which gives it the iconic double helix structure. (See Figure 1.)

An organism's instruction manual is known as its genome. Genomes vary in size and do not necessarily correlate with the size, or perceived complexity, of the organism. For example, the smallest known genome for a free-living organism belongs to the bacterium *Carsonella ruddii* and contains about 160,000 DNA base pairs. By contrast, one species of amoeba (*Amoeba dubia*) has some 670 billion base pairs, making it more than 100 times larger than our own genome, which is made up of ~3,200,000,000 base pairs. Organisms also vary in the number of copies of the genome that their cells carry: for example, male bees have only one copy whereas strawberries have eight. We humans have two copies.

Our cells therefore have a remarkable amount of DNA within them. The Wellcome Trust, which has funded the majority of the work on the link between surnames and genetics, provides a useful set of facts to put the size of the human genome in context: <http://genome.wellcome.ac.uk/doc_WTD020745.html>. For example, if all the base pairs in the human genome were spread out one millimetre apart, they would extend for 3,000 kilometres (or 1,864 miles), which is about the distance from the west coast of Ireland to the east coast of Canada or nearly the diameter of the moon.

The vast majority of our DNA is located in the nucleus, a special rounded structure within the cell, and for this reason it is known as nuclear DNA. Every cell nucleus in the body contains two copies of the genome and the same DNA is found in nearly every cell; the exceptions are red blood cells, sperm, and eggs. Mature red blood cells are thought to eject their nucleus in order to enable them to carry more oxygen in our blood, so they do not contain DNA, while eggs and sperm each contain just half the usual DNA; when they unite at fertilization the newly fertilized egg has two copies, ready for development to commence.

If we were to zoom in to look at the nucleus of a somatic cell (the word comes from the Greek *soma* meaning 'body') we would see that our DNA is tightly packaged into bundles known as chromosomes. We humans have 46 chromosomes arranged into 23 pairs. One half of each pair (representing one copy of the genome) is inherited from our mother and the other half (the second copy of the genome) from our father. The pairs are numbered according to size, with the largest pair of chromosomes known, perhaps not surprisingly, as Chromosomes 1 (each of which is 247 million base pairs long). The next largest pair is known as Chromosomes 2, and so on down to Chromosomes 22 (each of which is about 50 million base pairs long). These

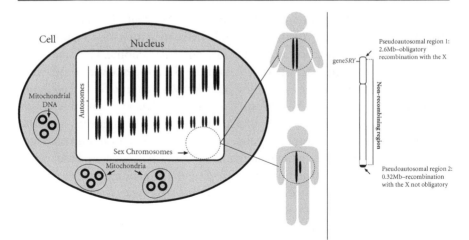

FIGURE 2 **Chromosomes**. We humans have 23 pairs of chromosomes. We inherit one half of each pair from our mother and the other half from our father. Chromosome pairs numbered 1 to 22 are known as our autosomes. Chromosome pair number 23 is known as our sex chromosomes. While men and women share the 22 pairs of autosomes in common, we differ in our sex chromosomes with women carrying two copies of the X chromosome. Men too carry an X chromosome but also carry a small chromosome known as the Y chromosome.

Note that both men and women also have mitochondrial DNA, contained within organelles in our cells known as mitochondria. To the right is an ideogram of the Y chromosome with its sex-determining gene *SRY*.

22 pairs of chromosomes are the same for men and women and are known as autosomes. (See Figure 2.)

The remaining pair of chromosomes, number 23, determines the sex of an individual. Unlike the other chromosomes, the sex chromosomes come in two types, known as X and Y. They differ from each other in size, with the X chromosome (155 million base pairs long) being similar in size to Chromosomes 7 and the much smaller Y chromosome being only about 60 million base pairs in length. However, clearly size does not matter, as the Y chromosome has an important job to do: it determines sex. Alongside one copy of each of the autosomes, a woman's eggs only ever contain an X chromosome. However, a man's sperm, with its one copy of each of the autosomes, comes in two different types: that containing X chromosomes and that containing Y chromosomes. It is the sex-chromosomal make-up of the single sperm that wins the race to fertilize the egg which determines the sex of the child. Even then, the default pathway of the foetus in the first few weeks following conception is to develop as a female. At around six weeks gestation something momentous happens: if the sex chromosome combination includes a Y chromosome, a gene thereon, known as *SRY* (for *sex-determining region Y*) turns on and triggers a train of events which causes the foetus to develop as a male. A foetus with the sex chromosome combination XX continues on its path to develop as a female. So, altogether, we have 24 types of chromosome, comprising 22 types of autosome, the X chromosome, and the Y chromosome. The Y chromosome is particularly unusual among them. We inherit our autosomes from both our parents, and the X chromosome can be inherited from either parent. But because the Y chromosome carries the gene for maleness, it has the unique property that it can only be inherited down the paternal line.

Inheriting DNA

For us to have offspring and for them to survive, grow, and go on to have children themselves, our instruction manual needs to be copied and passed down from generation to generation. Our DNA is able to direct its own replication and therefore pass on all the information it carries to any new cell. There are two different circumstances in which our DNA needs to make a copy of itself: first, when making new somatic cells (blood cells, skin cells, etc.), and second, when making gametes, which are either male sperm cells or female egg cells. For example, when a skin cell divides to make new ones, it passes on a full copy of all its genetic material to each new cell. This process is known as mitosis, and each new 'daughter cell' as it is called (regardless of the sex of the individual) is genetically identical to the original cell.

However, when our bodies make sperm or eggs (gametes), this time through a process known as meiosis, they need to halve the number of chromosomes in the resulting cells. If this did not occur, and all 23 pairs of chromosomes (two copies of the instruction manual) were passed down in each egg or sperm, then each embryo would have double the number of chromosomes of each of its parents, and with each generation the number of chromosomes would double again. Each person need have only two copies of the instruction manual in their cells and each parent therefore passes on just one of each pair of their chromosomes.

A process which is unique to meiosis, and which has tremendous ramifications for the parts of our DNA that we can use in genealogical studies, is that of recombination. This can be illustrated by a single pair of chromosomes, but the same process is true for all chromosome pairs except for the sex chromosomes (XY) in males. A pair of Chromosomes 1 (one of which came from the mother and the other from the father) line up next to one another and swap portions of their DNA. The outcome is that each Chromosome 1 is now a patchwork of the two that were inherited, with each 'new' Chromosome 1 having some parts from the mother and other parts from the father (see Plate 1). Following this process, one of each of the pair is randomly assigned to one sperm or egg cell. The sex chromosomes are different in that, in women, the X chromosomes are able to pair up and exchange information just as for the other chromosomes, but in men, only the tips of the X and Y chromosomes pair and exchange genetic information. The remainder of the Y chromosome is known to geneticists as the 'non-recombining region' (NRY).

Recombination increases genetic diversity and means that each child (save for monozygotic twins arising out of a single egg) receives its own unique blend of DNA from each parent. The vast majority (except for the non-recombining part of the Y chromosome) of the DNA that each of us has inherited is a mixture of the DNA of our parents, which is a mixture of their parents and so forth. Virtually all our DNA is a patchwork of that of our ancestors. However, we have also lost some of the genetic information of our ancestors: because we only receive one half of each chromosome pair from each parent, we have lost the information contained in the other half of each pair which we did not inherit. As we move back in time, the amount of DNA that we have inherited from each ancestor will not be equal because of the random way in which each chromosome is inherited. The Y chromosome is again unique in this respect. We know not only that each man can only have inherited his Y chromosome from his father, but that it has been passed down from his father virtually unchanged.

It is worth mentioning mitochondrial DNA (mtDNA) at this point. Mitochondria are small organelles found not inside the nucleus, but in the surrounding area inside a cell. Mitochondria contain their own DNA (mtDNA), which is a small circular piece of DNA, only 16,568 base pairs in length. Because we inherit our mitochondria through our mothers and mtDNA also escapes recombination, it is the maternal equivalent of the Y chromosome. It is passed down only through our maternal lineage and therefore not usually inherited with a surname, and so will not be discussed further in this book.

Mutation

Each pair of chromosomes (save the X and the Y) are almost identical. The differences that exist occur because mutations arise during the copying process which takes place when sperm and egg are being created. During this process, all the chromosomes in the progenitor cell are copied. To make a copy of the human genome is like asking someone to make a copy of a three billion-letter text. And because there are two copies of the genome in each cell, this would have to be copied twice. With all the care in the world, the small mistakes which are bound to be made from time to time provide the differences in our DNA. After copying, one of each chromosome, with any mistakes, is passed down into each sperm or egg cell. These differences are known as DNA polymorphisms, from two Greek words meaning 'many forms'. It is these polymorphisms which make each of us unique. They affect the DNA sequence, including the specific forms of the genes that we carry. Without polymorphism, we would all be the same and life would be very boring indeed.

Genes

Although genes will not be discussed in detail in this book, it is worth pointing out at this stage what a gene is and what it does. Rather like the way that letters of the alphabet, written in a certain order, create words and sentences, it is the particular order of the four bases which makes up the instructions in the manual in the form of genes. Genes are specific sections of our DNA, each of which acts as an instruction to make a specific protein. The proteins themselves are made up of twenty different amino acids, which are assembled in various combinations. The order of bases tells the cell which amino acids to use, and in which order to assemble them, so as to make a particular protein. By this means, our genes determine what proteins are made in our cells. This is crucial because proteins are involved in every process that occurs in a cell. They make up the very structure of our bodies, such as our bones, skin, and eyes; they also act as enzymes to allow chemical reactions to take place; they can be hormones which act as chemical signals for other cells; and they can act as receptors that allow us to taste and smell. And that's just for a start. Without them, we would not exist.

A gene can come in different forms, known as alleles of the same gene, with each allele coding for a slightly different protein. Because each cell has two copies of the instruction manual, everybody carries two copies of each gene (except on the X or Y in males). Two identical copies can produce a different effect from two different copies. Simply inherited traits, such as ABO blood types or dimples in cheeks, come from a combination of alleles in just one gene, while other traits, such as hair colour, are determined by multiple genes working in concert. Other differences, such as height, are determined by a combination of many genes and the environment. Two technical terms that are worth remembering are genotype, for the particular allele combination carried at one gene or many, and phenotype, for the observable effects of genes, such as eye and hair colours.

Surprisingly, only around 2 per cent of our DNA is made up of genes. The remaining 98 per cent acquired the term 'junk DNA', as for a long time it was thought that it did not actually have a function, but now this term is thought to be inaccurate as a portion of this non-coding DNA is known to have a regulatory role which affects the genes. The parts of our DNA that we are interested in for the vast majority of genetic studies of events in the past are the parts which do not code for anything. Clearly the fidelity of the DNA sequence for genes is important: the wrong code can result in the wrong protein being made or a protein not being made at all. This can have varying effects: the fertilized egg may not develop at all, a foetus may not survive to term, a child may be born but not grow up to reproduce. Very deleterious genes are 'selected' against, so they are not passed on to the next generation. In this way, a functional genetic sequence is conserved: variation is not able to arise willy-nilly. But as geneticists want to be able to tell people apart using DNA, they welcome variation. For this reason, they tend to look at the neutral parts of our DNA that can accumulate mutations quite happily, in the non-coding regions, providing us with the genetic variation to tell individuals' DNA apart.

The Y chromosome

It should now be obvious that there is a piece of DNA, the Y chromosome, which has a number of unique features that make it a useful tool, not only for genealogists to complement traditional research but for scientists wishing to study human history. First of all, the Y chromosome has on it the gene which determines maleness and therefore can be inherited only down the male line. Secondly, because in men the sex chromosomes are comprised of an X and a Y, recombination takes place only at the tips of the chromosomes, and the Y chromosome does not undergo the reshuffling of information that the rest of our chromosomes do every time sperm and eggs are made.

The Y chromosome becomes the star of our show because, unlike the rest of the genome, it has the capacity to enter into a partnership which makes it useful for family historians. Because a surname, like the Y chromosome, is inherited from father to son these two pieces of information should travel hand in hand down through the generations. Where a surname acts as a cultural marker of common ancestry, the Y chromosome should act as a biological marker. Just as a father passes on his surname to all his children, so he passes on his Y chromosome type to all his male children. It follows that all men descended from this father should bear both his surname and his Y chromosome type and, theoretically, this should remain the case regardless of the number of generations and the 'width' of the genealogy. Professor Sir Alec

Jeffreys, renowned for having invented DNA fingerprinting, shares a surname with (and according to a long-running family story can trace being related to) Judge Jeffreys. Also known by his sobriquets the Bloody Judge or the Hanging Judge, Judge Jeffreys is best remembered for the ruthless sentences he handed down when he presided over the trials of those involved in the Duke of Monmouth's challenge to the throne of James II in 1685. Sir Alec, on the other hand, is much liked: while he might be known to be firm but fair, there any resemblances between him and the Judge seem to stop. In the absence of a genealogy which connects these two men, the only way to test the family story is to use genetics: if the surname inheritance is faithfully mirrored by the Y chromosome's inheritance, then Alec and the known descendants of Judge Jeffreys, all sharing the same Y chromosome type, should essentially form a very large family tree. We will return to Alec's story later in the next chapter.

Let's look at the Y chromosome in more detail. It is made up of approximately 60 million base pairs and is thought to contain between fifty and a hundred genes, including the *SRY* gene. It can be divided into two regions: the tips where exchange of genetic information takes place during male meiosis with the formation of sperm; and the rest of the Y chromosome, some 57 million base pairs in length, where recombination does not occur, which is known as the non-recombining region of the Y (or NRY for short). Because the vast majority of the Y chromosome escapes recombination it is passed down from father to son virtually unchanged. The changes that do occur are the gradual accumulation of mutations. A modern man's Y chromosome contains within it a record of the mutational events that have occurred along his male lineages through time. These mutations generate the differences between Y chromosomes seen among men today, and the locations where these mutations have taken place are known as DNA markers. With new sequencing technologies, new markers are being found all the time. Geneticists look at the alleles that each man carries at a number of these markers in order to distinguish between Y chromosome types. However, because a man has just one copy of the Y chromosome and therefore just one allele for each marker, and no recombination takes place, all the markers are inherited together in one job lot as a single unit on a single chromosome. This job lot of linked markers is known as a haplotype.

The two main types of markers that are used to distinguish between Y chromosomes – binary markers and short tandem repeats (STRs, also known as microsatellites) – can be likened to the hands of a clock. The binary markers act as the hour hand, changing slowly, while the STRs act as the minute hand, changing more rapidly. Binary markers can take the form of insertions and deletions of DNA but single nucleotide polymorphisms (SNPs – pronounced snips) are the most common form of binary marker, with several hundred to choose from on the Y chromosome. A SNP is a difference

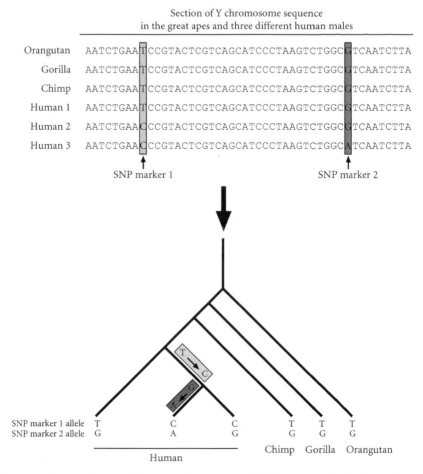

FIGURE 3 **Binary Markers.** Binary markers are so called because an individual will carry either of two forms. These different forms are known as alleles. The most common type of binary marker are single nucleotide polymorphisms (SNPs). Here there are two possible alleles at a single nucleotide position, and this location therefore becomes a marker we can use to distinguish between individuals. For example, at the position highlighed in light grey, the two possible alleles are a T or a C at this particular marker. At a second marker, highlighted in darker grey, the two possible alleles are G or A.

The mutations which produce these markers are very rare and this allows us to build an evolutionary tree of the Y chromosome types.

in the nucleotide (base) that we find at a particular location. In Figure 3, if we compare two men at the same SNP marker, one might have a C-allele and the other might have a T-allele.

Many binary markers can be considered to represent unique events in human evolution, due to their extremely low mutation rates: there is around a one in 100 million chance of any one base changing to another base as the Y chromosome is passed down from father to son.

Low mutation rates enable us to use these markers to generate a unique evolutionary tree of Y chromosome types, showing how all the Y chromosomes in the world today are related to one another. By comparing the human sequence at binary markers with the same sequence in the great apes, our closest non-human relatives, we are able to determine what the ancestral state for a marker must be. This in turn allows us to root the tree and determine the single Y-chromosomal ancestor of all men alive today: it is this position on the tree that has earned him the moniker of Y-chromosomal Adam and we can date him to have lived in Africa some 60,000–100,000 years ago. Binary markers, which tend to go by such non-intuitive names as P25 and M170, therefore determine the branches of the evolutionary tree and, ultimately, the branch tips of this tree, each of which represents a different type of Y chromosome known as a haplogroup. Each major branch (clade) of the tree is known by a letter and all the haplogroups are identified by using an alphanumeric string (literally a set of alternating letters and numbers) which defines where it is in the tree. Although recurrent mutations at Y-chromosomal SNPs are known, they are very rare and do not cause practical problems. Because many SNPs are typed in combination, this usually resolves any ambiguity as to where the Y chromosome type can be placed on the tree.

Binary markers therefore allow us to place men into these broad groups, haplogroups, based on the fact that they all share the same combination of alleles at a set of markers. Because these mutations arise infrequently, millions of men can share the same combination of alleles. For example, about 54 per cent of men in the UK and some 110 million men worldwide have the same combination of alleles which places them in haplogroup R1b1b2 (a rather unwieldy label!). The marker which defines this haplogroup is known as M269 and is thought to have originated in the Near East some 8,000 years ago around the start of the Neolithic era, and to have been brought to the British Isles by Neolithic farmers as they spread throughout Europe. These men can be typed by using more binary markers, so that the haplogroup can be subdivided into smaller and smaller haplogroups. Conversely, a new SNP allele can be found in just a few individuals or even in one man. As more and more markers are found, we are able to subdivide men into ever more discriminating haplogroups. The geographical specificity of haplogroups and their usefulness in the study of surnames will be discussed in a later chapter.

The very low mutation rates of binary markers imply that men who share an allele have a common descent. Conversely, males who differ at one of these places cannot share common ancestry within the last few thousand or even tens of thousands of years, let alone within the time of surname establishment. The tree presented in Figure 4, at the time of writing, is the latest scientifically-published version, but this tree will evolve as more markers are discovered.

As binary markers place men into broad groups, containing, at times, many millions of individuals, Y chromosomes are differentiated at a finer level by using short tandem repeats (STRs), which are often likened to being a stutter in the DNA sequence at a particular location (see Figure 5). STRs consist of units ranging from two to five base pairs in length, repeated in tandem, typically from ten to thirty times. Differences in the number of repeats found between men at the same marker are thought to be generated by mutations which resulted in the deletion or addition of a repeat unit. Each STR marker has its own specific mutation rate but not all of the different mutation rates are known accurately. An accepted average mutation rate for Y-STR markers does exist: it is calculated to be a one in 500 (0.2%) chance of a mutation occuring at a Y-STR marker as the Y chromosome is passed down from father to son. Because STR markers have much higher mutation rates, they can have many more alleles than a binary marker: they are said to be multi-allelic and are therefore more likely to differ between individuals. Indeed, it was when Alec Jeffreys noticed the variation at markers very similar to these (known as minisatellites, which have longer repeat units) that he had the 'eureka' moment which led him to develop the technique of DNA fingerprinting at the University of Leicester. We can use many of these rapidly mutating markers to give a much more specific, even unique (if enough markers are used), Y chromosome type, known generally as a haplotype. Because the Y chromosome is inherited down the paternal line, it follows that male-line relatives from the same family will have identical, or near identical (if a mutation has occurred), Y chromosome haplotypes. In general, the more distantly related two men are, the more differences we expect to see at these markers.

As the Y chromosome is inherited as one long piece of DNA, a new mutation at a binary marker (which will define a haplogroup) will arise on a Y chromosome which had its own Y-STR haplotype. The man with this new binary marker will now it pass and its associated Y-STR haplotype on to all

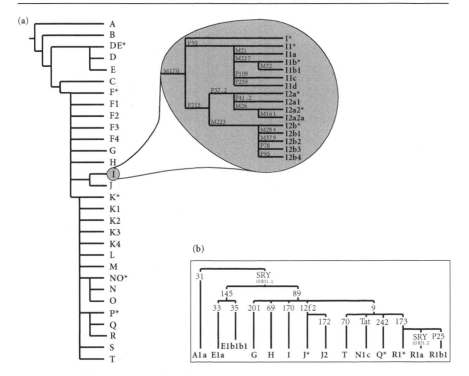

FIGURE 4 Evolutionary tree of Y chromosome types

(a) It is possible to use binary markers to construct an evolutionary tree of the Y chromosome types of all men alive today. Letters are used to name the main branches of the tree and these branches are further subdivided using additional markers. An alphanumeric string is used to name each branch- tip: these are broad groups known as haplogroups. Thus it is possible to type of the Y chromosome of any man and place his Y chromosome type in the tree according to the alleles that he carries at a number of these markers.

(b) Usually, due to economic constraints, Y chromosomes are not typed down to a specific branch-tip but to a particular branch such as I. Y chromosomes are then further subdivided using Y-STR markers. These are the markers typed in the 40 surnames part of the study.

his sons. Over succeeding generations, mutations will gradually occur at the Y-STR markers such that some of his descendants will still carry his original Y-STR haplotype, whereas others will have slight differences (see Figure 6). It follows that all men who belong to a particular haplogroup will carry Y-STR haplotypes that are variants of the haplotype of the founder of the haplogroup. The older a haplogroup is, the more variation will be found in

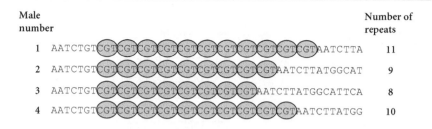

Male number		Number of repeats
1	AATCTGT CGT CGT CGT CGT CGT CGT CGT CGT CGT CGT CGT AATCTTA	11
2	AATCTGT CGT CGT CGT CGT CGT CGT CGT CGT CGT AATCTTATGGCAT	9
3	AATCTGT CGT CGT CGT CGT CGT CGT CGT CGT AATCTTATGGCATTCA	8
4	AATCTGT CGT CGT CGT CGT CGT CGT CGT CGT CGT AATCTTATGG	10

FIGURE 5 **Y-STRs.** Y-STRs (also known as microsatellites) are often likened to a stutter in the DNA code. A short DNA sequence is found repeated many times and the number of repeats at a particular marker can vary greatly. These types of markers are rapidly mutating: during the DNA copying process a mistake is made and a repeat (or even two repeats - though this is rarer) is added or deleted. By using a number of these markers in combination, it is possible to differentiate between Y chromosome types on a much finer scale. They are recorded using the marker name and number of repeats, e.g. DYS390 = 26.

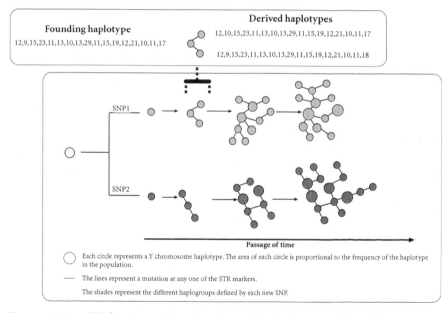

FIGURE 6 **How STR haplotype diversity arises within haplogroups.** Two SNP mutations occur on an ancestral chromosome resulting in two chromosomes, in two different haplogroups, with no diversity at linked STR markers. As time passess mutations occur at the STR markers, creating new haplotypes, and diversity within the haplogroup increases.

the Y-STR haplotypes and the more likely it is that men's Y chromosome types will differ from one another: they have simply had more time to accrue mutation. Conversely, the younger a haplogroup is, the more likely it is that men will share the same Y-STR haplotype, for there has not been enough time for mutations to accrue and for them to differentiate from one another. Each haplogroup therefore has its own characteristic set of Y-STR haplotypes and the more closely related two haplogroups are, the more likely it is that they will share some Y-STR haplotypes.

To study the link between surname and Y chromosome haplotype, the two different types of marker, binary and Y-STR, are used in combination (see Figure 7). Among men sharing the same surname, we are seeking groups of them with Y chromosome types that are the same or similar enough to mean that they could share a common ancestor within the time of surname establishment.

Combined haplotypes

Individual	Haplogroup	Y-STR haplotype	Mutational step differences
1	R1b1	12,16,10,10,12,14,12,18,23,9,15,11,12,15,13,10,17	
2	R1b1	12,16,10,10,12,14,12,18,23,9,15,11,12,16,13,10,17	1 step from individual 1
3	R1b1	12,17,10,10,12,14,12,18,23,9,15,11,12,15,14,10,17	2 steps from individual 1 2 steps from individual 2
4	R1b1	14,16,10,10,13,14,12,18,23,9,16,11,12,15,14,10,17	5 steps from individual 1&2 4 steps from individual 3
5	I	11,15,10,11,12,14,12,19,23,9,15,10,12,15,13,11,17	
6	E1b1b1	11,15,10,10,11,14,12,18,22,9,15,11,12,14,13,10,17	⎫
7	E1b1b1	11,15,10,10,11,14,12,18,22,9,15,11,12,14,13,10,17	⎬ Identical haplotypes
8	E1b1b1	11,15,10,10,11,14,12,18,22,9,15,11,12,14,13,10,17	⎭

FIGURE 7 **Combined haplotypes.** Y chromosomes are typed using both binary and STR markers. For surname studies, haplotypes are compared to look for individuals whose Y chromosomes are identical or near identical and therefore indicate possible common ancestry within the time of surname establishment. Men who differ at a binary marker and therefore fall into different haplogroups cannot share a common ancestor within this time period. Among men who fall within the same haplogroup, an assessment of the number and nature of the differences among their Y-STR haplotypes must be made to determine whether they could share a common ancestor through their surname.

Lab procedures

So, how do we go about typing Y chromosomes (or indeed looking in detail at any sequence of DNA) in the lab? In the first instance, labs and most commercial companies use cheek swabs or saliva samples to collect DNA. Rubbing the brush or swab on the inside of the cheek, or spitting into a collection tube, will collect cells, known as buccal cells, which contain sufficient DNA for analysis. Once the sample arrives in the post, it undergoes a number of steps to extract the DNA. While the exact method may differ from lab to lab, the central process remains the same. Because the DNA lies within the nucleus of the cell, the first task is to break open the cell and nuclear membranes to release the DNA. This is done by using a solution with a detergent, similar to the detergent used in shampoo and washing liquid, which breaks down the cell and nuclear membranes. An enzyme is used to break down proteins in the cell. These steps release all the cell contents, including DNA and protein, into the solution in one gloopy mess. Adding salt to the solution will cause proteins and carbohydrates to clump together and precipitate out of the solution while the DNA will remain dissolved. Spinning the solution at high speed in a centrifuge causes all the unwanted material to collect at the bottom of the tube while the DNA remains in solution. This solution is then transferred to another tube, where alcohol is added causing the DNA to come out of solution. On spinning the tube again, the DNA settles as a small pellet to the bottom of the tube so the liquid can be removed. The DNA can then be re-dissolved in water and kept in the freezer for later use. A newer, automated method of DNA extraction breaks up the cells and passes the whole lot through a sort of silica gel matrix in a tube, but loses some of the magic of the earlier method: it can be a wonderful experience to add alcohol to the solution and, hey presto!, see a whitish, stringy substance appearing in the tube - millions and millions of strands of a person's DNA.

The next step is to determine which alleles the donor carries at particular markers. Because cells contain over six billion base pairs, however, and the markers we are interested in can be in the case of a SNP marker a difference at a single base, or in the case of Y-STRs differences in the number of repeats in a stretch of only a few hundred base pairs or less, geneticists need a way of focusing on the particular sequences of interest. This is done by using a technique known as PCR (Polymerase Chain Reaction) (see Figure 8), which allows the production of many millions of copies of a particular section of DNA.

Three main components are required for the process of 'amplifying' the region of interest. First, the PCR technique makes use of a naturally occurring enzyme known as polymerase, which catalyzes the formation (or repair) of DNA and which can withstand the high temperatures which the PCR reaction

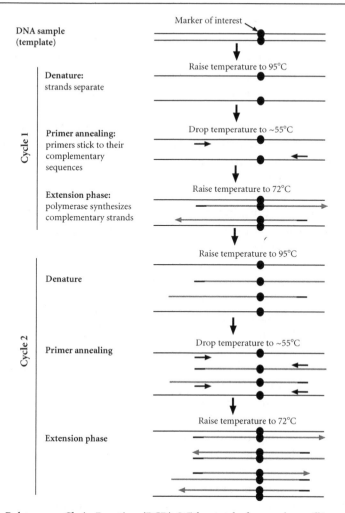

DNA sample (template)

Marker of interest

Denature: strands separate

Raise temperature to 95°C

Cycle 1

Primer annealing: primers stick to their complementary sequences

Drop temperature to ~55°C

Extension phase: polymerase synthesizes complementary strands

Raise temperature to 72°C

Raise temperature to 95°C

Denature

Cycle 2

Primer annealing

Drop temperature to ~55°C

Extension phase

Raise temperature to 72°C

FIGURE 8 **Polymerase Chain Reaction** (PCR). With a total of ~30 cycles, millions of copies of the template are generated

requires. Then short sequences of DNA, known as primers and just twenty or so base pairs in length, are generated to act as a short complementary strand to a specific sequence either side of the marker of interest. The primers are designed so that a copied DNA section incorporates the marker we wish to examine. Finally, the donor's DNA is added to the mix. As outlined above, human DNA is like a ladder (or zip) and, if heated, the two strands of DNA will separate: a process that is known as 'denaturing' the DNA. If the temperature is dropped, the strands of DNA will find their complementary strands again and stick (in technical jargon 'anneal') to one another. However, during PCR, the short DNA primers will anneal to their complementary strands close to the marker we are interested in. In the final step, known as the extension phase, the temperature is raised slightly. The DNA polymerase then starts at each primer and synthesizes a new complementary DNA strand, thus making a copy of the region of interest, using the genomic DNA as a template. This cycle of denaturing, annealing and extension is carried out a number of times and, after the first cycle, both the genomic DNA and the newly generated copies (amplicons) of the marker region act as templates for further copies to be made. The process is exponential with the number of copies doubling each time. In the space of a couple of hours, many millions of copies of our region of interest are generated, thus making it far easier to analyse the marker we wish to examine. It is possible to look at more than one marker at a time, in reactions known as multiplexes. In practice, the numbers of markers typed in one reaction are typically around eight to ten for binary markers and around twenty for Y-STR markers. New technologies, however, are beginning to increase these numbers dramatically (see Chapter 9).

Once the DNA is amplified, a way of visualizing which allele is present at each marker is needed. This can be done by using an ABI Genetic Analyser (or ABI as it is known) which allows two parameters to be adjusted to allow accurate identification of the particular allele that a person has at a particular marker. The ABI first draws up the PCR products' amplicons through a substance which acts to separate them by size. Different colours have been introduced by tagging one of each pair of STR marker primers with a fluorescent dye during the PCR step. The amplicons then pass, in size order, in front of a laser that emits light, which in turn causes each dye to fluoresce. Both the colour emitted and the size of the fragment are then recorded by the ABI and can be turned (using further software) into an image known as an electropherogram or trace (see Plate 2). The software that is used can even be primed to output the number of repeats at each STR marker, though the researcher needs to check each allele call manually for any anomalies. SNPs can be analyzed using a wide variety of methods with modern techniques that also use fluorescent dye technology to detect the different alleles.

The link between surnames and genetics

The idea that a link between a surname and genetics exists is not a new one. In 1875 George Darwin, the son of Charles Darwin, examined the frequency of marriages between people with the same surname to estimate the frequency of inbreeding. In societies which have patrilineal surnames, the Y chromosome and surname are usually inherited together and therefore one might expect a direct link to exist between the two; that is, a patrilineal surname would be expected to correlate with a type of Y chromosome. Indeed, the idea of surnames being compared to a genetic marker was first put forward in the 1930s.

The first evidence that this link between a Y-chromosomal lineage and a surname could be made in practice came to light in 1972 following the cytogenetic study (that is, looking at the structure of chromosomes, usually down a microscope) of a French-Canadian family with a pedigree extending back ten generations. During the analysis of a member of this pedigree for an unrelated cause, Dr Paul Genest, a pathologist working at McGill University in Montreal, discovered a male individual who had a type of Y chromosome known as a 'satellited' Y chromosome (or Yqs), that is one where a detached part of another chromosome has become attached (translocated) to the end of the Y chromosome. Such translocations do not appear to have any harmful effect and can be detected simply by looking at the chromosomes down a microscope. A further fifty men sharing the same surname (given only as 'R') were contacted from among the staff and students at the university, and testing identified seventeen of them who shared a Yqs that was assumed to be identical by descent with the original example. Genealogical research showed that all of these men were descended from Antoine R., a French barrel-maker ('tonnellier') who had emigrated to Canada in 1665, the trans-location having arisen prior to his arrival some 300 years previously. Further research found another French-Canadian family with a different surname but carrying an apparently identical Yqs. This new family was eventually con-nected to the 'R' family through a non-paternity event which must have occurred around 1830.

In the following decades it became possible to examine differences between Y chromosomes at the DNA level. With the advent of the PCR method in 1985 and the subsequent discovery of polymorphic DNA markers on the Y chromosome over the following years, geneticists had a set of techniques and markers with which to tell Y chromosomes apart in much finer detail. Finally, in 1997, Professor Mark Jobling and others published a paper which included a small paragraph suggesting that, given the potential link between surname and Y chromosome type and the emergence of these new techniques, it might be possible to use a Y chromosome haplotype to predict a surname, though it was thought that the link might be so weak as to be uninformative.

What followed was a set of small but intriguing studies which showed that a link may indeed exist. Evidence that this link between a Y-chromosomal lineage and specific putative descendants living today could be made using polymorphic molecular markers was shown in a study of the Jewish Cohanim priesthood. In biblical tradition, all Cohanim are patrilinearly descended from Aaron, the brother of Moses, reputed to have lived about 3,000 years ago. If this were true, and if there had been no subsequent non-paternity, they would be expected to share a Y chromosome haplotype - so 306 Jewish males (Cohanim, Levite, and Israelite) from Israel, Canada, and the United Kingdom were recruited and their Y chromosomes were typed using six Y-STRs and six binary markers. Though not all of the Cohanim males shared surnames, many were called Cohen or they had related names such as Kahn and Kane. As might be expected, a common modal haplotype (the most frequently occurring haplotype in the set) was found in the Cohanim. The frequency of this haplotype and haplotypes that differed from the common haplotype by one repeat unit at any of the STR markers was over 60 per cent, compared to below 15 per cent in control groups. Hence, this study showed that Y-chromosomal analysis could be used to demonstrate patrilineal descent within a group.

The Jefferson study

A very convincing link between surname and Y chromosome was shown in a study of a single famous surname, Jefferson, borne by the third president of the United States, which revealed that males sharing the Jefferson surname shared a Y chromosome. It also showed that a time delay of several generations did not preclude the possibility of paternity testing.

Following the death of his wife, Martha Wayles Skelton, Thomas Jefferson is said to have had a long-standing relationship with his slave, Sally Hemings, Martha's half-sister following her father's liaison with one of his own slaves. An excellent and detailed exploration of the history, rumours, and the evidence supporting the theory that Thomas Jefferson had fathered children by his slave Sally Hemings can be found in Annette Gordon-Reed's fascinating book *Thomas Jefferson and Sally Hemings: An American Controversy* (1997); meanwhile a retired American pathologist, Eugene Foster, had become interested in the idea that the mystery might be solved by typing the Y chromosomes of the surviving male line descendants of Sally's male children and comparing them with the Y chromosomes of the Jefferson family. Dr Foster interviewed and collected blood samples from individuals from four relevant lineages. The first of these lineages was that of Thomas Woodson, whose surname was derived from his later owner. Thomas was the first child born to

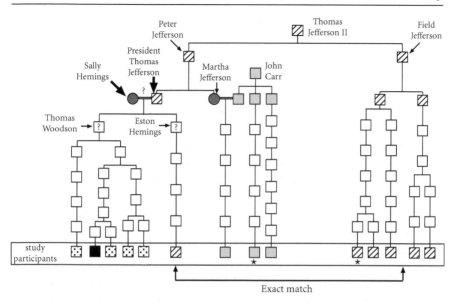

FIGURE 9 **The Jefferson study.** The family trees of the participants. The Y chromosome type of the descendant of Eston Hemings exactly matched that of the family of President Thomas Jefferson. The slight mutations within each family are represented by a star below the square representing the family member. The black square represents the haplotype which contains too many mutations to be closely related. In each case it is not possible, without further testing, to determine where the mutation or non-paternity took place within the family tree.

Sally Hemings and was said to have been fathered by Thomas Jefferson when he and Sally were in France together while he served as minister. The present-day members of Thomas Woodson's family believed the family story that Thomas Jefferson fathered their ancestor. Five male-line descendants of Thomas Woodson agreed to take part in the test.

Sally Hemings had several more children, again thought to be by Thomas Jefferson, Her last son, Eston (born 1802), who was said to have borne a striking resemblance to Thomas, eventually entered white society as Eston Hemings Jefferson. It was suggested by others, however, that this resemblance was due to the fact that he had been fathered by one of the nephews of Thomas Jefferson: Samuel or Peter Carr, the sons of Thomas's sister. To explore this claim, the male-line descendants of two further lineages were tested: the Y chromosome of one of Eston Hemings Jefferson's male-line descendants, and three male-line descendants of the Carr lineage through John Carr, grandfather to Samuel and Peter Carr. Finally, male-line representatives of Thomas Jefferson's lineage were required to provide a 'Jefferson Y chromosome type' against which the others could be compared. While Thomas Jefferson had six children with his wife, including a son, all his children, save his eldest daughter, died in childhood, leaving the modern-day DNA detectives with no direct male-line descendant to provide a Y chromosome to type. However, because the Y chromosome is passed down patrilinearly, Dr Foster turned to other male-line relatives of Thomas Jefferson. Five male-line descendants of Field Jefferson, Thomas Jefferson's paternal uncle, agreed to take part in the study.

Following extensive testing of the Y chromosome types of all of the study participants, some of which was carried out in Mark Jobling's lab at the University of Leicester, it was discovered that the Y chromosomes of four of the descendants of Thomas Woodson shared a haplotype (with one carrying a mutation) which was European in origin but, crucially, did not match any of the other three lineages. The fifth Woodson descendant had a very different Y chromosome type (most often seen in Africa) indicating a break in the surname/Y chromosome link along that lineage, the origin of which was unknown.

The Y chromosome types proved the close relationship between the individuals in the Carr lineage. As the Carr Y chromosome type differed markedly from those of any of the other lineages, the Carr brothers were ruled out as potential fathers of either Thomas Woodson or Eston Hemings Jefferson. The Y chromosomes carried by the five patrilineal descendants of Field Jefferson were all very closely related and, crucially, the core Jefferson haplotype was identical to that carried by a patrilineal descendant of Eston Hemings Jefferson, Sally Hemings' youngest son. The Jefferson/Hemings, Carr, and Woodson lineages all carried Y chromosomes that were very different from one another. To cap it off, the Jeffersons and the Hemings-Jefferson lineages shared a Y chromosome type which is very rare in the general population: at the time of the study it had never been seen outside the Jefferson family when compared with known Y haplotypes. Even now, with ever-increasing Y haplotype databases and published results, it remains a very rare haplotype. This rarity made it extremely unlikely that anyone other than a Jefferson could have fathered Eston Hemings Jefferson. The genetic evidence is compatible with Thomas Jefferson being Eston's father, but it cannot exclude other contemporary patrilineal relatives of Thomas, such as his brother, Randolph, from being the father. However, combined with the historical evidence, it supports the theory that Thomas was the father of at least one of Sally's children.

Surnames as a means to subdivide a population

An examination of Y-chromosomal haplogroup diversity in Ireland (Hill et al., 2000) used surnames as a way to define the samples in the set geographically. The Y chromosomes of a general sample of Irishmen were subdivided by surname into seven groups based on the known historic and prehistoric (Gaelic) origin of these names. Four of these groups were Gaelic in origin and corresponded to the four ancient provinces of Ireland (Ulster, Munster, Leinster, and Connaught). The remaining three were thought to be diagnostic of incursions from outside: Scottish, Norman/Norse, and English. When the Gaelic-surnamed men were separated from the overall set, it was found that they had a higher frequency of 'haplogroup 1' (now known as P*[xR1a]) than when the set was considered as a whole. When the Gaelic surnames were further subdivided according to the four regions of Ireland in which they originated about 1,000 years ago, a further pattern emerged. The four groups were significantly different, and a gradient within the Irish samples was revealed with the westernmost group (Connaught) showing near fixation (98.5 per cent) of these P*(xR1a) chromosomes.

The Sykes surname study

The results of the first true single-surname study were published in the same year. This examined the diversity of haplotypes defined by four Y-STRs in 48 men bearing the surname Sykes and 160 control non-Sykes men. Because the Sykes men in the study all lived within three neighbouring counties, the possibility arose that they could all share the same or a similar Y chromosome type because it was a type that happened to be common in the region. This could result from unknown historical circumstances and is referred to as geographical structuring: that is, particular types of Y chromosome being found in a region due to past events. The control for this non-Sykes group included 21 different-surnamed men who were neighbours of the Sykes men. Twenty-one (43.8 per cent) of the Sykes Y chromosomes belonged to a single haplotype and this haplotype was not found in any of the control group. A number of different haplotypes were found in the remaining Sykes chromosomes; two of these haplotypes (carried by four individuals in total) were one mutational step away from the 'core' Sykes haplotype. The authors of the paper interpreted their results as showing a single origin for the name Sykes approximately 700 years ago. Any Sykes chromosomes which did not belong to the core haplotype were considered to be due to non-paternity events (estimated at 1.3 per cent per generation), rather than to multiple founders for the surname, or to Y-STR mutations. The study had low haplotype resolution and highlighted some of the difficulties in interpreting the patterns of Y chromosome types seen within a surname but, nevertheless, it was ground-breaking and the findings were intriguing.

The results from the scattered studies regarding the connection between surname and Y chromosome were encouraging: it appeared that some link did exist. But the questions remained. What is the nature of the link between a surname and a Y chromosome type? We know that there are a number of confounding factors that can affect it, or even break it (see Plate 3). Where the link is weak or absent, is this because of the multiple independent founders for many names, mutation on the Y chromosome, or the non-patrilineal transmission of a surname through adoption, illegitimacy, maternal surname inheritance, or name-changes? If the link exists, is it the same for all surnames? What do we see if we look at a number of surnames in depth? And are there any general conclusions that can be drawn?

It was also apparent that genetic testing had to be informed by historical research into the origins and spread of surnames. In 2001 George Redmonds presented a BBC Radio 4 series, *Surnames, Genes, and Genealogy*, which started with the Sykes study, and drew upon the expertise of historians and geneticists alike to look at surnames from different parts of the country. The present book is a development from this early initiative.

8

The Link between Surname and Y Chromosome Type

Modern advances in genetics have made it possible to carry out surname studies at a much higher resolution. In recent years, a large in-depth study of British surnames has been made by Turi King in the lab of Professor Mark Jobling at the University of Leicester and a similar one of Irish surnames has been undertaken by Brian McEvoy in Professor Dan Bradley's lab at Trinity College Dublin. Both these studies sought to examine, in detail, the Y chromosome types that are associated with a number of surnames by collecting large numbers of samples. Fortunately, as both studies used the same set of Y-STRs and typed a set of binary markers, the results can be compared. The British study had another component which was simple in its aim: to assess the general link between surname and Y chromosome type.

So, how to test this general link? With a perfect correlation between surname and a type of Y chromosome, two same-surnamed men taken at random from anywhere in Britain, who did not already know themselves to be related, should have identical or (if mutation had occurred) nearly identical Y chromosome types. Given the factors that can break the link between surname and Y chromosome, a perfect connection was not expected: but does that link exist at all, or has it been weakened or even obliterated over the centuries since surnames became established because of high instances of non-patrilineal transmission events such as non-paternity, adoption or maternal transmission of surname? What factors need to be considered when deciding the strength of this link? The researchers really had no idea what they would find.

The sampling of pairs of same-surnamed men at random from around the country was done in two stages. First, 150 men with different surnames that covered the frequency spectrum of the most common 40,000 names in Britain were chosen: from Smith (over 560,000 carriers) down to Rivis (50 carriers). The lower limit avoided the increased risk of accidentally sampling men who were closely related when others were recruited to form a pair for each surname. Second, each of the 150 men was paired with another man who had the same surname. To avoid bias, both members of a surname pair were sampled geographically randomly and a questionnaire asked all the men to list their known male-line relatives so as to avoid pairs who already knew themselves to be related.

The next step was to type the Y chromosomes with eleven binary markers in order to place them into the broad haplogroups. Binary markers mutate very slowly, so the mutations which have occurred to produce them are ancient and predate the time that surnames were formed, sometimes by many thousands of years. It follows that if two men's Y chromosome types are not in the same haplogroup, they cannot share a common ancestor through their surname. The binary markers immediately ruled out close relationships between some of the surname pairs, but 85 of the 150 pairs did share the same haplogroup, and so were potentially showing a sign of sharing a Y chromosome type because of their shared surname.

The next task was to examine the 17 Y-STR haplotypes, which differentiate Y chromosomes at a much finer level. Only 16 of the 150 pairs had identical Y-STR haplotypes within the same haplogroups. Some of these haplogroups are common in Britain, so was this sharing just due to chance? How often did men in the set who did not have the same surname share a Y chromosome type? To answer these questions, all of the Y chromosomes from the first 150 men were compared with one another. No matches were found, so it was clear that any matches that might be discovered within same-surnamed pairs would be significant. Given what is known about surname history, it is likely that the rarer names had fewer founders, perhaps just a single one, and therefore a stronger link between the surname and the Y chromosome type should exist. Perhaps not surprisingly, 15 of the 16 pairs carrying identical haplotypes carried surnames that fell into the lower half of the frequency spectrum (the rarer 75 names) in the national population, that is with 5,600 carriers or below.

Men can share a common ancestor through their surname but may not share an identical Y chromosome type if a mutation has occurred on either of their lineages in the time since they shared that ancestor. The likelihood of finding that a mutation had occurred between two lineages depends on the number and properties of the Y-STRs that are analysed, and the number of generations between the individuals tested. So what about those pairs of men who shared an identical surname but who did not share an identical Y chromosome type? First, it was necessary to make an estimate, based on the genetic data, of the time to the most recent common ancestor (TMRCA) of the two men, to see whether this fitted within the time since surnames became established.

Calculating TMRCA

All men share a common paternal ancestor: the ancestry of every man alive on the planet today can be traced back to a male in Africa some 60–100,000 years ago who is known as Y-chromosomal Adam. Since that time, Y chromosomes have diversified considerably. All men are patrilinearly related, but at varying time depths. Men who share both a surname and a Y chromosome type could have a common ancestor within the last few hundred years, whereas men with the same surname but very different Y chromosome types had a common ancestor who lived long before the time of surname formation.

As a general rule, the more similar two Y-STR haplotypes are, the more recent their common ancestry (see Fig. 7 in the previous chapter). It should thus be possible to convert the number of differences that exist between the haplotypes (the mutational distance) of the two men in the same-haplogroup pair into the time of their most recent common ancestor (TMRCA), and then to ask if this estimate is younger than the time since the surname was established. This would allow an estimate of the proportion of same-surnamed individuals who share similar Y-STR haplotypes through surname-related co-ancestry.

The adoption of hereditary surnames was not a uniform process: many surnames became hereditary earlier than others and surnames in general have various time depths in different parts of Britain. To allow for analysis however, it is necessary to define an average age of establishment to provide a cut-off date against which to compare the TMRCA dates. An average date of 1300 AD, at a mid-point between 1066, when surnames were first introduced into England, and 1500, the point by which most surnames had become established, was chosen. Two other parameters were needed: mutation rate and generation time. The average Y-STR mutation rate was taken to be the commonly accepted 0.2 % per locus per generation. Next, the length of a generation had to be determined.

In human population genetics, 20 and 25 years are often used as the average generation time over the span of human evolution, but it is difficult to determine generation length in the era in which surnames were formed in Britain, as we have no documentary sources that provide direct demographic information. It becomes easier after 1558, when parish registers began, and we are on much firmer ground after 1837, when the civil registration of births, marriages, and deaths was introduced by the state. Two books from the Cambridge Group for the Study of Population and Social Structure (CAMPOP) – Wrigley and Schofield (1981) and Wrigley *et al.* (1997): see Bibliography – provide a synthesis of this information, based on a variety of techniques that were used to establish demographic rates and processes. The authors suggest that the mean age at maternity was about 33 years in the period 1550–1725 and 31.3 years for the period 1775–1850. No corresponding value is available for mean age at paternity, but it is possible to estimate this by taking into consideration the calculated mean age gap between marriage partners, giving a mean age at paternity of approximately 39 years and 36 years in these two periods. This would put average generational span (the difference between mean ages at paternity and maternity) at about 35 years.

For the period before 1558, the evidence is very patchy and we are faced with the additional problem of the plagues of the fourteenth century, which devastated the national population. There is much debate about the timing of marriage during this period, but the general belief is that the mean age was in a person's early to mid-twenties. However, due to the plagues, which were endemic, mortality rates were higher than for the post-1558 period and they may have shortened the natural period of reproduction. Thus, the fertility phase in this period was probably more concentrated in a person's twenties and early thirties than it was from the Elizabethan period onwards. As populations were more vulnerable to higher mortality, shorter fertility durations resulted in unstable time differences between generations. The mean generation time since surname adoption was lower than that of the post-1558 period, but it is difficult to determine by what amount. For this reason, a conservative approach was taken for the study and the generational age fixed at 35 years across the entire period. Given the 700-year time depth of surnames that was adopted, the maximum number of generations to a same-surname co-ancestor is therefore twenty.

Estimating TMRCA for a pair of Y-STR haplotypes

The method that was used to estimate the TMRCA of two haplotypes was that proposed by Bruce Walsh in 2001. This takes into account the number of Y-STRs tested and some knowledge of the mutation rate of Y-STRs, and it makes an assumption about the process by which mutations arise. The version implemented here assumed that when a Y-STR mutates it has an equal chance of gaining or losing one repeat unit. This method provides a distribution and median value of all the possible dates of the TMRCA for two haplotypes, but it is not possible to determine the exact date as the mutation rate itself is simply an estimate, based on what has been observed in previous studies. As some Y-STRs mutate more rapidly than others, and the mutation rates for many of the markers are not known, it was estimated that the chance of a mutation at a particular locus was 0.2 % with each generation. To put it another way, during 500 generations it is expected that a Y-STR will have gained or have lost a repeat unit. It is usually impossible to say precisely when a mutation occurred in a single person's lineage. Indeed, the only way it can be done is in conjunction with a large genealogy. If other male members of an extended family are tested and, for example, only the original man in the sample and his close relatives carry the mutation it might be possible to pin it down to a particular father-to-son transmission. Without this, we simply cannot tell; the mutation could have occurred 500 generations ago or in the sperm that produced the individual whose Y chromosome is being examined, or anywhere between these two extremes.

This TMRCA method works best when many markers are used and the number of differences between individuals is small. In practice, however, difference between the earliest and most recent possible times to the most recent common ancestor tends to be very large. For example, for a pair of haplotypes identical for the 17 Y-STR markers used in this analysis, the possible number of generations between them ranges from 0.4 to 60 with a median of 11 generations. The method is far from perfect, but at present it is the only one available that deals with pairs of haplotypes; and it does at least give some indication of TMRCA.

The TMRCA was estimated for the 85 same-surname pairs who fell into the same haplogroup. For the 16 surname pairs that had identical haplotypes, the median value for TMRCA (11 generations) lies well within the time of surname establishment. For an additional 20 surname pairs, the median lies outside this time, but as the lower bound of the TMRCA is less than 20 generations, up to 24 % of the sample of surname pairs plausibly share co-ancestry through both their Y chromosomes and their surnames. So what can be said about these 36 pairs? Only five of them are amongst the 75 most frequent surnames; the remaining majority have only 4,500 bearers or fewer. The rarer the name, the more likely it is that its bearers will share a common ancestor. If a surname is of a frequency below 5,000 bearers, the probability of two same-surnamed men sharing a common ancestor through that surname is nearly 50 %. This was a relief! It meant that the link between surname and Y chromosome existed and appeared strong among rarer names.

Surnames in depth

The second part of the Leicester study analysed 54 British surnames in more detail. These names were chosen to give a range of types and frequencies. Men bearing the name, or a recognized spelling variant, were recruited randomly from around the country in large numbers. The questions asked were: What were the patterns of Y chromosomes associated with surnames? How diverse were the Y chromosomes associated with any one name? Were there any conclusions that could be made generally about the link between surname and Y chromosome type? Could any conclusion be drawn about the number of founders for a surname based on the Y chromosome data?

The intensive sampling for each surname increased the chances of close relatives being included, which could amount to paternity testing! So, various measures were taken to exclude relatives closer than second cousin, such as sampling geographically randomly, and asking participants to fill in a questionnaire about their known male-line relatives. A problem that soon became apparent was that varying frequencies of names meant that it was impossible to get even representation. For example, DNA testing of 5 % of men carrying the surname Hey required just over 90 samples, whereas testing the same proportion of Smiths would have needed over 23,000. Clearly, this was not feasible and adjustments were made during the analysis to compensate for these differences. Over 2,500 men took part in the study, which was eventually reduced to 40 surnames, where the sample sizes for each were large enough to make a reasonable analysis.

Some of the questions that were asked were the same as those that were posed in the first part of the study. But new problems arose with the interpretation of the results. How can groups of men who share a common ancestor through their surname be defined? Can the genetic data provide any information about the number of founders for the surname? Can any surnames be said to have a single origin with all male bearers being related to one another and descending from one man? What cannot be achieved through DNA analysis?

The sample of 40 surnames

In the more detailed study of 40 British surnames, the Y chromosomes were typed to a higher resolution with up to 20 binary markers and with the same 17 Y-STRs. A control group, considered to represent the general population, was also assembled consisting of 110 men all with different surnames. Once the haplotypes had been identified for each surname and for the control group, the patterns in the same-surname groups were explored in more detail in order to draw some general conclusions.

A variety of methods can be used to get a picture of the strength of the link between a surname and a Y chromosome type. If all the haplotypes associated with each surname are taken and each surname's set is compared against all others, and against the control group's, significant differences among them emerge. The haplotype sets of the majority of the surnames were significantly different from those of the controls (though those for Smith, King, Stead, Feakins, Tiffany, and Chubb were not) and, significantly, the surname sets also differed from each other. What this tells us is that each surname (save for more common ones) tends to have its own characteristic, non-random set of Y chromosome types associated with it.

Another method is to explore the probability that two randomly sampled men sharing a surname have a matching haplotype. While this is similar to the pairs study, it differs in that it asks how likely it is, if each man is taken in turn, that he would share an identical Y chromosome type with someone else within the same surname set. It might be expected that if a surname had a single or limited number of founders it would contain higher frequencies of a small number of specific haplotypes linked to that surname. Multiple-founder surnames would be expected to show the opposite: low frequencies of many different haplotypes. For example, in a very simplified scenario, if the surname had a single origin and just one Y chromosome type, then the chances of one man matching another with the same surname in the set is 100 %. The closer the value is to 100 % the more the surname is dominated by a single Y chromosome type. This condenses into one simple value the effect of the number of different haplotypes and how grouped they are. The average probability of a man sharing an identical Y chromosome haplotype within a surname set across all the 40 surnames studied was 12.8 %, compared to only 0.1 % in the control group. This means that the chance of sharing a Y chromosome type amongst people with the same surname is 100 times greater than within the population as a whole. Large differences exist between different surnames: the range extends from 0.1 % within Smith to 53 % within Herrick. The rarer the surname, the more likely that two men taken at random with the same name will also share a Y chromosome type. These probabilities were based on perfect matches, but men can be related through their surname yet not share a perfect match. The approach in this study was a conservative one that did not allow for mutations since the period of surname formation. If we were to allow for a mutational difference of two STR steps, the values would rise to 4 % for Smith, and up to 79 % for Herrick. Again, the correlation between surname and Y chromosome is shown to be strong.

The next step in the study was to look for patterns among the Y chromosome types that were associated with each surname. This was done by using Network, a computer program which provides graphic displays of the relationships between haplotypes and which analyses the diversity of the Y chromosome types seen within a surname. Network takes all the haplotypes together and reconstructs the shortest and least complex links between them (see Plate 4).

Some Y-STR loci have higher mutation rates than others and so are prone to recurrent mutation which can produce reticulations (where the lines interlace and resemble a net) and thus cause confusion. We therefore need a way of weighting the Y-STRs to reflect the fact that some mutate more frequently than others: a mutation at a marker that rarely mutates is more significant than a mutation at another which mutates more frequently. As not all the individual mutation rates for each of the Y-STR loci were known, the number of alleles at a particular locus had to be used as a proxy for the rate of mutation: the more alleles seen, the higher the mutation rate. Other sophisticated techniques are also used to enhance the accuracy of the network.

Given the perfect scenario of a single surname ancestor and all the bearers of the surname today carrying his Y chromosome type, it might be expected that a network would consist of a single haplotype borne by every man who was sampled. In practice, mutation will act to diversify some Y chromosome types during the time that men have shared a common surname ancestor, so we might expect to find 'descent clusters' within surnames. These clusters consist of groups of men whose ancestors originally shared a common haplotype, perhaps that of an original founder of the name, but some of whom now bear closely related Y chromosomes, having undergone some diversification through mutation.

Perhaps the most difficult part of carrying out an analysis of surname groups is determining precisely what constitutes a descent cluster. What criteria should be used to define a core haplotype within the name? Which haplotypes are related to the core haplotype because the individuals share a common ancestor through their surname? Which of the haplotypes around the core are considered to have too many mutational steps difference and therefore cannot share a common ancestor within the time of surname history? If a large group of men share a similar Y chromosome haplotype, then the problem is to determine where the edge of the descent cluster lies. The issue of whether a true core exists arises when just two individuals share a haplotype which is not connected to a larger core. Can a group consisting of two individuals be considered as a 'core' haplotype within a surname? Do these two individuals share a haplotype by descent or simply by chance?

Haplotype sharing by chance

In this study, the researchers were interested in defining groups of men who share a common ancestor through their surname. However, within haplogroup groups which are very frequent in Britain, such as the 50–60 % of indigenous British men who fall into haplogroup R1b1, the possibility of two men sharing a Y chromosome type by chance, and not through their surname, is increased. A situation could have arisen whereby two men who happened to have the same (or a very closely related) Y chromosome type happened to take on the same common surname. Or a non-paternity event could have brought in a Y chromosome type which is very similar to that already carried by bearers of a particular surname. It is therefore necessary to examine the frequency with which men can share a haplotype within a haplogroup by chance and then to make adjustments to the criterion that are used to define a core haplotype.

The control set of 110 men with different surnames allows us to estimate the amount of haplotype sharing that occurs in the general population, and it provides a network against which to compare the patterns that are seen in the same-surname groups (see Plate 5). The control group was overwhelmingly made up of singletons: 102 haplotypes were unique and only four pairs shared a haplotype, each of which were within the most common haplogroups, R1b1 and I, to which 50–60 % and 30 % of indigenous British men belong, respectively. This finding suggests that within these very common haplogroups we should sometimes expect to find identical or closely related haplotypes within surname groups purely by chance rather than as a true signal of surname-related descent. However, because sample sizes are usually smaller within surname groups than within the control group, the significance of any haplotype sharing within the set will be increased. Within rarer haplogroups it follows that Y haplotype sharing purely by chance is rare and therefore a core could consist of just two individuals. However, because haplogroups R1b1 and I are the two most common haplogroups in Britain, a conservative approach, which may miss some true cores, is to disregard clusters that contain only two individuals as a core haplotype within these haplogroups only, and to increase the number that constitutes a core to three.

The next step is to determine where to expect the edges of a descent cluster to lie. The aim is to include closely related haplotypes which have arisen through mutations that have occurred since the sharing of a common surname-ancestor, but to exclude those Y chromosomes which have too many differences to indicate a common ancestor within the time-depth of surname development. In determining who should be considered to be part of the descent cluster and who should not, the argument is in danger of becoming circular. We need to include individuals with Y chromosomes that may be slightly different from the core but whose mutations could have occurred within the time since surnames were established, but ultimately we want to be able to calculate the time to the most recent common ancestor for all the men in the cluster which itself should fall within the time since surname establishment.

So how do we know when a cluster is a true cluster? How many mutational step differences do we allow from the core while remaining confident that the cluster contains true descendants from the founding haplotype? At what point are we beginning to include individuals in the cluster who happen to have the same surname but have Y chromosomes that are similar by chance, rather than because they share a common ancestor through their surname? Determining where the edge of a cluster lies is extremely difficult within the most common haplogroups, as a core haplotype may sit within a sea of similar Y chromosome types purely because they are all of a type which is common in Britain.

A way of determining what a true descent-cluster might look like is to look within surname groups for closely related Y chromosome types belonging to haplogroups that are rare in the UK. This greatly reduces the possibility of someone being included in the cluster who is not descended from the same-surname founder. If, for example, more than one person took on the surname, or there was a non-paternity event which brought in a new Y chromosome type, the chances of it belonging to the same rare haplogroup is small. If any of these events were to bring in a new Y chromosome type, good money could be put on the second surname founder or non-paternity event bringing in a Y chromosome that belongs to haplogroup R1b1 or I rather than one belonging to the same rare haplogroup as the first.

A good example of this sort of surname is Ketley (and spelling variant, Kettley), which has a cluster dominated by twenty individuals with the same haplotype and a further seven individuals having Y chromosome types that were very closely related to the core group (see Plate 6). This can be interpreted as a group of men who all descend from a common ancestor through their surname. The fact that this cluster is made up of individuals whose Y chromosomes fall into haplogroup J2, which is rare in the general population (only 1 %), makes the chance of a non-paternity event bringing in another J2 type 1 %. All members of this cluster probably descend from a common ancestor through their surname. Repeating this process for other surnames with clusters within rare haplogroups produced a set of ad hoc rules as to the definition of a true descent cluster, which was then applied to all the surnames studied.

The control group provided a set of chromosomes against which the diversity of Y chromosomes found within a surname group can be compared. Perhaps the most interesting surname to compare with the controls is Smith, the most common name in Britain, and one that is so frequent that it must have had many 'founders'. So, do we see any structure in the network groups of men who share Y chromosome haplotypes? A random sample of 58 men from around the country produced a network of Smiths that is remarkably similar to that encountered in control men all having different surnames. A statistical test showed that the set of haplotypes associated with the Smiths was not significantly different from that associated with the controls. The same is true for some other common surnames that were examined, such as King and Bray. What these tests tell us is that so many people have taken on the very common names that there is little structure to see; no obvious patterns of Y chromosomes, randomly-scattered haplotypes within the haplogroups, and haplotypes are not grouped together into clear descent clusters within the names.

Tests on most of the other surnames show that one or more haplotypes were shared by several men. Moving down the frequency spectrum from the most common names to those whose bearers number under 10,000, the patterns begin to change. We see clear groups of men whose Y chromosomes constitute descent clusters. If we take, for example, the surname Jefferson, a patronymic which might be expected to have more than one founder, we find clear descent clusters of men who must share a common ancestor. The signal of surname co-ancestry crosses surname types. It can be found, for example, in diminutives such as Jobling, nicknames such as Chubb, or occupational names such as Sacker.

The Wadsworth surname provides a further element which speaks of a strong, clear signal of co-ancestry. It is one of those names that are dominated by a cluster of men whose Y chromosomes belong to a haplogroup which is generally very rare in Britain. It is also an example of a surname which answered the general question of whether or not accepted spelling variants of a surname were derived from a common ancestor, or whether each new variant reflected a new founder. In the majority of cases, spelling variants were found within the descent clusters of the main version of the name. One haplotype was shared among some Wadsworths and some Wordsworths, while another was shared among some Grewcocks, Grocotts, and Groococks. Accepted spellings for surnames were fixed only in recent times, long after spelling variants had become surnames in their own right.

For surnames with just a few thousand carriers the amount of sharing can be even more striking (see Plate 7). Hey is dominated by three large clusters and Ravenscroft has just two. By contrast, although Jeffreys has few carriers, the degree of haplotype sharing is not as great as that found within surnames of a similar frequency. Clearly other factors are at play. Jeffreys is a patronymic, derived from the Norman personal name Jeffrey, so given its age and its popularity as a first name a number of founders might be expected. Then it has a strong Welsh focus, and since Welsh surnames are largely derived from personal names many people will have taken on this name. Most surnames, except the very common ones, show some descent clusters. The rarer the name, the more likely it will be dominated by a single cluster. Although the rarity of a surname does not guarantee it to be of single-family origin, the surnames that are dominated by a single cluster occur among those with fewer than a thousand bearers.

Are there any general correlations that can be drawn between the frequency of a surname and the patterns that we find? One way to discern a trend is to look at a surname and ask how many of the haplotypes within it belong to a descent cluster, regardless of the number of clusters. The average proportion of men with Y chromosomes belonging to any cluster within a surname across the set was 62 %, with values ranging from zero for the surname Bray to over 90 % for the surname Herrick. This trend was strongly correlated to the frequency of the surname; in other words, the rarer the name the more likely men are to belong to a descent cluster. On turning to how many individuals belonged to the largest descent cluster for each name, the correlation with frequency was even stronger, with an average of 41 %. This suggests that most surnames have more than one descent cluster associated with them but that the rarer the name, the more likely it is to be dominated by a single large descent cluster. Bray and Herrick again had the lowest and highest values respectively.

This gives a general indication of the patterns of diversity within surnames, and in most cases it shows the complexity of the link between the name and Y chromosome types. For example, a surname might have many clusters, with none of them dominant. Some surnames, such as Butterfield and Ravenscroft, have two large but distinct clusters. In five other cases, where the surname was rare, more than 70 % of men with the surname belonged to one cluster, which was also the largest cluster. So what do these summary statistics mean? Can descent clusters be equated with founders? Could these findings indicate that rarer names had single founders?

Part of the answer to these questions comes from estimating the ages of the descent clusters, this time by using the program Network, which is able to do this calculation for large numbers of haplotypes. 62% of the TMRCAs of the 74 clusters in all the surnames were found to be within the time of surname establishment; if those within the lower bounds of the dates are included, the proportion increases to 95 %. Tellingly, the three instances where even the lower limits of the dates predated the time of surname establishment all occurred in clusters belonging to the most common haplogroup, R1b1; this suggests that some of the haplotypes within the cluster were not related to the core through a shared common ancestor by surname, but were included in the cluster simply because of their chance similarity.

Some TMRCAs for the descent clusters turned out to be surprisingly recent. In the case of the Ravenscrofts it was only 190 years, though the name is known to be much older. What these very young dates for descent clusters tell us is that some lineages have expanded relatively recently and that genetic drift – the stochastic differences in the number of male offspring each man has, and consequently the number of times his surname and Y chromosome are passed on to the next generation – greatly affects the frequency of Y chromosome types that we find associated with any one surname today.

Six case studies

The idea that a very large number of English surnames may have had single-family origins was contentious when it was first advanced by George Redmonds in *Yorkshire, West Riding* (1973), volume I of the *English Surname Series*. This was not what the dictionaries of surnames had told us. The conclusion was based on intensive genealogical research, distribution maps of surnames at various points of time, and a detailed knowledge of the history of the local communities in which the names were formed and flourished. In many cases, however, the patchy survival of medieval records meant that definite proof was lacking: the earliest links in the chain could not be demonstrated beyond all doubt. With the publication of the Sykes and Irven article 'Surnames and the Y Chromosome' in 2000, however, the exciting possibility arose that genetics might solve this problem (see Plate 8).

The reality is that non-paternity events and drift have often so clouded the picture that the results of DNA analysis can offer only general support for the supposition that a name has just one founder. With rare names, the genetic evidence can be unequivocal, but in such cases the historical evidence often already seemed firm. One of the clearest examples is Attenborough, a surname that was derived from a south Nottinghamshire village that was only a small settlement in the Middle Ages. At the time of the 1881 national census the 621 Attenboroughs and the 192 people bearing twenty variant spellings of the name lived mostly in the Trent Valley, in the neighbouring counties of Nottinghamshire, Derbyshire, and Leicestershire, not far from their ancestral home. The name was particularly concentrated in the adjacent registration districts of Nottingham (147) and Basford (90). Only the 42 people who lived in London, or their ancestors, had moved far. Two centuries earlier, all the eight householders who were recorded in the Nottinghamshire hearth tax returns lived within three miles of the village of Attenborough; at that time, none had moved over the border into Derbyshire. The genetic evidence endorses the view that the Attenboroughs share a common ancestor. Furthermore, it hints that the surname could indeed have had a single founder who belonged to a haplogroup that is very rare in Britain.

DNA results can sometimes confirm that just one founder was responsible for a name that now has many different spellings. In 1881 the surname Haythornthwaite was borne by 259 people and by 53 others with nine different spellings that were very close to the original. They were mostly recorded in adjoining registration districts in north Lancashire: Burnley (47), Lunesdale (30), Preston (28), Blackburn (27), Clitheroe (22), Fylde (20), and Lancaster (15). There can be no doubt that the surname was derived from a small place of that name in the parish of Lancaster. But what about the 74 Hawthornthwaites and the 15 others with four variant spellings who were also recorded in 1881? They too lived mainly in north Lancashire. The genetic evidence resolved the matter by proving that they shared a common ancestor with the Haythornthwaites. Further tests are needed to see whether names such as Haythorne and Hawthorne are shortened versions.

Genetics has also confirmed that the surnames Swindlehurst and Swinglehurst have a common origin from a tiny place called Swinglehurst ('the wood on the hill used for feeding swine') on the edge of the Forest of Bowland. Adam de Swynleyhurst was recorded there in the late twelfth century. The names became interchangeable when they spread across the Yorkshire border into Lancashire, but Swindlehurst was already the preferred spelling by the fifteenth century. The 1881 census listed 605 Swindlehursts, mostly in Lancashire (455) and neighbouring parts of Westmorland (50) and the West Riding (47), with the highest numbers in Preston (117) and Blackburn (96). All the 62 Swinglehursts also lived in the northern half of England, with 32 in Lancashire. DNA tests show that most men with either spelling of the name are related and belong to a haplogroup that is rare in Britain.

Sometimes, the genetic evidence points to a single-family origin for a surname when the historical evidence is not clear-cut. A good example is provided by Herrick, a surname that was derived from a Viking personal name. A notorious bearer of this personal name was Eric Bloodaxe, the tenth-century warrior, but the surname was not formed until a few generations after his time; the personal name must have remained in use long after the Norman Conquest. It is no surprise to find it used as a surname in the thirteenth century in Leicestershire, an area of intense Danish settlement, when Henry Eyrig or Eyrek witnessed charters in Wigston Magna. The Herricks remained in Wigston until the twentieth century. Other members of the family were recorded nearby, at Great Stretton in the thirteenth century, and at Houghton-on-the-Hill 200 years later. Thomas Herrick, son of Robert Herrick of Houghton, moved into Leicester, where he was borough chamberlain in 1511. His sons, Nicholas and John, both became mayors of Leicester, while William, the youngest of his five sons, became a goldsmith in London and such a prominent figure in the capital city that he was knighted in 1605. William's cousin, Robert Herrick, was the well-known poet.

The Leicestershire origins of at least one family named Herrick are certain. Eighty-one of the 435 Herricks who were recorded in the national census of 1881 lived in the county, and 47 of these were resident in the borough. However, the census also recorded 115 Herricks in Lincolnshire (including 66 in the county town), another 55 in Nottinghamshire, and 78 in London. The Londoners can be accounted for as migrants, but at first sight it seems that Lincolnshire (another county with a strong Viking presence) was a second home of the name. The DNA analysis, however, pointed to a single-family origin. This finding prompted a more thorough search of the documentary evidence. First of all, the absence of any Herricks in the Nottinghamshire hearth tax returns of 1664–74 suggested that the surname was not established there until later. The Lincolnshire hearth tax returns are not yet in print, but an alternative source is provided by the protestation returns of 1642, which named thousands of men over the age of eighteen. No Herricks appear in the Lincolnshire lists. A search of the International Genealogical Index proved that in the sixteenth and seventeenth centuries the surname was overwhelmingly found in Leicestershire, with odd ones scattered far and wide. The earliest reference in Lincolnshire was to John Hericke, who in 1627 was baptized at Folkingham, ten miles south-east of Grantham and only twelve miles from the Leicestershire border. The strong presence of the name in Lincoln, about 34 miles further north, in the 1881 census must have arisen from later migration. The historical evidence in the case confirmed the genetics, rather than the other way round.

The results of the analysis of the Y chromosomes of men with the surname Butterfield also prompted a re-think of the historical evidence for the name. Butterfield has always been thought of as a Yorkshire Dales name that migrated into the West Riding textile towns. In 1881 about half of the 4,001 Butterfields lived in the West Riding, with a particularly strong presence in Bradford (623) and Keighley (421), but also with over 100 each in Dewsbury, Leeds, and Hunslet. The minor place-name which gave rise to the surname has not been identified, but it may have been situated just across the border in Lancashire, where a Simon de Butterfield was recorded in the mid-thirteenth century. By 1379 the family were well established in Bowland, with branches in Newton, Mitton, and Slaidburn, which suggests that they may have been there for some time. So, when the genetic evidence pointed to two concentrations of the surname, one in the West Riding in the R1b1 haplogroup and the other in and around London in the I haplogroup, the obvious solution was that the southern Butterfields were descended from an illegitimate line when a Yorkshire girl migrated to London. The capital city has always attracted young people and distribution maps of surnames are often skewed by this effect.

However, further historical enquiry, stimulated by the genetic findings, came up with an unexpected result. The southern Butterfields seem to have originated in Buckinghamshire. A militia return for the county in 1798 noted them in three parishes, and a hearth tax return for 1671 recorded them in four. Further back in time, a muster roll of 1522 listed them in seven places, with the highest concentration in Chalfont St Peter, and an earlier, but undated, charter of Missenden Abbey recorded the minor place-name of 'Buterfeld in Chalfhunte', which is possibly the present Butterfield in Wooburn Green, five miles west of Chalfont St Peter. There seems little doubt that the two hap-logroups represent two separate origins for the surname in different parts of the country.

In cases such as these, DNA analysis has clearly become an important new tool for the study of surnames. But in many other instances it has failed to provide definite evidence to prove or disprove whether a name has a single founder. The main reason for this disappointment seems to be that the issue is obscured by non-paternity events (mainly illegitimacy, but also adoption, or maternal transmission, or change, of name), which are not always discernible in the documentary record. If the genetic tests reveal two or three clusters for a name, there is no way of telling whether they signify separate founders or non-paternity events within just one family.

This problem is illustrated by the surname Hey. A hey was a medieval hedged enclosure taken in from the edge of a moor or a wood. The poll tax returns of 1379 name several people with this name, but some of these may have been simply by-names and others may have failed in the male line. The documentary evidence points to all the present bearers of the name sharing a common descent from the tenants of a farm, now known as Hey Lathe, in the moorland township of Scammonden to the west of Huddersfield. The boundary of this eighteen-acre smallholding is drawn on an estate map of 1607 and is perfectly preserved in the landscape by a dyke, a continuous wall, and a prominent bank thrown up from a well-defined ditch. Alan del Heye and Thomas, his son, paid an entry fine for this property in 1333. All the farms in Scammonden were created piecemeal by taking in new land in the years leading up to the Black Death, which brought a sudden end to this period of expansion. Perhaps Thomas was one of the victims of this plague, for on 18 May 1350 his younger brother, Richard, became the new tenant. Richard's descendants continued to live there until at least 1577, but junior branches moved elsewhere. Most of them stayed in the West Riding, no more than twenty miles or so from Scammonden, but others crossed the Pennines into east Lancashire. The problem that has not been solved by historical research is whether or not all the Heys who were recorded in Lancashire in late medieval and early modern times were descendants of the Scammonden family or whether any belonged to separate families who had taken their name from one, or perhaps more, of the heys that served as minor place-names in Lancashire.

DNA tests have not made us any the wiser. The sample revealed three distinct clusters, but we cannot tell whether they represent three separate origins or whether non-paternity events have taken place. Other names in the Leicester study produced similar results. We can conclude that names such as Hey had very few founders, but we cannot say with any certainty that they had only one. We are back to square one.

The general conclusion from the Leicester study is that if we take two men with the same surname from any part of the British Isles there is a one-in-four chance that they will be related to the extent that they had a common ancestor in the last few hundred years, and that if the most common surnames are removed the chance increases to 50 per cent. But in individual cases, the question of whether or not a name has a single-family origin cannot be answered definitively.

Genetic drift

Genetic drift can have some dramatic effects. We need look no further than Jane Austen's *Pride and Prejudice* to see one extreme case, albeit a fictional one. Mr and Mrs Bennett, so the story goes, continued to have children in the hopes of having a boy to whom they could leave their estate, but gave up after having five daughters, so in this one generation, Mr Bennett's surname and Y chromosome were not passed on; in genealogical circles his lineage is said to have 'daughtered out'. At the other end of the spectrum in recent times, a Lionel Felton from Birmingham and his wife continued to have children in the hopes of producing a girl, but gave up after having eleven sons. In this one generation, a surname and Y chromosome type have ramified; if the sons go on to have sons of their own, they will ramify even further. Such fluctuations in the number of male offspring, and therefore Y chromosome type, will ultimately affect the types of Y chromosome associated with a surname today.

Further evidence that drift is playing an important role in the history of a surname comes from comparing the results of the British study with that carried out in Ireland. Irish Y chromosomes, in general, show much lower diversity in terms of haplogroup; 90 per cent fall in haplogroup R1b1 and therefore it is predominantly the Y-STRs which act to differentiate Y chromosome types. As with the British, the Irish controls showed few shared haplotypes. The average proportion of haplotypes that fell into a descent cluster within surnames (61 per cent) is almost identical to the British study (62 per cent), but is different in that the proportion does not correlate with surname frequency. Even very common Irish surnames, such as Ryan and O'Sullivan, which are found at frequencies of 1 per cent of the Irish population, can be dominated by a single descent cluster: a phenomenon which was not seen among common surnames in Britain. One reason for this striking difference could be increased drift within the Irish population as a whole. In the first instance, Ireland is known to have had a system of medieval patrilineal dynasties, meaning that some men and their male offspring had greater reproductive success over long periods. Further factors that could result in increased drift in Ireland stem from events such as the potato famine and the impact of epidemic disease in different parts of the country.

To get a sense of the amount of drift, one of the authors of the British surnames study carried out simulations of surname and Y chromosome descent. Factors such as exponential population growth (and decline, where appropriate) within Britain from 1300 AD up to the present were built in. This allowed an estimation of growth rate and therefore an average number of male offspring per father per generation, around which the number of offspring could be chosen (male offspring ranging from 0 to 6) randomly during the simulation. Non-paternity events were also incorporated into the simulation, at a rate of 2 per cent per generation, to assess the impact on the types of haplotypes seen at the end.

The results of these simulations were revealing. It appears that drift has an extremely important role to play. Not only did some lineages ramify greatly, purely by chance, but around a third of lineages became extinct in each generation. The chance of a surname founder some twenty generations ago having offspring surviving today was only about 10 per cent. It was entirely possible for any genetic trace of an original founder to dwindle to extinction or near-extinction, only for the surname to be dominated by the result of a non-paternity event.

What the simulations show is that it is likely that not all the founders of a surname will have surviving offspring and that the number of descent clusters that we see today is probably a very poor reflection of the true number of founders. Drift is acting to blur, or possibly even overwrite, the original genetic picture of a surname's origins and, with it, a true indication of the number of founders that a surname had. Genetics can act only as a guide in this matter, and DNA analysis alone cannot determine the number of founders. The bottom line is that while general trends exist, each surname has its own complex history.

This brings us to the issue of what constitutes a founder. Given that genetic lineages can be extinguished, even though the surname survives, the term 'founder', as it stands, is wrong. From a genetical point of view, a non-paternity event, especially one that took place in the early history of a surname, may have produced a Y chromosome type which came to dominate a surname. The original founder's Y chromosome type may persist but cease to form the dominant haplotype seen within the surname today. Does the usurping haplotype become a 'founding' haplotype in it's own right? It seems more appropriate to widen the definition of 'founder'. The genetic evidence points not to a specific number of founders for surnames but to surviving lineages, encompassing 'founders' from varying times and becoming 'founders' through differing circumstances. It is here that we find a discrepancy between what genealogy might show – a single origin surname – and what the genetic patterns look like today. Genetics cannot provide all the answers – indeed, it can add more questions – and it is only through a combination of genetics, surname, and family history research that we can gain a clearer picture of the true history of a surname.

Finally, let us return to Sir Alec Jeffreys' family story. Alec, being at Leicester, and his invention of DNA fingerprinting allowing all such work as this to take place, was one of the first to volunteer for the surnames study and it was at this point that he was keen to know if he was related to the family of Judge Jeffreys. During the course of the study, a participant came forward with an extensive family tree tying him back to the judge's family. However, his Y chromosome type did not match that of Alec; they belonged to two different haplogroups, and therefore are not related through a shared surname-ancestor (see Figure 10). But the story does not end there. Once again, genetics cannot provide a definitive answer. A non-paternity event down either lineage may have broken the link: if the non-paternity was down through Alec's lineage then he cannot be related genetically. However, if

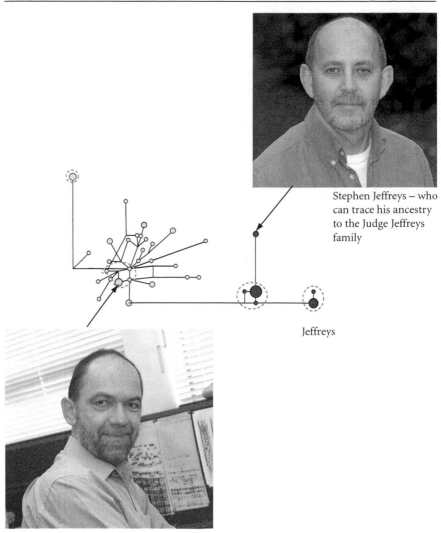

Stephen Jeffreys – who can trace his ancestry to the Judge Jeffreys family

Jeffreys

Alec Jeffreys

FIGURE 10 **The Alec Jeffreys story.** One Jeffreys participant could trace his ancestry back to Judge Jeffreys family. Unfortunately, his and Alec's Y chromosome type did not match. Here is an example of a case where genetics cannot provide the final answer to the question. It is possible that their Y chromosomes do not match because there has been an NPT event in either of their lineages. Only further Y chromosome testing of members of both their family trees and genealogical research could provide a conclusive answer.

the non-paternity was down the lineage of the other participant then the possibility of a genetic link remains. Typing of further individuals from the extended family trees of both individuals would tell us if either of these two men differed from their relatives and give us the consensus haplotype for both trees to compare. Once again, the genetic results have led to more questions than answers and further work involving both genetics and genealogy offers the only way forward.

9

The Wider Picture

While the study described in the previous chapter was not intended to be a genetic genealogy project, the surname/Y choromosome link has had its biggest and most enjoyable impact in the area of genetic genealogy. Y chromosome analysis can help to prove or disprove old family stories and to illuminate connections between individuals that were previously unknown. Where the paper trail has gone cold in joining two family trees, analysing the Y chromosomes of individuals from both trees can connect them or indicate that they are indeed separate genealogies.

The genetic research outlined in this book has taken place within a pure research laboratory, with all the constraints that that entails, but a number of companies have brought genealogical research into the realm of genetics by offering genetic genealogy testing. The comprehensive Cyndi's list http://www.cyndislist.com/dna.htm, one of the top genealogy websites, lists numerous services involving genetics and genealogy. What is readily apparent is that these tests can be expensive for the consumer, with an average price of around £150 per person and with varying degrees of resolution, but this is clearly not enough to deter enthusiasts. At present, Family Tree DNA, based in the USA and by far the largest genetic genealogy company, lists over 179,422 records in its database and 5,838 surname projects. The largest company in Britain, Oxford Ancestors, is headed by Bryan Sykes, author of the first single-surname study, and has about 40,000 records in its database.

The Sorenson Molecular Genealogy Foundation is a non-profit organization which takes the link between genetics and genealogy one step further. Since its inception in 1999, it has sought to connect both DNA and family trees by collecting the pedigrees of all testees. Its freely accessible database allows individuals to conduct a search by using either the genetic or genealogy strands and enables them to connect and build deeper and wider family trees all on one site. The genealogy websites <www.ancestry.co.uk> and <www.ancestry.com> now provide similar services. The combination of DNA analysis with standard genealogical research is becoming routine.

An exciting area of research that has been opened up is the possibility of finding distant branches and connecting family trees in far-flung parts of the world. Beyond Britain, genetic genealogy has been particularly popular in the USA, Canada, Australia, and New Zealand. It allows families whose heritage can be traced back to Britain to connect to older family branches and perhaps to locate the original home of their surname.

Distant cousins once lost can now be re-found through the power of DNA. Sometimes, this happens by chance. When men were recruited for a study of the surname Jefferson, two were found with an identical Y chromosome type to that of the third President of the USA, though neither of them knew themselves to be related to Thomas Jefferson; they traced their ancestry back to Yorkshire and the West Midlands, respectively. Thomas Jefferson's family tradition held that the family originated from Snowdon in Wales, but no evidence has yet come to light to support this claim; when some Welsh Jeffersons were tested no matching Y chromosomes were found. Thomas Jefferson, the great-grandfather of the President, is generally believed to have been the man recorded in Henrico County, Virginia in the 1670s, but further genetic and genealogical research is needed to pinpoint a common ancestor between the English Jeffersons and the family of Thomas Jefferson. Genetic testing companies, armed with the knowledge of the Presidential Jefferson's family haplotype now provide a service which enables anyone to compare their Y chromosome with that of the Jefferson family.

Distant relatives can also be found by design. News of typing the Herricks, a local Leicestershire name, as part of the surnames project, reached members of the Herrick Family Association (HFA) based in the USA who were keen to find connections to Herricks in Britain. The Herricks who form the HFA claim descent from Henerie Herrick, originally believed to be the fifth son of Sir William Herrick of Beaumanor Hall (Leicestershire). It was known that around 1629 this Henerie arrived in Salem, Massachusetts, where he married the daughter of a doctor and raised five sons and a daughter. However, another Henry Herrick was found to have emigrated to the USA in the early seventeenth century and to have settled in York, Virginia in 1641. In the following year this Henry was documented as having a wife, Ann, and further research placed *him* as being the fifth son of Sir William. While there is no evidence pertaining to whether he and Ann had any children, it led the descendants of Henerie from Salem on a quest to find his ancestral family and homeland. After extensive research by members of the HFA, it is now thought that the two Henrys share a common ancestor in Thomas Eyrick of Houghton on the Hill, Leicestershire, in the late fifteenth or early sixteenth century. Testing the Y chromosomes of descendants of Henry of Virginia and/or

English descendants of Sir William and comparing them with the descendants of Henry of Salem could solve the mystery as to whether the two Henrys were indeed related. To date, the genetic research carried out in Leicester has found identical links with a dozen individuals in England, most of whom can trace their ancestry to north Leicestershire and south Nottinghamshire, close to Beaumanor Hall, but the English families do not have genealogical information connecting them to either of these two Henrys. The Y chromosome certainly connects virtually all the participants and Henry of Salem, but the proof of the link to Henry of Virginia, and therefore Sir William Herrick, remains elusive. DNA analysis has the power to connect family trees and although it points to the neighbourhood of the home of the surname, it is only through a combination of good old-fashioned genealogical research and genetics that the problem can be solved.

The growth of interest in genetic genealogy has inspired a group of individuals outside the academic arena who are passionate about the subject and who have an impressive grasp of the research issues. Two focal points for this group are the International Society of Genetic Genealogy and the *Journal of Genetic Genealogy*. The ISOGG is a non-profit, non-commercial organization that provides resources and maintains one of the most up-to-date, if not completely academically verified, phylogenetic trees of Y chromosome haplogroups. The *Journal of Genetic Genealogy* is its online journal, and while it does not abide by the standard system of scientific peer-review, it has attracted contributions from academic geneticists and will no doubt go on to become an important forum through which academics and the public can interact.

The rise of the internet has greatly facilitated genetic genealogy studies. Datasets of Y chromosome and surname data are now freely available on a variety of websites. Large databases from the academically-led Y Chromosome Haplotype Reference Database <yhrd.org> to the numerous databases (some private and some public) associated with DNA testing companies now allow individuals to search for Y haplotype matches and/or look for potential genetic relatives at a speed which has revolutionized genealogical research. The informality of the web allows people to find and contact potential relatives more quickly and easily. Though there is probably a bias in who has been recruited to take part in many of the surname studies by including many people already known, or suspected, to be related, the fact that the data is online allows for collaboration again between academics and the public. For instance, a recent academic study that used online genetic genealogy databases uncovered fifteen new SNPs in haplogroup G.

An early example of the public's use of genetic genealogy concerns American genealogist Susan Meates, who has a surname that is very rare in the USA but which is found in Ireland, England, Wales, Australia, and New Zealand. She began with a genealogical study that traced her ancestry from Ireland via Canada to the USA. Five Irish families called Meates were unable to prove a connection or to trace their lines back beyond 1800, though they knew of a Meates who was recorded in 1708. The paper trail had come to an end, for the registers of the parishes where some of the families had lived had been burned in the Dublin fire of 1922. She also established that the most distant ancestor of one Meates line had lived in Worcestershire before moving to London, and that another Meates line resided in Wales. Further genealogical work proved that the New Zealand families share a common Irish ancestor and those in Australia have their origin in London.

Traditional genealogical methods had revealed much of interest but they could not answer the question: are all these Meates and others with similar-sounding names related? Susan Meates turned to the commercial company Family Tree DNA, which offered first of all a 25-marker test, then later the use of 37 markers. All five lines with Irish progenitors were shown to have a 37/37 match, with one mutation in family 5 and two mutations (suggesting a more distant common ancestor) in family 2. However, the Meates line from Worcestershire and London was not related to the Irish families.

The next step was to look at possible variant spellings of the surname, starting with Mates, a name that has multiple origins in different countries. All the Irish Meates were shown to be related to the Irish Mates, except for a line in County Kildare. The Meats, who were first recorded in Derbyshire, before spreading to Nottinghamshire, Herefordshire, and Gloucestershire also share a common ancestor with the Meates of Ireland, but neither the Meates of London nor the Meates of Wales showed this genetic connection. This, of course, leaves open the possibility of a genealogical connection obscured by a non-paternity event. Mate, Mates, Meates, Meats, and, less obviously, Myatt were also proved to be surviving variant spellings of the name. This one-name study is one of many that combines genealogy with DNA testing to show which families are related and which are not, and which surnames are spelling variants, including some that at first seemed unlikely.

The public's growing interest in genetics and the reduced costs of many technologies have led companies to offer more detailed analyses of people's genomes. Up to one million genome-wide SNPs can now be tested in one go and several hundred Y chromosome SNPs can be investigated to provide much more detailed information about Y chromosome lineages. There are problems in confirming the authenticity of some of these Y-SNPs and how they fit into the academically-accepted phylogenetic tree of Y chromosome types, but the sharing of data among genetic genealogists is going some way to addressing these issues and even confirming SNPs which might prove useful in population studies. For example, it was precisely this sort of work by genetic genealogists which identified a marker (S116) which has been demonstrated to be of use in subdividing haplogroup R1b1b2, the most common haplogroup in Western Europe. This marker is now used in academic labs that carry out population studies and by commercial companies that offer Y chromosome SNP typing for ancestry testing.

In the past few years a number of books and articles on the subject of conducting a single-surname genetic genealogy study have appeared, not all of which get the facts straight. Common mistakes include the assertion that the tests look at certain places in selected human genes (as opposed to the majority of markers falling outside genes); that geneticists like working with the Y chromosome because it has only two active genes on it and so is made up of mostly 'junk DNA' (which is incorrect, and where the actual gene numbers are irrelevant); or that just a small portion of the Y chromosome is passed down from father to son virtually unchanged (when it is the bulk of the Y chromosome which escapes recombination). Such statements contribute to public misinformation regarding the scientific background to this sort of study and can be frustrating to geneticists trying to ensure that the public receives accurate information about the research. While it might be suggested that this is because these books are often written by genealogists rather than geneticists; but *Trace your Roots with DNA* (2004) by Megan Smolenyak and Ann Turner proves that they need not be misleading. These authors provide a comprehensive guide as to how to conduct a genetic genealogy project, going into technical detail about genetics and inheritance, how testing is carried out, who to sample (including the issues surrounding possible multiple origins for a surname, surname adoption, and so on), and the calculation of time to the most recent common ancestor for participants. Importantly, they address in great depth the disruptive impact that illegitimacy has on a genetic genealogy study (and the necessity of typing more than one individual per family tree), whereas some writers seem rather reluctant to tackle this issue.

Ancestry testing

Commercial companies have been quick to react to the public's appetite for claiming a well-known person as part of their family tree. Tests on offer include those seeking matches with the Y haplotypes of Thomas Jefferson, Niall of the Nine Hostages, and Genghis Khan. The ancestry net is cast wider when companies offer to test whether individuals belong to an ethnic group. People who use the genetic testing companies usually want their results to tell them something about where their distant ancestors came from and to whom they are related. Questions commonly encountered are: 'Am I a Viking/Anglo-Saxon/Celt/Jew/Native American/African/Huguenot/Barbarian/Mongol warrior?'. Certain testing companies will provide participants with a certificate of 'ancestry' based on their results, but some of these conclusions are more robust than others. The Y chromosome is highly geographically localized at the continental level and can give an indication as to ancestry on a broad scale, (though there are exceptions to this - see the Revis story below) but what is not often explained to the customer is the lack of certainty inherent in many of these results, which leads to mistaken beliefs as to what is, or is not, possible using genetic data. At least five factors ought to be explained. First, given that the theoretical number of ancestors each of us has far exceeds the population in existence at the time when the Celts/Viking/Anglo-Saxons lived in Britain, it is safe to say that everybody in Europe or with European ancestry is likely to have ancestors in each of these groups. Second, the Y chromosome (and mitochondrial DNA) is inherited from just one parent, and so the ancestry being explored is only one lineage out of the many that each person has. Third, predictions are based on the frequencies of haplotypes in different parts of the world today, using databases of often unknown size and provenance. For example, a haplotype may be found at a higher frequency in a certain part of the world and therefore labelled as 'Viking' or 'Celtic' depending on the location, but this is not to say that these haplotypes are not found elsewhere, or may have arisen separately in different areas. Fourth, modern haplotype frequencies may have been affected by drift, and are conditional on sampling, which is often patchy and limited. Fifth, tying a Y chromosome type based on location in a database cannot guarantee its link with a particular (often historical) cultural group; for example, a problem arises when we try to identify Anglo-Saxon, Danish Viking, and Norman ancestry, because these historical groups were separated by just a few generations in the same part of Europe. It is frequently not possible to say definitely where a man's Y-chromosomal cultural ancestry originates; but the general public often do not wish to hear about 'grey areas', and some commercial companies do not illuminate them.

Idea of identity

What is compelling about this research is the degree to which some people equate the results of their genetic testing to how they feel about themselves: their identity in the world. It can be disturbing to find that you are not genetically part of the family tree that you thought you were. This can extend to a feeling of belonging to a surname. One individual who was told that he did not actually belong to the main descent cluster within a surname said, 'I have always felt like a fill-in-surname': he felt he was not truly a member of the surname by not belonging to the main group. Conversely, people who have long suspected (possibly because they were adopted or the father was not listed on a birth certificate) that their ancestry is linked to a particular person and surname have said that they feel a sense of 'homecoming' and peace to find that they now know that they are truly a member of that family and a bearer of that name. For others there can be an instant feeling of connection with someone of the same surname even before they are known to be related to one another. Clearly, for many individuals their surname forms an essential part of who they are.

This sense of identity is sometimes tied to belonging to a wider community. On taking DNA samples, geneticists speak to hundreds of people who passionately believe themselves to be descended from a particular historical group. Judging by these enquiries, the Vikings are by far the sexiest people to have had as ancestors! From personal stories of having blond hair and blue eyes (despite the fact that these traits have complex patterns of inheritance and are not transmitted through the Y chromosome), or feeling an affinity for the sea, or hearing old family stories of Norse heritage, people feel a strong pull towards Vikings, regardless of their violent reputation. Though most Europeans can expect to have Viking ancestry somewhere in their family tree, what is fascinating is the number of people for whom this is not good enough: they want it to be down the paternal line, through the Y chromosome, and, ideally, they would like a certificate to prove this is the case. Whether enabling people to know if they are related to one another, or that they have ancestry which appears to be tied to a particular area of the world, for some the research results unquestionably have a tremendous resonance, and it can be a very moving experience to be able to provide them with this information.

Perhaps because people move around so much in the world today our sense of who we are and where we fit in now comes less from our extended family and its stories and from living in small communities where many people are related. We no longer have those ties to our families and ancestry that we once had and so we turn to genetics for another layer of connectedness with certain groups. The social impact of DNA testing is the subject of a project being carried out by Wendy Roth at the University of British Columbia, Canada. She is exploring how the receipt of information about ancestry from genetic genealogy or DNA testing affects an individual's feeling of identity, ethnicity, and attitudes.

Unexpected results

DNA has brought a fascinating and exciting new angle to the core family history and surname research techniques, but it can provide some unexpected information. Among the samples studied for genetic research, four haplogroups (A1a, E1, T, Q*), which were previously undetected in samples from the British Isles, might point to exotic ancestors. Two of these, A1a (in the surname Revis) and E1 (in Bray), are normally found only in Africa. The hgT and Q* chromosomes are found at low frequency in several names: Feakes, Jobling, Jefferson for T; and Butterfield, Hey, Jefferson, Mallinson, Ravenscroft for Q*. Haplogroup T is found in the Middle East at its highest frequencies, and in Western Europe (in particular the Iberian peninsula) at low frequencies. Haplogroup Q is normally associated with Native Americans, where it is found at very high frequencies; however, the version found here, Q*, is not typical of the Americas and is poorly characterized in world populations. Both haplogroups have been reported in Middle Eastern, and particularly Jewish, populations, so their presence in Britain could be due to the Jewish diaspora. The presence of these 'exotic' lineages among indigenous British men represents a cautionary tale for those who would predict ethnic origins from Y-chromosomal haplogroups, and instances such as these can be surprising for the participants involved.

One interesting discovery made during the research outlined in Chapter 8 was the finding of a rare African lineage among men with a Yorkshire surname. As indicated above, Y chromosome haplotypes can be highly geographically localized, particularly at the intercontinental level. We can say in broad terms that a man's Y chromosome indicates, for example, that he has African, Asian, or European ancestry. Some haplotypes are so specific to particular continents or regions that they can be used to assign a Y chromosome type to a region of origin. It was expected that the individuals taking part in the British surnames study would have Y chromosomes typical of those found in Europe. Imagine the surprise and excitement when, during the routine testing of a man carrying a Yorkshire surname, it was discovered that he had an extremely rare Y chromosome type (haplogroup A1a) that was previously found only in Africa. Haplogroup E3a is by far the most frequent Y chromosome lineage in Africa and therefore one might expect that any African Y chromsomes found in Britain would have belonged to that haplogroup. As it turned out, not only was this the first trace of African ancestry among any 'indigenous' British samples, but it happened to belong to one of the two deepest-rooting branches of the Y chromosome tree.

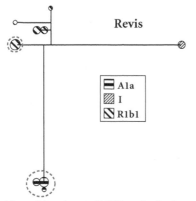

Revis

■ A1a
▨ I
◩ R1b1

Network based on 17 Y-STR marker haplotype

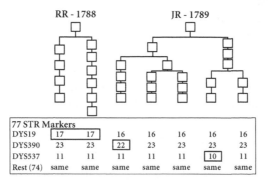

77 STR Markers							
DYS19	17	17	16	16	16	16	16
DYS390	23	23	22	23	23	23	23
DYS537	11	11	11	11	11	10	11
Rest (74)	same	same	same	same	same	same	same

FIGURE 11 **The Revis surname**. John Revis took part in the early stages of the study and was found a very rare Y chromosome type. Collecting further men with the surname, and a spelling variant, found a further six men with the surname Revis who carried the same Y chromosome as John. Genealogical research was able to connect them into two family trees dating back to 1788 and 1789, respectively, but was not able to join the trees. Typing the men with the standard 17 Y-STRs used in the rest of the study revealed only three haplotypes (see network above). Typing with a further 50 Y-STRs revealed only one further mutational step, indicating that these men are likely to share a common ancestor some time in the early eighteenth century.

The first step was to contact the bearer of this intriguing Y chromosome, John Revis, and ask him if he could tell us anything about his ancestry (see Figure 11). In particular, we wanted to know if he knew of any African ancestry in his family. As he lived locally and because, being indigenous to Britain, the information we had to give him might have been a bit of a surprise, we invited him to come for a chat. John very kindly obliged and was as intrigued as we were. He had carried out a great deal of genealogical research before taking part in the study and knew of no African ancestry in his family. Clearly very knowledgeable, he suggested the possibility that his ancestry could go back to the Vikings having brought people from North Africa to Britain in the ninth century.

So the detective work started. How had this Y chromosome type come to Britain and how did it become associated with the Revis surname? Aside from the small numbers allegedly brought to Britain by the Vikings, Africans entered Britain in two main groups. The first of these was in the Roman period: for example, it is known that a garrison of African soldiers was guarding Hadrian's Wall around 200 AD. Much later, from 1555 onwards, the Atlantic slave trade brought the first West Africans to Britain in large numbers: during the Tudor period it was fashionable to have African servants, musicians, and entertainers. An estimated 10,000 black people lived in Britain by the latter part of the eighteenth century, mostly in the cities. We might expect to find a genetic trace of these Africans among the British population today, but no previous study had discovered any.

The first step was to determine if any other men with the surname had the same exotic Y chromosome type. Revis is a rare name with only 121 individuals bearing it in the 1998 British electoral rolls and another fifty named Rivis, a recognized spelling variant. When an extra seventeen men with these names were recruited for the study, six (all with the Revis spelling) were found to carry the African Y chromosome type. The next step was to see if we could find out when these men shared a common ancestor by using genealogical research. Professional genealogist Geoff Swindfield placed the men into two family trees, dating back to Yorkshire in 1788 and 1789, respectively, but these trees could not be joined. Interestingly the patterns of forenames in the two trees were quite distinct and so could indicate that a common ancestor was not shared in the recent past. The mutational differences among the men using the standard 17 Y-STR loci did little to help give an indication as to TMRCA. Individuals belonging to one tree all shared a single step difference at one marker compared to the men belonging to the second tree, and one individual differed from all the others by a single step mutation. Bearing in mind that the date could not be before the time that hereditary surnames were introduced to England in the eleventh century the 17 Y-STR loci and Network were used to calculate the TMRCA for these men. The predicted time to their most recent common ancestor was 440 $\pm$ 330 years, which was a little too wide for what we were trying to ascertain.

In a further effort to pin down a date before which the Y chromosome type must have become associated with the surname, twelve unrelated men bearing the surname Revis who lived in North America were recruited. We hoped to find Revis men who carried the African Y chromosome type and whose families had emigrated to the New World before 1788, to give us an earlier date where the surname must be associated with the Y chromosome type. But as none of these men carried the A1a haplotype we hit another brick wall.

Finally, we turned to what a more detailed genetic study could do in terms of refining the TMRCA dates in order to inform us about when the two trees could have shared a common ancestor. Each of the seven men were typed to a very high resolution using an additional 60 Y-STR loci, yet the number of mutational differences increased by just one, where an individual had a single mutational step difference. However, the lack of mutation in the additional markers tells us that these trees are unlikely to have been separated from one another by many generations. The TMRCA dates given were 140 $\pm$ 80 years. If we add this to the average age of the participants, the oldest likely date is 1734, which overlaps the previous dates that were calculated by using the lower resolution data. The dates still equate to an approximate five-generation window. By using genealogical data we can obtain an indication of when all these men shared a common ancestor and a date before which the Y chromosome type must have become associated with a surname.

This case again highlights the conclusion that genetic testing will not always provide a definitive answer. DNA analysis is not always the magic bullet it is made out to be. It does not provide a date when this unusual Y chromosome type became associated with the Revis surname. Indeed, the common ancestor could have arrived in Britain before the use of hereditary surnames; perhaps a male-line descendant acquired the name later on? The man arriving in Britain may not have been 'African'; he could have been an individual with recent or distant mixed ancestry when he arrived carrying the A1a Y chromosome. Unfortunately, at present, genetics is not able to resolve these issues for us.

Unwanted information

On some commercial companies' sites it can be difficult to discover the names of the markers that are tested, for this information is generally not made available until a person has undergone the testing procedure. One very important issue is the possibility that some of these markers lie in areas where genes important for male fertility exist. If while testing one of these markers no result can be obtained, this may indicate a deletion on that part of the Y chromosome and therefore the possibility that a man could be infertile. An example of this came to light during the course of this research when three individuals were found who were deleted for the binary marker P25 which defines the most common haplogroup in Western Europe, R1b. P25 lies within the AZFc region of the Y chromosome and its deletion is the commonest class associated with infertility. Though binary markers are not routinely tested by genetic genealogy companies, at least two Y-STR markers, found in the same region, are tested: DYS464 and CDYa,b. One company involved states (at the time of writing) on its FAQ page that no markers tested will inform testees of the presence of a disease. While infertility may not fall strictly into the definition of a disease, as a person may not be unhealthy with the condition, the fact that the possibility of infertility may come to light through this testing should be acknowledged. One can imagine the potential emotional impact this might have on an individual prior to his wishing to start a family, or indeed the situation where a person may believe they have fathered children, only to find out that it was not physically possible; so it would be prudent for companies to provide a warning that a diagnosis of infertility may be a by-product of the testing procedure.

An interesting recent case suggests that another warning ought to be posted on genetic testing companies' websites: that of the discovery of a person's biological father even though he was an anonymous sperm donor! The 3 November 2005 issue of *New Scientist* reported such a case, when an anonymous sperm donor was traced on the Internet. Though the case is an unusual one in that the boy was aware of his biological father's date and place of birth and his college degree, the Y chromosome testing he had carried out with Family Tree DNA provided him with the missing surname he needed. The boy was contacted by two men who had also had their Y chromosomes typed through the same company, who had very similar Y chromosomes to his own and who carried spelling variants of a surname. Equipped with the surname, he then used Omnitrace.com to search for all people born with that surname on the day and place of his father's birth. There was only one match for the surname and he was able to make contact with his biological father within a few days, even though his father had never submitted his Y chromosome for testing. This story has led some companies to offer to help people who were adopted by comparing their DNA results with those on their database. While the potential is there for some wonderful family reunions, there is the inherent possibility of conflicting interests for the parties involved. It does lead to interesting questions surrounding the identification of sperm donors and the possibility of being found when perhaps they wish to remain under the conditions under which they gave their sperm: as anonymous donors.

Some uncertainties within genetic genealogy testing

Questions from people wanting to know whether their Y chromosome results might indicate that they are related to Prince Charles (through the female line!) or King Cnut notwithstanding, many genetic genealogists are carrying out a surname study or are trying to link family trees for which the paper trail has gone cold. They wish to know how closely they are related to people bearing the same name, and when this relationship began. The company Family Tree DNA, for example, has a proprietary tool, known as Family Tree DNA Time Predictor, which notifies its customers of the probability of a range of generations within which two people shared a common ancestor, providing they have an exact match for a given number of Y-STRs (this is the Walsh method, used in the research discussed in the previous chapter). However, many of these ranges can be so large as to be unhelpful to a genealogist who wants to know where and when to look for a paper confirmation of a common ancestor. If the number of markers used is low, the time ranges returned can reach to a period which predates surname establishment in the western world, and so this information is unlikely to be of any use to a genealogist. Even with the highest resolution tests the results returned can be expressed only in terms of probabilities. For example, if two men differ by one marker on a higher resolution test (37 markers) then the chance of them sharing a common ancestor within the last four generations is 59 per cent and within twelve generations is 97 per cent. Unfortunately, this is a probable time span of about 400 years and it is not certain that the common ancestor will fall within it. However, this tool is certainly the most advanced of those available and it does take into account as much information as possible regarding the mutation rates of individual markers. Even higher resolution tests of 67, and the rumoured soon to be available 110, Y-STR marker tests should be able to provide more precise time-estimates for participants; Family Tree DNA are certainly the leaders in the field.

The numbers and types of markers that are tested are also critical to questions surrounding haplogroup prediction. Few testing companies make standard use of binary markers to determine haplogroup, preferring instead to use haplogroup prediction based on Y-STR haplotype. This method is not without its errors. Closely related haplogroups can be difficult to distinguish from one another and can share identical haplotypes even when many STRs are typed. The increasing number of Y-STR markers that are typed does provide greater resolution of haplotype and increases the confidence with which people with identical haplotypes and the same surname can expect to share a common ancestor since the time of surname establishment. However, it also increases the probability of typing error and of finding a mutational difference among close relatives which could be interpreted as excluding a person from a family tree.

DNA and the past: using surnames to get at the Y chromosomes of the past

There is a great deal of interest in determining whether or not we can ascertain signals of the genetic legacy of such groups as the Celts, Anglo-Saxons, and Vikings. Debate revolves around whether they migrated in large numbers or whether various regions came under the control of a ruling elite comprised of relatively few individuals. People have turned to genetics as another way to approach the question, but trying to ascertain the genetic make-up of a region in the past by looking at the people living there today is rather like disentangling a palimpsest. We want to read the genetic text of the population that existed hundreds of years ago, for example at the time of the Vikings. However, since the time of the Vikings, this text has been overwritten by the population movements and growth that have occurred subsequently. So can we find genetic evidence of where these Vikings settled and what was their contribution to the gene pool in the past?

We can attempt to answer these questions and read the genetic text of the past in two ways. First, we can do what might be likened to a direct reading by carrying out archaeological excavations and attempting to extract DNA from skeletons from the period of interest. But this means finding an appropriate site and working in extremely clean conditions to ensure that the DNA sequence retrieved is from the skeleton and not from an excavator or a lab member. Sample sizes are usually small and what DNA is available may be very degraded with the result that it isn't possible to choose which parts of the DNA we wish to examine: we can only examine what is left. Finally, these individuals may not have left any descendants alive today. Techniques are improving all the time, however, so this route certainly seems to be becoming more feasible.

The second way to read the 'text' is by sampling modern populations: an indirect reading that has the advantage of the ease of collecting samples. The lure of free genetic testing attracts an overwhelming response. By using modern DNA, geneticists are able to examine the parts they are interested in, unconstrained by DNA degradation. But this method of proceeding is not without its own problems. Who should be sampled to best answer the questions? Should people be selected by where they live now or where their grandparents lived? By proximity to towns, or by county? And what allowance should be made for population movements such as that which occurred in the wake of the Industrial Revolution? Where people live now, or even where their grandparents lived, may not be where their ancestors lived several hundred years ago.

The link between surname and Y chromosome type now provides us with an indirect link with the past, allows us to leap-frog over periods such as the Industrial Revolution, and opens the door for studies using surnames as means to determine the genetic make-up of a past population. A study carried out at the University of Leicester sought to test the theory that surnames could be used as a means to sample men in order to provide an indication of the genetic legacy of the Norse Viking migration in the Wirral Peninsula and west Lancashire, where a great deal of historical, archaeological and place-name evidence indicates a Viking presence in the past, but where heavy immigration has blurred the genetic signal of their settlement. What we wanted to know was whether surnames could provide us with a 'lens' through which to examine the types of Y chromosomes that were present during the period a few hundred years after the Vikings arrived.

To test this theory two groups of men were collected. The first was comprised of those who had at least two generations of ancestry in the region, thus ruling out recent immigrants. The second group of men also had two generations of ancestry but were sampled on the basis of their surname. The aim was to collect men who had surnames that were tied to the Wirral and west Lancashire as far back as possible. To find such names a search was made of old lists: for example the 1545 subsidy rolls that recorded householders in the Wirral and the names of individuals from west Lancashire who promised to contribute to the stipend of the priest of the altar of Our Lady at Ormskirk in 1366. Names from smaller sources and some derived from local place-names were also included. These names did not necessarily have to be Scandinavian in origin (though some of them came from place-names with Scandinavian elements) as surnames did not become established until long after the Vikings had been there. The expectation was that by choosing old-established surnames, we were getting significantly closer to the genetic make-up of the population at the time of the Vikings and just afterwards.

The study found that the Y chromosomes associated with the surname-sampled men carried a significantly different set of chromosomes from those of the men who had only two generations of residence in the area. For example, both the Wirral and west Lancashire surname-sampled men had higher frequencies of a Y chromosome type R1a1 which is frequent in Norway ($\sim$ 35%), but rare in most mainland English and Welsh samples. An admixture analysis, whereby it is assumed that the population is a mixture of two parental populations, was then carried out in the expectation that in this instance it would be a mix of British and Norse. To represent the types of Y chromosomes that might have characterized the population of Britain before the Viking incursions, some were chosen from previous investigations in central Scotland and central Ireland, areas that had had little or no Viking contact. The Vikings were represented by samples taken from modern Norwegian populations. A computer program then examined each Wirral and west Lancashire Y chromosome type from the two sets of men to determine which of the two parental populations it belonged to. While the modern samples showed some Norwegian input, among the medieval-surnamed men the proportions were significantly higher. The results are tantalizing and the project is currently being expanded, using the same methods, with samples from Cumbria, Yorkshire, Northumberland, and Durham.

Turi King is also a collaborator on the People of the British Isles project, based at Oxford, headed by Professors Sir Walter Bodmer, Peter Donnelly, and Lon Cardon, and run by Bruce Winney. Samples are taken from men from different geographical locations, based on the criteria that all four of their grandparents were born within thirty miles of one another, ideally in rural locations, so as to increase the likelihood that their ancestry is from that area. The aim of the study is to look at the genetic differences across all of the genome between people from around Britain and to look for variations within and between different parts of the country. The main aim of the project is a medical one. When searching for the genetic basis for a disease, what scientists look at are sections of the DNA that differ in people who have the disease from those of a control group of people who do not. The control group is supposed to represent the regular population; but what are the implications if you are looking at people with a disease in Scotland but your control group is from southern England? How are scientists to know that the bits that are different in the disease group as opposed to the control group are significant and related to the cause of the disease? What if the samples differ genetically because the people of Scotland have different population histories from the populations in the south? London for example has a much more mixed population than elsewhere. What the People of the British Isles study aims to create is a control group for each region and, crucially, it will look for differences between regions.

What also emerges from the project is the possibility to look for genetic differences among the different regions of the British Isles. The project will examine, among other things, Y chromosome types that are common in particular regions of the country. It aims to assess the impact of historical population movements, such as the Viking incursions, and to use the geographical localization of some surnames. In collaboration with the team behind the National Trust Surnames website, individuals will be assigned an ancestral location based on their surname history and the patterns will be compared to see if particular Y chromosomes are found in different parts of the country. These results will be compared with those seen by linking people to locations based on their grandparents' place of birth. A much smaller, but very similar study, was carried out in the Leicester surnames project, when men were assigned to an area based on the places of birth of paternal grandfathers and then, where possible, to a region based on surname history. The results from both approaches showed very little structure of Y chromosome types, but the study reconfirmed the observation that the proportion of R1b Y chromosomes increases the further west one travels in the British Isles. The new, much larger study has the capacity to reveal in much greater detail the types of Y chromosome found around Britain.

Two slightly different studies linking surname with Y chromosome types tied to past populations came out of Dan Bradley's lab in Dublin. The first was a small study which again used the geographical information regarding origin inherent in many surnames and attempted to use them to look for a signal of Viking ancestry in Ireland. This involved sampling forty-seven men who bore one of twenty-six surnames, including Thunder, Sweetnam, Doyle, and Nelson, that are thought to be of Norse Viking derivation. Typed with 13 Y-STRs and up to six binary markers, their Y chromosome types were compared with other Irish, British, and Scandinavian data, but they were not found to carry a signal of Norse ancestry; instead, they were more closely related to the Irish samples. It is possible that the genetic contribution of the Norse Vikings was low and the contribution of surnames was cultural rather than genetic. Some of the Norse Viking migration predates surname foundation in Ireland, so the link between modern surname and Viking Y chromosome type could have been broken.

The second, much larger, study provided striking evidence of a link between a well-known dynasty of early medieval Ireland, its allegedly related surnames, and a Y chromosome type. The researchers used surnames to identify and sample the putative descendants of Niall of the Nine Hostages, who was High King of Ireland at the beginning of the fifth century. Legends tell that his eight sons became the founders of the Uí Néill lineages that dominated Ireland from the seventh to the eleventh centuries. The Irish surnames that started in the tenth century AD were often derived from lineages such as these. The Y chromosomes of fifty-nine men, each bearing one of the twenty-five surnames associated with Uí Néill, were analysed and over 50 per cent were found to belong a single, or closely related, Y chromosome haplotype. The TMRCA for the cluster was estimated at 1,700 years, a time approximately consistent with the period of Niall's reign. Interestingly, in a study of unrelated men from north-west Ireland (the seat of the Uí Néill dynasty's power), which was carried out as part of the same research, this lineage was also found at a very high frequency. About one in five of the Y chromosomes in north-west Ireland belong to this or a closely related haplotype, which is found at lower frequencies in the rest of Ireland and also found in many North American samples, probably because of the well-documented high rates of Irish emigration. Given the rates of the haplotype in these populations, it was estimated that as many as 2–3 million males worldwide could carry the Uí Néill haplotype. Much less evidence of co-ancestry was found when studying multiple surnames that were thought to descend from two further clans: the Eóganacht and Dál Cais in the south of Ireland. This suggests that perhaps not all clans had a single founder and/or that the link between the founder and associated modern surnames has been broken.

What is startling about this study is the demographic impact of a single lineage. At the time, Ireland was a polygynous society (in which a man has more than one legal wife), with a strong patrilineal system and with considerable emphasis on family relationships, where land and titles were handed down through male lineages. A man of power, wealth, and prestige could have had more than one wife and therefore more children. Members of the Uí Néill clan such as the O'Donnells were certainly a case in point: Lord Turlough O'Donnell (d. 1423) sired eighteen sons with ten wives and had fifty-nine grandsons down the male line. A feature of Irish custom was that illegitimate sons were claimed and had rights protected by law – they were included in the clan.

Polygyny is a practice that, interestingly for geneticists, ensures that a man's surname and his Y chromosome are passed on together. This can be contrasted with the other means whereby men could have had offspring outside marriage but where there was no provision for illegitimate sons. If the woman involved was married then it is presumably more likely that the child would have the genealogical father's surname but the biological father's Y chromosome type. If the mother was unwed, then again there is no guarantee that the child would have the biological father's surname; indeed, it could be much more likely that the child would have the mother's surname. Both instances are seen as straight non-paternity events in terms of the resulting broken link between Y chromosome type and surname. The practice of polygyny perhaps goes some way to explaining why, even for some very common surnames in Ireland, there is a single large descent cluster of related individuals; something which is not seen for very common names in Britain.

Forensics

The signal of co-ancestry in up to 24 per cent of the pairs in the Leicester study, constituting powerful evidence for the common patrilineal origins of men sharing the same surname, also has forensic implications, for it could allow the prediction of a surname from crime-scene samples. To test how this might work in practice the pairs were split, with the Y haplotype of one half of each of the 150 surname pairs becoming the crime-scene sample and the other half of the pair becoming a surname-linked Y haplotype in a simulated forensic database. Forensic investigators do not analyse binary markers on the Y chromosome as a matter of course, but Y-STR haplotyping using commercial kits is now widespread and so only these were considered. A computer program was then written to take each crime-scene Y haplotype in turn and assign it the most closely related haplotype(s) in the surname/Y haplotype database. Matches of up to three mutational steps difference were allowed.

The average number of surnames that a crime-scene haplotype matched was 1.3, though the range was up to six. The correct surname emerged in 28/150 cases (19 per cent). As expected, given that we know the link between surname and Y chromosome type is stronger the rarer the name, the great majority of these (26/28 matches) occurred within the lower-frequency group of surnames and only Major, with 5,600 carriers occurred above rank 71. This corresponds to a 34 per cent chance of correct prediction of surname in this sub-sample of 80 surnames. If we look at the number of surnames which fall between these two frequencies (5,600 and 50 bearers, respectively) in the population of Britain we find ~40,000 surnames within this frequency range.

These results are intriguing. While it would not be expected that a perfect surname-prediction system would emerge for forensic use, it could prove to be a useful investigative tool. If a large database of surnames and associated Y-chromosomal haplotypes were available, a Y haplotype from a crime scene could be compared with the database to yield a list of surnames, which could then be combined with other intelligence information to identify a suspect pool. Additional refinements such as statistical adjustments, based on local demographic factors, could be applied to these predictions: for example, if local knowledge had been required by the perpetrator to commit the crime then local surnames could be prioritized. Y-STR weighting schemes could be used to judge the significance of closely related haplotypes.

Although such a database could never be more than an investigative tool, there are cases where it might prove useful. An estimated twenty-five to sixty-five no-suspect murders and three to four hundred no-suspect rapes each year in the United Kingdom include unidentified DNA samples. An ideal database that included the frequency range outlined above of about 40,000 names with associated Y-STR haplotypes could contribute to the intelligence-led investigation of such crimes. Using the figure of a 34 per cent chance of correct prediction of surname from Y haplotype, the number of cases in which surname prediction could contribute usefully is ten no-suspect murders and fifty-seven no-suspect rapes per year. A surnames database also has a deterrent value because, given the sharing of surname and Y haplotype, individuals need not be represented on the database themselves for the link between their Y chromosome haplotype and their surname to already exist in the database. This could conceivably allow perpetrators to be apprehended early in their criminal careers. Though this study has been carried out in Britain, DNA-based surname prediction would, in principle, be applicable in any society having diverse patrilineal surnames of reasonable time depth.

There are two caveats regarding this proposal. The work was carried out using a set of samples that is atypical of those normally encountered by police forces investigating serious crime. The surnames analysed were all British, and individuals who had changed their names or were adopted were excluded. Three generations of residence in Britain was also required. It remains to be seen how well the surname prediction approach would work in the typical (and much more complex) urban British population. Far more importantly, the ethical issues surrounding such a database need to be considered. Quite rightly, much debate revolves around the composition and number of individuals whose DNA profiles are registered on the National DNA Database, and the policies regarding whose profiles are retained and when they are removed. While this could only ever be an investigative tool, and while it is a database containing genetic information linked to nothing more than a single surname, it could potentially be considered to contain personal information. As such, the keeping of a database would have to be debated and ethical issues considered and addressed. DNA-based surname prediction would, in principle, be applicable in any society that has diverse patrilineal surnames of reasonable time depth. Current work in this area involves testing the hypotheses on more forensically relevant samples. Would social factors surrounding the people who commit crimes make it less likely for a link between surname and Y chromosome to exist, thereby making a database far less applicable to typical forensic case work?

The future of genetic genealogy and surnames

There are now well over 200 Y-STRs available: a comprehensive survey of human Y-chromosomal STRs will allow far greater typing resolution than before and enable surname histories to be studied on a much more recent time scale. It will also lead to greater precision in estimating the time to most recent common ancestor between individuals. The 1000 Genomes and the Cancer Genome Projects, both of which are carrying out sequencing and using the results to look for differences between a large number of individuals, will each provide a wealth of data about human genomes and include sequence information about the Y chromosome. Indeed, the amount of new Y-SNP data will probably make the current method of Y chromosome nomenclature unwieldy. New technologies are making it more much more affordable for the public to have partial Y Chromsome sequencing carried out by commercial providers. This will allow still further Y-SNP discovery and although it is currently impractical to sequence the Y chromosome of many individuals within a surname group it should in principle be possible to find SNPs that are unique to particular surname lineages in the near future (private SNPs). Indeed, the expense of whole genome sequencing is within reach of greater numbers of private individuals. Certainly as more and more people are having their whole genomes sequenced for recreational purposes and, like Craig Venter and James Watson, making them available online, databases of such information will grow. The databases resulting from the expansion of genealogical DNA testing and whole genome sequencing will produce an explosion of new information, and provide increasingly powerful resources for genealogical research.

Conclusion

The study of surnames was once the preserve of the specialist in old languages. The dictionaries that are still consulted on the shelves of public reference libraries were compiled by philologists in a long tradition that culminated in the work of P.H. Reaney and R.M. Wilson. Knowledge of Old English, Old Norse, Norman French, Middle English, and other languages that have influenced the ways that surnames have been formed is clearly an essential component of a proper understanding of the subject. As with the study of place-names, it is essential to establish the earliest recorded spellings of a surname and to place them in an appropriate linguistic context. But only a small group of scholars who are interested in surnames possess these specialist skills and so the etymologies that have been derived from them have been readily accepted by the public at large.

It is now clear that this approach remains valid only if it takes account of other methods of enquiry. It is not the sole way to the truth. Linguists have often failed to provide correct etymologies because they have not linked the earliest recorded examples with present forms. Although the linguistic approach is usually effective in explaining medieval by-names, it often lacks credibility when dealing with modern surnames, for it has taken little or no account of how very many names have changed over the centuries, often radically, and it has had no interest in the past and present geographical distributions of surnames. Time and time again, compilers of dictionaries have quoted medieval evidence from counties far distant from the present concentration of a name and for which there are no later records. No attempt has been made to show that the early by-names that they unearthed ever developed into hereditary surnames. What Reaney and Wilson produced was not a dictionary of current surnames, but a useful compilation of etymologies of numerous English by-names during the main period of surname formation.

Linguistic analysis remains an important component of the study of surnames, but it needs to be subsumed in a multi-disciplinary approach that uses the techniques of genealogy and the knowledge of local historians. Each family name, even if it is one shared by numerous families across the land, should be treated as having a unique history that must be traced back in time step by step. Only by the use of such painstaking methods can we be sure whether a name has retained its early form or has been altered, either subtly or out of recognition, over the centuries.

Genealogical methods can also establish whereabouts a particular surname was formed, or they can at least demonstrate that a distinctive name was confined to a particular locality in the late Middle Ages or by the beginning of parish registration in the mid-sixteenth century. One of the greatest advances in the study of surnames has been through mapping their distributions at various points of time, starting with modern electoral rolls and telephone directories, then going back in time to the 1881 census, the hearth tax returns of the 1660s and 1670s, and possibly to the poll tax returns of 1377–81. Such maps show immediately that the surname Ashurst, for example, was derived from a minor place-name near Wigan and that the bearers of this name have no historical links with similar place-names quoted by Reaney and Wilson in Kent, Surrey and Sussex. If any of the medieval by-names that were formed from these other Ashursts became hereditary surnames, they must have died out quite early.

The local provenance of numerous British surnames, as revealed by distribution maps and genealogical research, suggests that very many of them are of single-family origin. Historians have often been thwarted in their attempts to prove this claim because of the relatively sparse nature of the documentary evidence at the time when surnames became generally adopted. This is why they have welcomed the new technique of DNA analysis of the male Y chromosome with such enthusiasm. Some spectacular results have been achieved and the case for single-family origins of many surnames has undoubtedly been strengthened. Yet this approach alone does not always resolve the problem, for it is often frustrated by what scientists call non-paternity events, chiefly high rates of illegitimacy. The results of investigations into DNA structures are often not sufficiently certain on this point to stand on their own. They have to be considered alongside those of linguistic, genealogical, and historical research.

Genetics has much more to offer family historians than the resolution of this particular problem, however. It can provide a way of determining whether or not two or more names shared a common ancestry, as seemed possible or even likely from the historical evidence. This is not just a matter of connecting names with variant spellings; it can also demonstrate a complete change of a name through the use of an alias, or show that illegitimacy, adoption, or some other form of non-paternity event has occurred. Proving a link between different names has been a particularly exciting new development when different forms of a surname appeared thousands of miles away across the Atlantic. Genealogists have turned to this new technique with enthusiasm and have quickly become the best informed amateurs about the implications of the genetic structure of the male Y chromosome.

The study of surnames is of particular interest to family historians, but it also has wider implications. Surname distributions have much to tell us about the stability and mobility of the British population as a whole over the past few centuries. They demonstrate that, despite the mobility of numerous individuals, most families remained within the neighbourhood or 'country' that had been familiar to their ancestors. London was exceptional in attracting a continuous flow of migrants from far and wide. The larger provincial cities, such as Norwich and York, also provided opportunities for the more adventurous, but the majority of the population – even after the coming of the railways – did not venture beyond their nearest market towns. The 'core families' that stayed put for generation after generation and who had well-established connections with similar families within the neighbourhood were the ones that shaped the character of the place: its speech, customs, attitudes, forms of religion, styles of vernacular architecture, working practices, and all the other matters that cemented a local society. These links are not as strong as they were, but even today a surname can locate a person within the territory where it was formed several centuries ago.

Surnames also provide vital evidence for the movement of populations overseas, particularly across the Atlantic. They can suggest whereabouts in Britain a family originated and they can sometimes indicate that a group of neighbours went on the long voyage together or perhaps followed each other when the first adventurers reported the success of their journey and the rewarding prospects that lay ahead. Genetics has been highly successful in demonstrating the movement of human populations in prehistoric and early medieval times. In tracing the movements of people in recent centuries, it has the benefit of drawing on other methods of enquiry. The cooperation of scholars across the disciplines is a very welcome development in all such studies. It is clearly necessary for a true understanding of surnames.

Bibliography

General works and dictionaries

Bardsley, C.W. 1901. *A Dictionary of English and Welsh Surnames*. London: Henry Frowde.

Bell, R. 1988. *The Book of Ulster Surnames*. Belfast: Blackstaff Press.

Black, G.F. 1946. *The Surnames of Scotland*. New York Public Library.

Camden, W. 1605; 1974 reprint. *Remains Concerning Britain*. Wakefield: EP Publishing.

Charnock, R.S. 1870; 2009 reprint. *Patronymica Cornu-Britannica: or Etymologies of Cornish Surnames*. Kissinger, USA.

Dorward, D. 1995. *Scottish Surnames*. Glasgow: HarperCollins.

Dunkling, L.A. 1998. *Dictionary of Surnames*. London: HarperCollins.

Fellows Jensen, G. 1968. *Scandinavian Personal Names in Lincolnshire and Yorkshire*. Copenhagen: Akademisk Forlag.

Fishwick, H. 1889. *History of the Parish of Rochdale in the County of Lancaster*. Rochdale: James Clegg.

Fryer, P. 1984. *Staying Power: the History of Black People in Britain*. London: Pluto Press.

Goose, N. and Luu, L. (eds) 2005. *Immigrants in Tudor and Early Stuart England*. Brighton: Sussex Academic Press.

Guppy, H.B. 1890. *The Homes of Family Names in Great Britain*. London: Harrison.

Hanks, P. and Hodges, F. 1988. *A Dictionary of Surnames*. Oxford: Oxford University Press.

Harrison, H. 1912–18. *Surnames of the United Kingdom*. London: Clearfield.

Herber, M.D. 1997. *Ancestral Trails*. Stroud: Sutton.

Hey, D. 1997. The Local History of Family Names. *The Local Historian*, 27, no. 4, Supplement.

—— 1998. The Distinctive Surnames of Staffordshire. *Staffordshire Studies*, 10: 1–28.

—— 2000. *Family Names and Family History*. London: Hambledon & London.

—— (ed.) 2008. *The Oxford Companion to Family and Local History*. 2nd edn. Oxford: Oxford University Press.

—— and Redmonds, G. 2002. *Yorkshire Surnames and the Hearth Tax Returns of 1672–73*. York: Borthwick Papers, 102.

Hooke, D. and Postles, D. (eds) 2003. *Names, Time and Place: Essays in Memory of Richard McKinley*. Oxford: Leopards Head Press.

Hoskins, W.G. 1946. Leicestershire Yeoman Families and their Pedigrees. *Transactions of the Leicestershire Archaeological Society*, XXIII, part I: 3–28.

Kneen, J.J. 1937. *The Personal Names of the Isle of Man*. Oxford: Oxford University Press.

Lasker, G.W. and Mascie-Taylor, C.G.N. 1990. *Atlas of British Surnames*. Wayne State University Press.

Laslett P. 1980. Introduction: Comparing Illegitimacy over Time and between Cultures, in P. Laslett, K. Oosterveen, and R. Smith (eds) *Bastardy and its Comparative History*. London: Edward Arnold.

L'Estrange Ewen, E. 1931. *A History of Surnames of the British Isles*. London: Kegan Paul.

—— 1938. *Origin of British Surnames*. London: Kegan Paul.

Lower, M.A. 1860; reprint 1996. *Patronymica Britannica*. Maryland, USA: Heritage Classic.

MacLysaght, E. 1985. *The Surnames of Ireland*. 6th edn. Blackrock, County Dublin: Irish Academic Press.

McClure, P. 1998. The Interpretation of Hypocoristic Forms of Middle English Baptismal Names. *Nomina*, 21: 101–31.

—— 2003. The Kinship of Jack: 1, Pet Forms of Middle English Personal Names with the Suffixes *-kin*, *-ke*, *-man* and *-cot*. *Nomina*, 26: 93–117.

—— 2005. The Kinship of Jack: II, Pet Forms of Middle English Personal Names with the Suffixes *-cok* and *-cus*. *Nomina*, 28: 5–42.

McKinley, R. 1975. *Norfolk and Suffolk Surnames in the Middle Ages*. London and Chichester: Phillimore.

—— 1977. *The Surnames of Oxfordshire*. London: Leopards Head Press.

—— 1981. *The Surnames of Lancashire*. London, Leopards Head Press.

—— 1988. *The Surnames of Sussex*. Oxford: Leopards Head Press.

—— 1990. *A History of British Surnames*. Harlow: Longman.

Morgan, T.J. and Morgan, P. 1985. *Welsh Surnames*. Cardiff: University of Wales Press.

Ó Murchadha, D. 1985; 1996 reprint. *Family Names of County Cork*. Cork: Collins.

Parkinson, E. 2008. *The Establishment of the Hearth Tax, 1662–66*. Kew: List and Index Society.

Plant, J. 2005. Modern Methods and a Controversial Surname. *Nomina* 28: 115–33.

Pooley, C. and Turnbull, J. 1998. *Migration and Mobility since the Eighteenth Century*. University College, London.

Postles, D. 1995. *The Surnames of Devon*. Oxford: Leopards Head Press.

—— 1998. *The Surnames of Leicestershire and Rutland*. Oxford: Leopard Heads Press.

—— (ed.) 2002. *Naming, Society and Regional Identity*. Oxford: Leopards Head Press.

—— 2009. *The North through its Names*. Oxford: Oxbow.

Quilliam, L. 1989. *Surnames of the Manks*. Peel, Isle of Man: Cashtal Books.

Reaney, P.H. 1967. *The Origins of English Surnames*. London: Routledge & Kegan Paul.

—— and Wilson R.M. 1997. *A Dictionary of English Surnames*. Oxford: Oxford University Press.

Redmonds, G. 1973. *Yorkshire, West Riding: English Surnames Series I*. London and Chichester: Phillimore.

—— 1990. *Yorkshire Surnames Series, Part 1: Bradford and District*. Huddersfield: GR Books.

Redmonds, G. 1992. *Yorkshire Surnames Series, Part 2: Huddersfield and District.* Huddersfield: GR Books.

—— 1994. *Holmfirth, Place-names and Settlement.* Huddersfield: GR Books.

—— 1997; 2002. *Surnames and Genealogy: a New Approach.* Boston: New England Historic Genealogical Society. Facsimile copy. Bury: Federation of Family History Societies.

—— 2001. *Yorkshire Surnames Series, Part 3: Halifax and District.* Huddersfield: Author.

—— 2004a. *Christian Names in Local and Family History.* Kew: The National Archives.

—— 2004b. *Names and History: People, Places and Things.* London: Hambledon & London.

—— 2005. The Sagars of Cliviger. *Lancashire Local Historian*, 18: 1–7.

Roderick, T. 2000. The Y-Chromosome in Genealogical Research. *National Genealogical Society Quarterly*, 88: 122–43.

Rogers, C.D. 1995. *The Surname Detective.* Manchester: Manchester University Press.

Rowlands, J. and S. 1996. *The Surnames of Wales.* Birmingham: Federation of Family History Societies.

—— 2006. The Distribution of Surnames in Wales. *Nomina*, 29: 97–113.

Scott-Bannister, S. 1997. *Names and Naming Patterns in England, 1538–1700.* Oxford: Clarendon Books.

Smolenyak, M.S. and Turner, A. 2004. *Trace Your Roots with DNA.* New York: Rodale.

Sykes, B. 2003. *Adam's Curse.* London: Bantam.

Titford, J. 2002. *Searching for Surnames.* Newbury: Countryside Books.

—— 2009. *Penguin Dictionary of Surnames.* London: Penguin Books.

Tooth, E. 2002, 2004. *The Distinctive Surnames of North Staffordshire,* vols 2 and 3. Leek: Churnet Valley Books.

Tucker, K. 2004. What Happened to the UK 1881 Census Surnames by 1997. *Nomina*, 27: 91–118.

—— 2008. Reaney & Wilson Redux: an Analysis and Comparison with Major English Surname Data Sets. *Nomina*, 31: 5–44.

Wagner, Sir A. 1983. *English Genealogy.* 3rd edn. Chichester: Phillimore.

Weekley, E. 1914; 2009 reprint. *The Romance of Names.* Cornell University Library.

Wrightson, K. 1980. The Nadir of English Illegitimacy in the Seventeenth Century, in P. Laslett, K. Oosterveen, and R. Smith (eds) *Bastardy and its Comparative History.* London: Edward Arnold.

Wrigley E.A., Davies R.S., Oeppen J.E., and Schofield R.S. 1997. *English Population History from Family Reconstitution 1580–1837.* Cambridge: Cambridge University Press.

—— and Schofield R.S. 1981. *The Population History of England 1541–1871.* London: Edward Arnold.

Record Publications

The information about individual family names and by-names that is quoted in the text comes from a wide variety of published and archival sources that are far too detailed to be quoted in full here. The list below notes printed sources that have been particularly useful. They are also intended to provide typical examples of the variety of sources that are available in print.

Archer, S. 2003. *The British 19th Century Surname Atlas*. Archer Software, www. archersoftware.co.uk.

Arkell, T. and Alcock, N. (eds) 2010. *Warwickshire Hearth Tax*. British Record Society.

Beckett, I.F.W. (ed.) 1985. *The Buckinghamshire Posse Comitatus 1798*. Buckinghamshire Record Society, 22.

Chibnall, A.C. (ed.) 1973. *The Certificates of Musters for Buckinghamshire in 1522*. Royal Commission on Historical Manuscripts, JP 18.

Collins, F. (ed.) 1896. *Register of the Freemen of the City of York, vol. I, 1272–1558*; 1900. vol. *II*. Surtees Society.

—— (ed.) 1887, 1902. *The Parish Registers of Kirkburton, 1541–1711*, 2 vols. Exeter: W. Pollard.

Edwards, D.G. (ed.) 1982. *Derbyshire Hearth Tax Assessments, 1662–70*. Derbyshire Record Society.

Evans, N. and Rose, S. (eds) 2000. *Cambridgeshire Hearth Tax Returns Michaelmas 1664*. British Record Society.

Fenwick, C.C. (ed.) 1998. *The Poll Taxes of 1377, 1379 and 1381: part I Bedfordshire–Leicestershire*. The British Academy.

—— (ed.) 2001. *The Poll Taxes of 1377, 1379 and 1381: part 2 Lincolnshire–Westmorland*. The British Academy.

—— (ed.) 2005. *The Poll Taxes of 1377, 1379 and 1381: part 3 Wiltshire–Yorkshire*. The British Academy.

Franklin, P. 1993. *The Taxpayers of Medieval Gloucestershire*. Stroud: Alan Sutton.

Fraser, C.M. (ed.) 1991. *Durham Quarter Sessions Rolls 1471–1625*. Surtees Society CXCIX.

Green, A., Parkinson, E., and Spufford, M. (eds) 2006. *County Durham Hearth Tax Assessment Lady Day 1666*. British Record Society.

Harrington, D., Pearson, S., and Rose, S. (eds) 2000. *Kent Hearth Tax Assessment Lady Day 1664*. British Record Society.

Haswell, F. and Jackson, C.S. (eds) 1938. *The Register of St Andrews Parish Church, Penrith, 1556–1604*. Cumberland and Westmorland Antiquarian Society.

Hatley, V.A. (ed.) 1973. *Northamptonshire Militia Lists*. Northamptonshire Record Society.

Hey, D., Giles, C., Spufford, M., and Wareham, A. (eds) 2007. *Yorkshire West Riding Hearth Tax Assessment Lady Day 1672*. British Record Society.

Hughes, E. and White, P. (eds) 1991. *The Hampshire Hearth Tax Assessments for 1662 and 1670.* Hampshire Record Series, II.

Hunnisett, R.F., (ed.) 1996. *Sussex Coroners Inquests, 1558–1603.* Kew: Public Record Office.

Kettle, A.J. 1976. A List of Families in the Archdeaconry of Stafford, 1532–33. *Collections for a History of Staffordshire.* Staffordshire Record Society.

Knafla, L.A. 1994. *Kent at Law, 1602.* London: HMSO.

Longstaffe, W.H.D. and Booth, J. (eds) 1889. *Durham Halmote Rolls 1296–1384.* Surtees Society, LXXXII.

Lutt, N. (ed.) 1992. *Bedfordshire Muster Lists, 1539–1831.* Bedfordshire Historical Record Society, 71.

Marshall, L.M. 1990. *The Bedfordshire Hearth Tax Returns for 1671.* Bedfordshire Historical Record Society, 16.

Meekings, C.A.F. (ed.) 1951. *Dorset Hearth Tax Assessments, 1662–1664.* Dorset Natural History and Archaeology Society.

Parkinson, E. (ed.) 1994. *The Glamorgan Hearth Tax Assessment of 1670.* Cardiff: South Wales Record Society, 10.

Phillips, C., Ferguson, C., and Wareham, A. (eds) 2008. *Westmorland Hearth Tax.* British Record Society.

Reed, H.C. and Miller G.J. (eds) 1944; 1975 reprint. *The Burlington Court Book of West New Jersey 1680–1709.* New York: Kraus.

Spencer, C.J. and Postlethwaite, R.H. (eds) 1994. *The Registers of the Parish Church of St Andrew, Slaidburn 1600–1770.* Preston: Private.

Stavert, W.J. 1894. *The Parish Register of Skipton in Craven, 1680–1771.* Skipton: Craven Herald.

Webster, W.F. (ed.) 1988. *Nottinghamshire Hearth Tax, 1664: 1674.* Thoroton Society Record Series, XXXVII.

Williams, W.O. (ed.) 1956. *Calendar of the Caernarvonshire Quarter Sessions Records, vol. 1, 1541–1558.* Caernarvonshire Historical Society.

Genetics

Bandelt H.J., Forster P., and Röhl A. 1999. Median-joining Networks for Inferring Intraspecific Phylogenies. *Molecular Biology and Evolution,* 16: 37–48.

Bosch, E., Lee, A., Calafell, F., Arroyo, E., Henneman, P., de Knijff, P., and Jobling, M.A. 2002. High Resolution Y Chromosome Typing: 19 STRs Amplified in Three Multiplex Reactions. *Forensic Science International,* 125: 42–51.

Bowden, G., Balaresque, P., King, T.E., Lee, A., Roberts, S., Waite, P., Jesch, J., Bradman, N., Harding, S., and Jobling, M.A. 2008. Excavating Past Population Structures by Surname-based Sampling: the Genetic Legacy of the Vikings in Northwest England. *Molecular Biology and Evolution,* 25: 301–9.

Foster, E., Jobling, M., Taylor, P., Donnelly, P., de Knijff, P., Mieremet, R., Zerjal, T., and Tyler-Smith, C. 1999. The Thomas Jefferson Paternity Case. *Nature,* 397: 32.

Foster, E., Jobling, M., Taylor, P., Donnelly, P., de Knijff, P., Mieremet, R., Zerjal, T., and Tyler-Smith, C. 1998. Jefferson Fathered Slave's Last Child. *Nature*, 396: 27–8.

Genest, P. 1973. Transmission héréditaire depuis 300 ans d'un chromosome Y à satellites dans une lignée familiale. *Annales de Génétique*, 16: 35–8.

Giraldo, A., Martinez, I., Guzman, M., and Silva, E. 1981. A Family with a Satellited Yq Chromosome. *Human Genetics*, 57: 99–100.

Gordon-Reed, A. 1997. *Thomas Jefferson and Sally Hemings: An American Controversy.* University Press of Virginia, Charlottesville, VA.

Gusmao, L., Sanchez-Diz, P., Calafel, F., Martin, P., Alonso, C., Alvarez-Fernandez, F., Alves, C., Borjas-Fajardo L., Bozzo, W., Bravo, M., Builes, J., Capilla, J., Carvalho, M., Castillo, C., Catanesi, C., Corach, D., Di Lonardo, A., Espinheira, R., Fagundes de Carvalho, E., Farfan, M., Figueiredo, H., Gomes, I., Lojo, M., Marino, M., Pinheiro, M., Pontes, M., Prieto, V., Ramos-Luis, E., Riancho, J., Souza Goes, A., Santapa, O., Sumita, D., Vallejo, G., Vidal Rioja, L., Vide, M., Vieira da Silva, C., Whittle, M., Zabala, W., Zarrabeitia, M., Alonso, A., Carracedo, A., and Amorim, A. 2005. Mutation Rates at Y Chromosome Specific Microsatellites. *Human Mutation*, 26: 520–8.

Heyer, E., Puymirat, J., Dieltjes, P., Bakker, E., de Knijff, P. 1997. Estimating Y Chromosome Specific Microsatellite Mutation Frequencies Using Deep Rooting Pedigrees. *Human Molecular Genetics*, 6: 799–803.

Hill, E., Bradley, D., and Jobling, M.A. 2000. Y-chromosome Variation and Irish Origins. *Nature*, 404: 351–2.

Jobling, M. 2001. In the Name of the Father: Surnames and Genetics. *Trends in Genetics*, 17: 353–7.

—— Pandya, A., and Tyler-Smith, C. 1997. The Y Chromosome in Forensic Analysis and Paternity Testing. *International Journal of Legal Medicine*, 110: 118–24.

—— and Tyler-Smith, C. 2003. The Human Y Chromosome: an Evolutionary Marker Comes of Age. *Nature Reviews Genetics*, 4: 598–612.

—— —— and Hurles, M. 2004. *Human Evolutionary Genetics: Origins, Peoples and Disease.* New York: Garland Publishing.

Kayser, M., Caglià, A., Corach, D., Fretwell, N., Gehrig, C., Graziosi, G., Heidorn, F., Herrmann, S., Herzog, B., Hidding, M., Honda, K., Jobling, M., Krawczak, M., Leim, K., Meuser, S., Meyer, E., Oesterreich, W., Pandya, A., Parson, W., Penacino, G., Perez-Lezaun, A., King, T.E., and Jobling, M.A. 2009. What's in a Name? – Y Chromosomes, Surnames, and the Genetic Genealogy Revolution. *Trends in Genetics*, 25: 351–60.

King, T.E. and Jobling, M.A. 2009. Founders, Drift and Infidelity: the Relationship between Y Chromosome Diversity and Patrilineal Surnames. *Molecular Biology and Evolution*, 26: 1093–102.

—— Bowden, G., Balaresque, P., Adams, S., Shanks, M., and Jobling, M.A. 2007. Thomas Jefferson's Y Chromosome Belongs to a Rare European lineage. *American Journal of Physical Anthropology*, 132: 584–9.

Kings, T. E. Parkin, E.J., Swinfield, G., Cruciani, F., Scozzari, R., Roas, A., Lim, S., Xue, Y., Tyler-Smith, C., and Jobling, M.A. 2007. Africans in Yorkshire? The Deepest-rooting Clade of the Y Phylogeny within an English Genealogy. *European Journal of Human Genetics*, 15: 288–93.

—— Ballereau, S.J., Schürer, K., and Jobling, M.A. 2006. Genetic Signatures of Coancestry within Surnames. *Current Biology*, 16: 384–8.

—— Bosch, E., Adams, S., Parkin, E.J., Rosser, Z.H., and Jobling, M.A. 2005. Inadvertent Diagnosis of Male Infertility through Genealogical DNA Testing. *Journal of Medical Genetics*, 42: 366–8. http://jmg.bmjjournals.com/cgi/content/full/42/4/366.

McEvoy, B. and Bradley, D. 2006. Y-chromosomes and the Extent of Patrilineal Ancestry in Irish Surnames. *Human Genetics*: 119: 212–19.

Moore, L., McEvoy, B., Cape, E., Simms, K., and Bradley, D. 2006. A Y-chromosome Signature of Hegemony in Gaelic Ireland. *Amercan Journal of Human Genetics*, 78: 334–8.

Motluk, A. 2005. Anonymous Sperm Donor Traced on Internet. *New Scientist*, November 3: 6.

Piccinini, A., Prinz, M., Schmitt, C., Schneider, P.M., Szibor, R., Teifel-Greding, J., Weichhold, G., de Knijff, P., and Roewer, L. 1997. Evaluation of Y-chromosomal STRs: a Multicenter Study. *International Journal of Legal Medicine*, 110: 125–33.

Qamar, R., Ayub, Q., Mohyuddin, A., Helgason, A., Mazhar, K., Mansoor, A., Zerjal, T., Tyler-Smith, C., and Mehdi, S.Q. 2002. Y-chromosomal DNA Variation in Pakistan. *American Journal of Human Genetics*, 70: 1107–24.

Sykes, B. and Irven, C. 2000. Surnames and the Y Chromosome. *American Journal of Human Genetics*, 66: 1417–19.

Thomas, M.G., Skorecki, K., Ben-Ami, H., Parfitt, T., Bradman, N., and Goldstein, D. B. 1998. Origins of Old Testament Priests. *Nature*, 384: 138–40.

Walsh, B. 2001. Estimating the Time to the Most Recent Common Ancestor for the Y Chromosome or Mitochondrial DNA for a Pair of Individuals. *Genetics*, 158: 897–912.

Name Index

This does not include the names of places that became surnames.

Aberdeen 93, 129
Accrington 2
Adlingflleet 55
Africa 201–3
Airedale 116, 145
Almondbury 29, 101
Altofts 12
Alton (Staffordshire) 112
Amounderness 98–9
Angus 85, 93
Annandale 117
Argyllshire 90
Ascott-under-Wychwood 44
Ashford (Kent) 15, 146
Ashton-under-Lyne 8, 98
Aston (West Midlands) 60
Auckland 4
Australia 12, 195, 197
Ayrshire 85
Aysgarth 73

Bainbridge 73
Banbury 45
Banffshire 92, 109
Barforth-in-Teesdale 27
Barkisland 113
Barmby-on-the-Marsh 138
Barnet 70
Barnsley 7, 102, 142
Barrow-in-Furness 39
Barton-upon-Irwell 33
Basford 185
Batley 23
Bedfordshire 47, 97, 133
Belph 14
Benwick 122
Berkshire 33–4, 50
Berwick-on-Tweed 98–9
Betley 30
Beverley 22, 27, 123, 137
Bingham 95
Birkenhead 69
Birmingham 60, 86, 91, 98, 189

Birstall 70, 101
Birstwith 34
Bishopley 83
Blackburn 2, 8, 76, 85, 118, 186
Blackpool 80
Blean 15
Bolton (Lancashire) 6, 36, 85, 118
Bolton-by-Bowland 68
Bolton Priory 27, 32, 133
Bonsall 128
Bowland 125, 186, 188
Bowness 70
Brabant 22
Bradfield (Norfolk 23
Bradfield (Yorkshire) 70
Bradford (Yorkshire) 8, 31, 71, 73, 76, 99,
    100, 115, 118, 132, 187
Bradley Grange 8
Brailsford 14
Braithwell 14, 108
Bramley (Yorkshire) 30
Brandsby 28
Breconshire 89–90
Bredwardine 48
Breedon-on-the-Hill 58
Bridlington 118
Brighton 138
Bristol 91, 97
Buckenham 142
Buckie 109
Buckinghamshire 46, 97, 133, 188
Burley-in-Wharfedale 56
Burnley 8, 33, 69, 75–6, 132, 186
Burton Constable 27
Bury 6, 76, 112–13
Butterworth 19, 75

Caernarvonshire 87
Caithness 26
Calder Valley xi, 8, 75, 101
Calverley 23, 71
Cambridge 123
Cambridgeshire 11, 13, 17, 46, 122–3, 132, 144

Canada 197, 200
Canterbury 15, 122, 124
Carlisle 117
Carmarthenshire 49, 85, 89–90
Castleton (Derbyshire) 11
Caston 142
Cavan 94
Cawthorne 101
Chadlington 44
Chalfont St Peter 188
Charlesworth 12
Chatburn 2
Cheadle (Cheshire) 7
Cheadle (Staffordshire) 7, 112
Cheddleston 116–17
Chertsey 96
Cheshire 7, 12, 29, 36, 38, 48, 69, 82, 85–6,
    92, 99, 112, 114, 128, 131, 143
Chester 33
Chester-le-Street 4, 49
Childrey 33
Chipping 99
Chipping Norton 45
Chorlton 98
Clitheroe 69, 186
Clunbury 119
Cockerham 2
Cockermouth 97
Colchester 124
Colne 125
Colne Valley (Yorkshire) 110, 112
Colwick 116
Congleton 92
Connaught 172
Conisbrough 92
Cork 55, 95–7
Cornwall 1, 65, 77–9, 81, 86, 88, 96, 117
Crigglestone 31, 121, 139–40
Cuckfield 110, 138
Cumberland 29, 49, 64, 83, 97, 99, 104, 109,
    111, 117, 140, 209

Dalton 101
Danby 142
Darlington 4, 14
Derby 10, 127
Derbyshire 7, 10, 14, 30, 43, 52, 82, 85, 112,
    114, 122, 128–9, 133, 143, 185–6, 197
Devon 1, 47, 68–9, 86, 88, 121, 129,
    135–6, 144
Dewsbury 8, 14, 30, 99, 101–2, 187
Doddington 122

Doncaster 144
Dorset 1, 51, 65, 96
Dover 15
Drax 138
Drypool 122
Dublin 96, 123, 197
Dudley 60
Dumfriesshire 92, 99, 117
Dunbartonshire 92
Dungworth 12
Dunkeld 27
Durham 29, 50
Durham (County) 4, 11, 14, 49, 65, 71, 73,
    82–3, 85, 87, 91, 93, 97, 103–4, 111, 118, 124,
    140, 209

Easington (Durham) 14
Easington (Oxfordshire) 44
East Anglia 3, 47, 87, 124, 131
East Lothian 92
East Preston 80
East Rainton 49
East Riding 87, 111, 123, 138
Eastry 15
Eccles 12
Ecclesfield 52
Edale 12
Edinburgh 93
Eggborough 138
Elham 15
Elland 75, 113
Ellenhall 48
Ely 17, 132
Embsay 96–7
Endon 7
Essex 33, 40, 45, 60, 69, 89, 91, 100, 116, 123,
    133, 147
Evenwood 4
Ewcross 13
Exeter 3
Extwistle 33

Faversham 146
Felixkirk 25
Fifeshire 92, 133
Flanders 22
Flanshaw 69
Folkingham 187
Follifoot 23, 29
Fountains Abbey 26, 28
Foxup 56
Freeby 51

Frickley 101
Frismarash 56
Froghall 112
Fulstone 36, 101
Fylde 186

Garforth 34
Gargrave 69
Germany 34–5, 122–4
Giggleswick 13
Gisburn 2
Glamorgan 49, 53, 85, 88–9, 97, 123
Glasgow 87, 90, 124
Gloucester 89
Gloucestershire 11, 31, 49, 61, 122, 128,
    139, 197
Goathland 25
Gowthorpe 23
Graistock 107
Grantham 187
Gravesend 98
Graveship of Holme 100–2
Greasbrough 101
Great Dunham 142
Great Ouseburn 28
Great Stretton 187
Greenwich 98
Grinton 140
Griston 142
Guernsey 120
Guisborough 85

Halifax 8, 12, 23, 28–9, 74–5, 81, 101, 106,
    109, 115, 137
Halstead 140
Hallamshire 42, 81, 100
Hampole Priory 28–9
Hampshire 33, 86, 93, 109
Handsworth 29
Hanley 42
Hartlepool 85
Hartshead 74
Haslingden 8, 75–6, 118
Hayfield 11
Heaning 130
Hedon 56
Hemlingford 16
Heptonstall 75
Herefordshire 47–9, 87, 124, 197
Hertfordshire 89–90
Hessle 55
Hexham 92

Hickleton 112
High Ercall 48
Hindley 131
Hipperholme 24, 75
Holborn 69
Holderness 24, 27, 55, 88
Hollington 112
Hollym 111
Holmfirth 36–7, 100
Honley 132
Hope 12
Horbury 107
Horsham 138
Horton 116
Horton-in-Ribblesdale 130
Houghton-on-the-Hill 187, 195
Howden 33–4, 123, 138
Howgill 125
Huddersfield xi, 19, 76, 100–1, 132, 188
Hull 31, 34–5, 55, 91, 106, 122
Humbage Green 14
Hunslet 187
Huntingdonshire 11, 65, 90, 115, 122–3

Ightenhill 69
Ipsden 44
Ipswich 41, 85
Isle of Man 86, 98–9, 133
Isle of Thanet 15
Isle of Wight 84

Jersey 97

Keele 60
Keighley 8, 114, 118, 187
Kellington 138
Kendal 109, 118
Kent 15, 45, 47, 79, 86, 104, 108, 117, 123, 135,
    146, 216
Kerry 55
Kildare 96
Kildwick 69, 118, 145
Kilmalcolm 119
Kincardineshire 93
King's Norton 60, 86, 133
Kirkburton 132
Kirkheaton 101
Kirk Lonan 99
Knaresborough 34, 116

Lambeth 69
Lanarkshire 10, 64, 87, 91–2, 97, 117, 133

Lancashire 2, 7, 8, 10–13, 20, 29, 31, 33–4, 36–7, 39, 48, 60, 69, 71, 73–6, 80–2, 84–7, 91, 93, 97–100, 104, 106, 110, 112–15, 117–19, 123, 125–6, 128, 131, 140, 143, 186, 188–9, 208
Lancaster 2, 186
Langcliffe 13
Langsett 100
Leathley 35
Leeds 30, 35, 71, 73–4, 91, 97–9, 107, 118, 124–5, 129, 134, 187
Leek 7, 60
Leicester 33, 187, 196
Leicestershire 10, 48, 87, 90, 92, 97, 102, 112, 185, 187, 195–6
Leigh 11
Leinster 55, 172
Lepton 24, 132
Lewes 108, 138
Leyland 169
Lincoln 109, 187
Lincolnshire 11, 35, 50–1, 64, 87, 90, 103, 122, 144, 187
Linthwaite 74
Litcham 16
Liverpool 10, 11, 69, 91, 96–9, 133
Leek 7, 60
Llanllachaiarn 115
London 3, 11, 15, 45, 68, 70, 72, 84, 86–9, 92, 95–6, 98, 100, 103, 114, 117, 119, 121, 124, 133, 136, 146, 186–7, 197, 217
Longford 96
Long Preston 25
Longtown 117
Lonsdale 21
Louth (Ireland) 96
Low Countries 121–4
Lumley 49
Lunesdale 186
Lyonshall 48
Lythe 142

Macclesfield 143
Maidstone 124
Malton 25
Manchester 38, 91, 98, 123–4, 131, 143
Marsh Benham 33
Medway 98
Melrose Abbey 26
Meltham 110
Melton Mowbray 12
Merthyr Tydfil 97

Methley 29, 51
Middlebie 117
Middleham 108
Middlesex 46, 52, 79, 85–6, 91, 97, 104, 135
Midlothian 10, 85, 91–2
Milton 15
Mirfield 135
Missenden Abbey 188
Mitton 25, 188
Mixbury 46
Monk Bretton Priory 42
Monmouthshire 53, 89, 97, 118, 123, 129
Montgomeryshire 88, 115
Moray 26, 129
Mottram-in-Longendale 7
Munster 97, 172

Newcastle-upon-Tyne 91, 96–8
New Malton 35
New Mill 101–2
New Zealand 195, 197
Newton in Bowland 24, 130, 188
Nidderdale 36
Norfolk 21, 32, 45, 47, 86–7, 93, 97, 103, 109, 142
Northamptonshire 49, 79, 87, 90, 114, 123, 133
Northumberland 11, 14, 49, 65, 71, 83, 86, 91, 93, 103–4, 111, 118, 209
Norland 23
Norton (Derbyshire) 52
Norton (Yorkshire) 142
Norton-in-the-Moors 111
North Riding 64, 73, 85
Norwich 3, 124, 217
Nottingham 91, 185
Nottinghamshire 13–14, 28, 34, 47, 85, 90, 95, 112, 185, 187, 196–7

Offaly 95
Oldham 8
Ormskirk 12, 208
Ottringham 55
Oxford 34, 44
Oxfordshire 43–5, 79, 97, 133

Pagham 68
Patching 80
Peak District 11, 14
Peebleshire 90
Pembrokeshire 53, 85, 89
Penistone 70

Penrith 118
Penzance 97
Perthshire 11, 64
Petworth 80
Pevensey 124
Pipton 90
Pittington 49
Plymouth 98, 136
Pontefract 70
Portsmouth 98, 136
Preese 98
Prescot 126
Preston 2, 192, 186
Pulborough 138

Radnorshire 89
Ranah Stones 5
Ravenshaw 4
Redenhall 21–2
Redruth 97
Reeth 73
Renfrewshire 92
Renishaw 4
Renshaw 4
Ribblesdale 13, 73
Richmond 23, 25, 108
Ripon 22–3, 27, 51, 69
Rishworth 113
Rochdale 8, 36, 74–6, 81, 85, 114–15, 125
Roscommon 96
Rothwell 70
Rowley 24
Roxburghshire 71, 90
Rutland 45, 84, 97
Rye 108

St Cad's 120
St Ives 115
Saddleworth 27, 115
Salford 29, 75, 98
Salisbury 123
Sandal 24, 139–40
Sandtoft 122–3
Sandwich 124
Sandy 16
Scammonden 188–9
Scotton 25, 107
Seaford 46
Seamer 142
Sedgefield 14
Seighford 112
Selby 23, 33, 70, 116, 142

Selkirkshire 10, 90
Settle 20, 73
Shaftesbury 51
Sheffield 12, 14, 29, 43, 52, 56, 97, 115, 122
Sheinton 119
Shelley 36
Sheppey 15
Shetland 64
Shipton 108, 119
Shropshire 47–9, 87, 112, 117, 119–20, 123
Sibford 44
Silkstone 123
Skeeby 25
Skipperbottom 6
Skipton 73, 90–1, 109, 118, 130
Slaidburn 20, 24, 130, 188
Slaithwaite 110
Slindon 79
Snaith 31, 35, 70
Solway Firth 99–100
Somerset 1, 11, 61, 117, 129, 132, 136, 139–40, 144
Soulby 141
Sowerby 23, 25, 28
Southampton 124
Sprotborough 101
Stafford 48
Staffordshire 7, 11, 13, 14, 30, 46, 48–50, 82, 85–6, 91, 104, 111–12, 116, 119–20, 123, 143
Staincliffe 13
Stainland 12
Stanhope 83
Stanley 28, 32, 36
Steyning 138
Stockport 82
Stockton 4, 14, 98
Stoke Marmion 44
Stoke-on-Trent 11, 143
Stone 11
Stourbridge 60
Stretford (Herefordshire) 49
Strumpshaw 142
Stutton 40
Suffolk 21, 40, 47, 85, 90, 97, 100, 121
Surrey 15, 46, 79, 86, 91, 96–7, 103–4, 135, 146, 216
Sussex 45–7, 68–9, 79–80, 86, 89, 103, 108–10, 121, 123–4, 135–9, 146, 216
Swaledale 73, 140–1
Swillington 110
Swithland 58

Tadcaster 26
Tankersley 70
Tarbock 128
Thirsk 25
Thornbrough 107
Thorner 27
Thorney 122
Thornhill 30
Thornton 110
Tickhill 130
Tideswell 12
Tipperaray 55, 95
Todmorden 8
Tong 115
Totmanslow 7
Totties 37
Toxteth Park 96, 99
Troughburn 103
Tynemouth 33
Tyrone 55

Ulster 94–5, 119, 172
Ulverston 39
United States of America 20, 28, 33, 70, 81,
    95, 121, 138, 170–2, 195, 197, 201
Upholland 34

Wadworth 128
Waitby 141
Wakefield 12, 23–4, 28, 31–2, 34, 36, 69,
    100–2, 115, 121, 139
Wallingford 34
Walsall 111
Walton-le-Dale 2
Warminster 11, 61
Warwickshire 42, 45, 48, 50, 79, 86, 104, 112,
    117, 120, 123–4
Waterford 96
Wawne 27–8
Wear Valley 83
Wensleydale 73
Werrington 68
West Bromwich 60

West Derby 10, 98–9, 126
West Leake 35
West Midlands 47, 84, 98, 195
West Riding 2, 7, 8, 13, 20, 38, 55, 68, 71, 73,
    75–6, 85, 87, 91, 97–9, 104, 114–15, 118, 121,
    123–5, 134, 139, 186, 189
Westmorland 64, 70, 80, 118, 141, 186
Wexford 96
Whalley 98
Wharfedale 56
Whiston (Cheshire) 112
Whitby 24, 85, 142
Whitehaven 97–8, 133
Whittlesey 122
Whitwell 14
Wibsey 99
Wickhambreux 15
Wicklow 96
Wigan 11–12, 126, 216
Wigston Magna 102, 187
Wilberfoss 142
Willimoteswick 83
Wiltshire 11, 61, 66, 96–7
Winchester 109, 128
Wirral 208
Wistow 33
Withernsea 111
Withington 12
Wolsingham 83
Wolstanton 11
Wolverhampton 60
Wooldale 37, 101
Worcestershire 26, 45, 48, 86, 90, 112,
    124, 197
Worthen 89

Yeadon 128
York 22–4, 26, 33, 55, 85, 88, 99, 103, 108–9,
    116, 120, 128–9, 132, 134, 140, 142, 217
Yorkshire 2, 11–14, 20, 22, 24–5, 29, 33–8,
    42, 45, 52, 55–6, 64, 74, 80–2, 85, 93, 96,
    100, 103, 106, 112, 114–18, 123–5, 128, 131–2,
    134–5, 138–44, 186–7, 195, 201, 209

Surnames and By-Names

Abb 38
Abson 38, 130
Ace 88–9
Adam 61, 93
Adlam 11
Adlard 11
Agnew 97
Alabaster 17
Alfrey 80
Allen 72
Allpress 11
Anders 11, 126
Anderson 67
Aneslaymayden 50
Anketell 21
Annesley 40, 96
Apps 146
Argent 40
Armatrading 69
Armistead 13
Armitage xi, 110
Arnold 53
Ashburner 39
Ashton 76
Ashurst 216
Ashworth 76
Attenborough 66, 185–6; see plate 8
Ayckbourn 123
Aylwin 80, 86

Baildon 68
Bakstoneman 27
Balcombe 80
Bamford 89
Bamforth 110
Bantyngflyth 21
Barbour 41
Barraclogh 71
Barrow 71
Bathgate 79
Bathurst 80
Beard 127–8
Beardmore 112
Beardsell 76
Beddoes 54

Beeching 66
Behagg 122–3
Beharrel 122
Belchamber 79–80
Beldon 68
Belfield 76
Belk 13–14
Bell 91, 95
Benbow 89
Benjamin 88
Benson 58
Beresford 96
Bethurton 38
Bevan 53, 67
Bevers 108
Bibbe 131
Billeclyf 100
Billings; see plate 6
Billingshurst 80
Bingham 95
Black 95
Blacker 139–40
Blaxland 15
Blenkinsopp 14
Bloomer 30
Bochcollock 32
Bolebec 45
Bolstridge 86
Boltupright 31–2
Bonde 32
Boniface 80
Bonsall 89
Bonser 128
Bonwick 138
Boocock 125
Booth 74
Bordclever 23
Bordewright 23
Boteler 41
Botting 80
Bourner 80
Bowen 87
Bower 110
Brabon 22
Bradbury 82

Bradford 10
Bradley 74, 95
Bradwell 10
Bramhall 128
Bray xi, 183–4, 201
Breadnell 14
Breadseller 22
Brekefart 127
Brelsforth 14
Brewell 14
Bridges 63
Bridson 86
Brierley 76
Brigendermaker 22
Brigstocke 89–90
Broadhead 101
Brook 76
Brooksbank 29
Broomfleet 51
Brown 1, 66–7, 73
Brownell 51
Brownhill 51
Brownsword 143–4
Buckley 76, 95
Bufton 89
Bullyfrogge 32
Buntyngflyth 21
Burdekin 11–12
Burgh 42
Burke 96
Burton 74, 77
Busby 79
Butterfield 187–8, 201; see plate 8
Butterley 36
Butterworth 36, 75–6
Byk 45
Bythewater 51

Cadogan 49
Cadwallader 119–20
Callister 86
Cameron 90
Campbell 67, 90, 104
Campey 51, 112
Campinot 51, 112
Campion 112, 142–3
Camplejohn 141–3
Canon 68–9
Carpi 45
Carr 170, 172
Carruthers 117–19
Carter 50, 64

Carver 22, 51
Catchpole 47
Catrew 47
Chadwick 76
Chatfield 80
Cheesman 80
Cherriman 137–8
Cherryholme 138
Chesandbred 16
Chester 107
Chevauchesul 45
Child 41, 63
Childrey 33
Chiswick 114
Chobard 36–7
Choce 45
Chubb 179, 183
Churchyard 121
Cinnamon 133–5
Clark(e) 63, 66–7, 95, 121
Claxon 52
Cleese 66
Clegg 76
Cleghorn 79
Clockmaker 22
Clouter 23
Clulee 86
Clutterbuck 122
Cobbold 59
Cockehakel 32–3
Cockeshank 32
Cockrobin 106
Cockroger 106
Cockshott 69
Cohen 169–70
Cok 23
Cokerose 21
Cokespur 32
Cole 53
Comber 80
Comberkichyn 32
Combsmith 1, 23
Comper 80
Congleton 91–2
Cook 29, 52
Cooper 63
Corner 121
Corslett 123–4
Costelloe 94
Cotyler 41, 127
Cotyngham 41
Cowgill 20

Cowie 109–10
Cowper 52, 63
Cowperthwaite 109
Crabtree 14
Crawford 79
Creame 108
Croftes 52
Crowhurst 80
Crowther, xi, 76
Cudworth 41
Cunnick 85
Cusack 96
Cutler 41
Cutson 130
Cutt(s) 130

Daft 59
Dakin 38
Dalgleish 10–11
Davenport 96
David 88
Davidson 92
Davies 1, 66–7
Dawkes 38
Dawson 38, 96, 130
Dawtry 138
Day 48
Dearnley 76
Dender 108
Depledge 7
Derby 10
Derling 47
Dernelove 34
Derrick 122
Dewhirst 107
Dewse 107
Dickson 93
Dillon 96
Dimbleby 66
Dimock 96
Dishbinder 23–4
Dissher 23
Dodd(s) 11
Dorward 93
Doyle 55, 210
Drew 44
Drinkall 31
Drysdale 79
Dumbrell 80
Dunlop 79
Dutton 99

Dymhayt 68
Dynthard 31
Dyson 74

Earnshaw 101–2
Ebson 36
Eccles 95
Edgeworth 96
Edkins 86
Elkin 11
Ellel 2, 10
Elstob 14
Eltofts 110
Ely 132–3
Emsden 85
Ephraim 88
Esau 88
Evans 1, 53, 66–7, 86
Eversfield 80
Evershead 47
Exeter 21

Faber 41, 129–30
Fairchild 64
Fair-John 50
Farncombe 80
Farndon 86
Fazakerley 99
Feakes 201
Feakins 179
Feemister 26
Felicedoughter 50
Felton 189
Fenay 29
Ferguson 54
Fernihough 7
Ferrer 31, 127
Firth xi, 76
Flanshaw 69–70
Flathers 85
Fleming 22
Flippance 66
Floyter 23–4
Ford 73
Forrester 115
Fox 127
Franceys 51
French 41
Friday 46
Frobisher 12
Fulstone 102

Fundon 121
Fyndyrne 32
Fyssher 127

Games 89
Gander 80
Garforth 108
Garlick 30
Garrie 85
Garthwaite 108
Gaukroger 106
Geldgrise 25
Geldbird 25
Geldehogg 25
Geldeneye 41
Gemson 130
Gibb 93
Gilleson 121
Gittins 54
Glasier 127
Gledhill 63
Glovere 48
Godale 31
Godeyere 41
Godknape 21
Gofayre 33–4
Goforth 34
Goldsmyth 91
Golightly 83
Goodfellow 64
Gostalk 41
Gotobed 16–17
Gourdskyn 31
Graham 92
Grant 38, 73, 131
Grasshopper 111
Gratwick 80
Gravestone 106
Grayson 106
Greathead 109
Greaves 43
Green 51, 109
Greenhalgh 99
Greenwood 28, 75, 109
Grenow 49
Gressome 108
Grewcock 183
Grime 108
Grinstead 80
Grislibber 24
Grocock 183
Grocott 183

Grosvenor 52
Gryfyn 49
Guise 86
Guylyn 48
Gyllessone 42
Gylyot 91

Haddington 91
Hagger 28
Haigh xi, 76
Haldesworth 52
Halidaye 25
Hallomschire 100
Halsall 99
Hamer 76
Hampshire 10
Hancock 11
Hanson 76
Harbottle 14
Hardcastle 36, 64, 109
Hardy 109
Hargreaves 76
Harker 140–1
Harman 108
Harrison 91
Harry 88
Hartley 110
Hatfield 89
Hauteyn 45
Hawile 41
Hawthorn(e) 111, 186
Hawthornthwaite 186
Hay 53
Haythorne 186
Haythornthwaite 71, 186; see plate 8
Healey 76, 132–3
Hemings 170, 172
Hemingway 14, 36
Henderson 91
Heppenstall 52
Hepworth 100–1
Herber 106
Herrick 179, 184, 186–7, 195–6;
    see plate 8
Heselheved 41
Hetblak 31
Hey 183, 188–9, 201; see plate 8
Heynon 49
Heyr 21
Higgs 131
Higgins 131
Higginson 131

Higson 38, 131
Hill 41, 73–4, 76
Hinchcliffe 14, 52, 101
Hirst 76
Hobson 36
Hogben 15
Hoggesflesh 79–80
Hogley 102
Holden 76
Hollingworth 76
Holloway 108
Hollywell 108
Holman 108
Hoo 42
Hopkinson 63
Horcefent 41
Hordern 111
Horsfall 51
Horsfield 51
Horton 77
Houseman 116
Howell(s) 149
Howarth 76
Hoyle xi
Hughes 54
Hullin 89
Humpage 86
Hungerford 96
Huntbach 14
Hunter 93
Hurlbat 33

Ilhore 32
Impcroft 29
Issabell 37

Jagger 12
Jay 42
Jedd 47
Jefferson 168–70, 183, 191, 195, 198, 201;
    see plate 7
Jeffreys 157, 183, 191–3
Jehu 88
Jelfs 86
Jena 49
Jevons 48
Jobling 183, 201; see plate 4
Johnson 64, 66, 91, 109, 121
Jones 1, 54, 66–7, 72, 86–7
Joseph 88
Jupp 80
Justice 44

Kahn 169
Kain 169
Kamesmyth 23
Kavanagh 97
Kearney 97
Keefe 97
Keegan 97
Kellogg 69–70
Kember 17
Kendal 109
Keogh 97
Kermode 86
Kerr 92
Kershaw 76
Kerridge 59
Keswick 114
Ketley 182; see plate 6
Kigelpening 34–5
Kilton 107
Kilvington 107
King 95, 179, 183; see plate 5
Kingsnorth 15
Kinniburgh 92
Kirkham 99
Kirsop 111
Kittewritt 23
Klyngbell 21
Knewstubb 141
Knight 121
Knott 106
Kyd 91

Lamprey 44
Lanchester 107
Leaper 93
Leach 127–8
Lee 73
Lekeblade 32
Leth 91
Lickbarrow 70–1
Lightowler 76
Lillicrop 136–7
Litilannotson 50
Lincoln 109
Lindfield 80
Lindsey 92
Littlewood 64, 101, 109
Llewellyn 67
Lloyd 54
Lockey 107
Lockwood, xi, 107
Lodelowe 31

Lodwick 89
Lomax 36, 112–13
Longbottom 70
Longley 70
Lorimer 92–3
Loukes 102
Lucas 37

MacAloon 95
McCarthy 55
M(a)cDonald 67, 72, 90–1, 104
MacFarland 90–1
MacGowan 94
McKain 120
McLean 90
McLoughlin 107
McSporran 90
Madoc 48–9
Maddrell 99
Major 115
Malet 41
Malin 38
Mallinson 38, 201
Mangham 107, 130
Mannering 52
Manning 107
Manningham 107
Mappin 122
Mapother 96
Marchall 127
Markenfield 69
Markwick 46
Marriott 11
Marsay 85
Marsden 76
Masheder 31
Mashiter 31
Mates 205
Mather 99
Mawson 56
Mayberry 90
Maypowder 96
Meates 196–7
Mendham 21
Mercer 91
Mesquene 120
Metcalfe 73–4
Mexborough 70
Michael 88
Milne 93
Mirfield 51
Moffatt 79

Monday 95
Monkman 109
Mortimer 110
Mounteney 52
Moxon 56
Mucklebreed 95
Murfin 51
Murgatroyd 137
Murphy 97–8
Mylchreest 86

Nelson 210
Nevergelt 31
Neville 41
Nice 17
Nicholas 121
Norfolk 109
Northam 190; see plate 7
Norton 10
Nouthirde 25
Nutley 80

Oakes 5
O'Donnell 211
Ogden 76
Ogram 55–6
Oldeschreu 32
Onions 48
Organmaker 22
Ormanroyd 71
Orr 93
Osan 36
Osgathorpe 10
Osmond
O'Sullivan 190
Oulsnam 116
Owen(s) 67, 87

Pache 41
Pankhurst 135–6
Parkin 52
Passepays 44
Patching 80
Patel 124
Paternoster 49–50
Paterson 93
Paw 38
Pawson 38, 130
Penhaligon 86
Pengelly 86
Penny 51
Pennyman 144–5

Penrose 96
Pentecost 80
Pepercorne 31
Peregrine 89, 147
Perigo 124
Pester 129
Peston 66
Peterson 121
Pettigrew 93
Peyntor 127
Philip 37
Phimister 26
Pilgrim 89, 147
Pilmay 123
Pike 31
Pikescull 32
Pittaway 86
Plant 30–1
Plummer 127
Pogson xi
Polglaze 86
Polkinghorne 86
Ponderswoman 50
Ponfret 91
Porter 128
Postgate 52
Potter 91
Price 86
Primmer 80
Pritchard 53
Proctor 96
Pudsey 68
Punshon 49
Purpelot 45
Pyper 127

Quareour 27
Quayle 86
Quyhird 25
Quinlan 55
Quinn 55

Radcliffe 86
Ramsden 102
Ramsey 92
Ramshaw 4–5
Rankin 93
Ratcliffe 99
Rawnsley 14
Ravenscroft 183, 185, 201; see plate 7
Ravenshaw 4
Raybould 86

Redfe(a)rn 76, 85
Redihough 113–14
Rees 67
Reid 73, 92
Renderour 41
Renshaw 4–5
Renishaw 4–5
Revis, Rivis 173, 201–3
Rhodes 106
Richard(s) 53
Richardson 25
Ridehalgh 113–14
Ridsdale 108
Rigden 15
Riley 75
Rimmer 12
Roberts 1, 54, 66
Robertson 64–5, 67
Roblin 53
Robinson 64, 108
Robson 68, 108
Roke 44
Rossel 48
Round 60
Rourke 97
Roxburgh 71–2
Russell 95
Ryan 190
Rydefare 33

St Valery 45
Sacker 183
Sadeler 127
Sagar 131–2
Saffery 15
Saltmersh 34
Sayle 86
Scarfield 79–80
Schofield 75–6
Scone 53
Scott 67
Scrapetrough 31
Sedgewick 80
Sekilwethir 32
Seyr 48
Shakespeare ix
Shakeshafte ix
Shaftoe 14
Shardlow 127
Sharpe 31
Sharples 36, 84–5
Sharvell 108

Shaw 73–4
Sheard xi
Shearer 93
Sheldon 89
Shepherd 76, 106
Sherman 127
Sherwood 108
Shipyard 106
Shore 76
Shufflebottom 6
Sibson 58
Sidebottom 36
Sievewright 93
Silliman 134
Simmonite 135
Sim(m)s 106
Singleton 80
Skarf 31
Skeffington 96
Skillicorn 86, 98–9
Skyle 51
Sladdin 76
Slaidburn 69
Smallbehind 70
Smith 1, 12, 23, 41, 59, 64, 66, 94–5, 109, 127,
    173, 179, 183; see plate 5
Smithson 1
Snaghasel 28
Soutemogh 32
Souter 93, 129
Spicer 115
Spilsbury 86
Squire 51
Stancliffe 52
Staniforth 41
Stanley 99
Stansfield 52, 76
Stark 93
Startup 44–5
Stead 179
Stobart 66
Stonehold 123
Stooke 108
Stope 108
Stott 76
Straightbarrel 69
Stretford 48
Stribling 190; see plate 7
Strickett 25
Stringer 21, 30
Stringfellow 30
Strongbow 69

Strudwick 80, 108
Styrkhyrd 25
Sullivan 97–8
Sutcliffe 75
Sutton 96
Swankie 85
Swathe 41
Sweetnam 210
Swerdslyper 23
Swetliglade 32
Swindlehurst 186; see plate 8
Swinglehurst 186
Swinshed 112
Swynlibber 24
Sykes xi, 19, 51, 72, 74, 171–2
Synderhill 29

Talbot 106
Tallowpot 106
Talun 41
Tarelton 96
Taunteliry 32
Taylor 1, 12, 21–2, 41, 48, 59, 66, 72, 76, 110
Teare 86
Tellwright 111
Thackaberry 96
Thatcher 16
Thighul 131
Thomas 1, 54, 66, 127
Thom(p)son 25, 58, 93
Thorp 51
Threapland 71
Thunder 21, 108, 210
Ticklepenny 35
Tickner 80
Tiffany 179
Tillotson 145
Titchmarsh 190; see plate 7
Tomlin 47
Tomson 50
Tonks 86
Tookey 17
Tordoff 99
Tottenham 96
Totty 37
Townend 110
Treais 79
Trebarthen 79
Trebilcock 78
Tredinnick 78
Tredwell 44
Treen 78

Trefuswethen 77
Tregagle 79
Tregaskis 78
Tregear 78
Tregenza 78
Tregloan 79
Treglown 78
Tregoning 78
Tregunna 78
Trelawney 77, 79, 86
Trelease 78
Treleaven 78
Trelescyc 77
Treloar 78
Tremaine 77–8
Tremayne 77–8
Trembath 78
Tremenheere 79
Trenerry 78
Trengove 78
Trepress 79
Treredenek 77
Tresawne 79
Trescothick 79
Tresise 78
Tresize 78
Trestrail 78
Trethewy 78
Trethowan 78
Trevain 79
Trevarthen 78
Trevaskis 78
Treveen 79
Trevelyan 77–8
Trevena 78
Treverton 78
Trevethan 78
Trevivian 79
Trevithick 78
Trevorrow 78
Trewartha 86
Treweek 78
Trewen 79
Trewent 53
Trewhellla 78
Trewin 78
Treworgie 79
Trilontheberye 32
Trolisse 110
Trollope 103
Trumper 70
Tulloch 79

Tunstall 42
Turnagh 71
Turner 12, 21, 71–2
Twentipayr 32

Upwode 51
Urton alias Steven 52

Vaughan 54
Verrall 110
Vevers 108
Voisey 106

Wadsworth 183
Walder 80
Waldershelf 43
Walischemon 127
Walker 1, 66, 72
Wandehagger 27
Wardle 76
Wardlow 53
Warwood 86
Watchorn 12
Waterleader 22
Watkins 17
Watson 52, 67, 93, 132
Wayte 127
Webbere 41
Welikempt 45–6
Werldlay 23
Wheelwright 23
Whirle 32
Whirlinthecole 32
White 73, 95
Whitebrow 31
Whiteserk 32
Whitlokes 42
Whittaker 76
Whitworth 76
Whytyng 51
Wigley 89
Wilcock 17
Wilkinson 50
Williams 1, 54, 64, 66–7, 86–7
Wilson 1, 41–2, 58, 66–7, 73,
    93, 127
Wimpenny 51
Winchester 109
Winston 190; see plate 7
Winterbottom 5
Winyeat 47
Witefeld 45

Wogan 66
Wolstenholme 76, 114–16
Wood 73–4
Woodman 96
Woodson 170–2
Woolgar 80
Woosnam 115
Wordsworth 76, 183
Wormald 113
Worsnop 115
Wright 12, 59, 72, 127

Wrightson 112
Wrixon 111
Wynegod 45
Wyndelester 23–4
Wythehoundes 32

Yapp 17
Yates 128
York 109
Youll 52
Young 67, 73, 95

General Index

Aliases 51–2, 107–8
Archer, Stephen: *The British 19th Century Surname Atlas* 9–10, 62, 67, 84, 114

Black Death 3–4, 41, 49, 68, 72, 102, 189
Black, George F. 26–7, 90, 92, 109, 128, 133
Bradley, Dan 173, 210
By-names 3, 5, 21–39, 57, 68, 109–10, 127–33, 215

Census returns (1881) 1–2, 4–11, 14–15, 45, 47–9, 55, 62–80, 84–105, 113, 115, 117
Civil registration records 9
Commercial DNA companies 194–9, 204–6
Cyndi's list 194

Darwin, George 166
DNA 148–214
 alleles 155, 158–60, 164, 166
 amplicons 166
 binary markers 157–61, 163, 166, 173–4, 176–7, 180, 204–6
 chromosomes 151–8, 167, 169, 173
 descent clusters 181–5, 189, 199
 genes 155–7, 198
 genetic drift 174, 189–93; see plate 3
 haplogroups; haplotypes 159–63, 169–74, 177–85, 188, 190–1, 193, 196, 198–9, 201, 206, 211–12; see plates 4, 5, 6 and 7
 mitochondrial DNA 152, 154, 199; see plate 1 and 2
 mutations 154–5, 159–63, 174, 176, 178, 180, 202; see plates 3, 4 and 6
 NRYs 154
 nucleotides 149–50
 PCRs 164–7
 SNPs 158–9, 164, 166, 196–8, 214
 SRYs 153, 157
 STRs 157, 160–4, 166, 168, 172–80, 184, 202–6, 210, 212–13; see plate 4
 structure 149–53
 TMCRA 174–7, 184–5, 203–4, 210

Y chromosomes 18, 152–64, 167–214; see plates 1, 3, 4 and 6

Electoral registers 11, 71
English Surnames Survey and Series 5–6, 8–9, 31, 43–7, 50, 62, 74, 84, 121
Expansion of surnames 62–7, 72–81
Extinction of surnames 63, 67–72

Family Tree DNA 194, 197, 205–6
Forensics 211–13
French names 2, 45, 122–3, 128

Genest, Paul 167
Guppy, H.B. 9, 80

Hearth tax returns 7, 12–17, 35, 70, 186–7, 216

Illegitimacy 18, 52, 211
Immigration 53, 120–4
International Society of Genetic Genealogy 196
Irish names 54–5, 94–8, 171, 173, 190, 210–11

Jewish names 125, 168
Jobling, Mark 167, 173

Lay subsidy rolls 4, 41–2, 44
Leicester University Genetics Department 149, 160, 173, 177, 189, 211
Locative (place) names 2, 7, 13–15, 35–7, 64, 74–9

McClure, Peter 12, 18, 35, 38, 130
McEvoy, Brian 176
McLysaght, E. 94–6, 119
McKinley, Richard 6, 43–7, 57, 75, 79–80, 108, 110, 112, 120–1, 135, 138–9, 143
Manor court records 24, 31–2, 41, 57
Maps of surname distributions 1–2, 5, 7, 9–10, 12–13, 17–18, 20, 39–40, 60–1, 82–105, 125–6, 146–7, 216
Morgan, T.J. and Prys 67, 88, 120–1

National DNA database 213
Niall of the Nine Hostages 198, 210–11
Nicknames 2, 30–35, 44, 57, 109–10
Non-paternity events 52, 174, 176, 181, 185,
    190–1, 196–9, 201, 216

Occupational names 1, 12, 22–30, 129–30
Origins of surnames 1–3, 41–59
Oxford Ancestors 194
Oxford English Dictionary 22–3, 25–7, 29,
    32–4, 137–8, 142

Parish registers 16, 18, 48, 132, 138
Patronymics 47–9
People of the British Isles Project 209
Personal names 2–3, 11–12, 17,
    37–8, 53–7
Poll tax returns 2–3, 13, 16–17, 19,
    21–2, 27, 29, 48–51, 68, 70, 113, 131,
    141, 216
Polygyny 211
Postles, David 42–3, 47, 68, 121, 136, 144

Quarter sessions records 49, 135

Reaney, P.H. 4–5, 8, 11, 21, 26–7, 30–1, 50,
    69, 88, 98, 128, 133, 139–40, 215
Roth, Wendy 200
Rowlands, John and Sheila 53, 88–9, 115,
    119, 123

Scottish surnames 5–8, 10–11, 26, 54, 64–5,
    85, 90–4, 109–10, 117–19, 128, 133
Single-family surnames 2, 72–4, 79, 112,
    185–9
Sorenson Molecular Genealogy
    Foundation 194
Surname changes and variations 6, 106–20,
    132–45
Sykes, Brian 19, 72, 185, 194

Titford, John 122–3
Tooth, Edgar 48, 111–12, 116, 143
Tucker, D.K. 5, 71

Walsh, Bruce 176
Wellcome Trust 151
Welsh surnames 1, 48–9, 53–4, 66–7,
    85–90, 119–20, 184